First World War
and Army of Occupation
War Diary
France, Belgium and Germany

59 DIVISION
Divisional Troops
Royal Army Medical Corps
2/2 North Midland Field Ambulance
1 November 1916 - 2 August 1919

WO95/3018/2

The Naval & Military Press Ltd
www.nmarchive.com
Published in association with The National Archives

Published by

The Naval & Military Press Ltd

Unit 10 Ridgewood Industrial Park,

Uckfield, East Sussex,

TN22 5QE England

Tel: +44 (0) 1825 749494

www.naval-military-press.com

www.nmarchive.com

This diary has been reprinted in facsimile from the original. Any imperfections are inevitably reproduced and the quality may fall short of modern type and cartographic standards.

© Crown Copyright
Images reproduced by permission of The National Archives, London, England, 2015.

Contents

Document type	Place/Title	Date From	Date To
Heading	WO95/3018/2		
Heading	59th Division 2-2nd Fld Ambulance Feb 1917-1919 Jly		
Heading	War Diary Of O.C. 2/2nd North Mid. Field. Ambulance From February 1st, 1916, To Feb 29th, 1916 (Volume 2)		
War Diary	Walford	01/11/1916	21/11/1916
Miscellaneous	59th Div 2/2 N. Mid. F.A. Feb 1917		
Miscellaneous	Cover For Documents. Nature Of Enclosures.		
Heading	War Diary Of 2/2nd North Midland Fd. Ambulance From 23.2.17 To 28.2.17 Volume II		
War Diary	Qillingham	23/02/1917	23/02/1917
War Diary	Havre	24/02/1917	25/02/1917
War Diary	Glisy	26/02/1917	27/02/1917
War Diary	Bayon Villers	28/02/1917	28/02/1917
Miscellaneous	Appendix I	24/02/1917	24/02/1917
Heading	59th Div. 2/2nd N.M Field Ambulance Mar 1917		
War Diary	Bayon Villers	01/03/1917	08/03/1917
War Diary	Proyart	08/03/1917	31/03/1917
Miscellaneous	Operation Orders By Colonel H.H.C. Dent A.D.M.S. 59th Division	03/03/1917	03/03/1917
Miscellaneous	Scheme for the evacuation of wounded in event of heavy casualties. Appendix 2		
Miscellaneous	Appendix 3		
Miscellaneous	A Form Messages And Signals.		
Miscellaneous	March 23/17 to March 29/17. Appendix 7	23/03/1917	23/03/1917
Miscellaneous	March 15th to 22nd 1917. Appendix 6	15/03/1917	15/03/1917
Heading	59th Div. 2/2nd North Midland F.A. April 1917		
War Diary	Proyart	01/04/1917	09/04/1917
War Diary	Bouvincourt	10/04/1917	30/04/1917
Miscellaneous	30/3/17 to 5/4/17. Appendix I	30/03/1917	30/03/1917
Heading	War Diary Of 2nd/2nd. North Midland Field Ambulance From 1/5/17 To 31/5/17 (Volume 5.)		
War Diary	Bouvincourt	01/05/1917	30/05/1917
War Diary	Lechelle	31/05/1917	31/05/1917
Miscellaneous	Honours and Rewards. Appendix I	01/05/1917	01/05/1917
Operation(al) Order(s)	Special Orders No.1 By Lt. Col. J. Colley Burkitt Commg 2/2nd N.M. Fd. Amb.	03/05/1917	03/05/1917
Miscellaneous	2/2nd Nth. Mid. Field. Amb. Appendix 3		
Miscellaneous	2/2nd Nth. Mid. Field. Amb. Appendix 5	06/05/1917	06/05/1917
Miscellaneous	2/2nd Nth. Mid. Field. Amb. Appendix 6	07/05/1917	07/05/1917
Miscellaneous	2/2nd Nth. Mid. Field. Amb. Appendix 7	08/05/1917	08/05/1917
Miscellaneous	2/2nd Nth. Mid. Field. Amb. Appendix 8	09/05/1917	09/05/1917
Operation(al) Order(s)	Operation Orders No.2 by Officer Commanding 2/2nd Nth Mid Fd Amb	11/05/1917	11/05/1917
Miscellaneous	2/2nd Nth. Mid. Field. Amb. Appendix 10	10/05/1917	10/05/1917
Miscellaneous	2/2nd Nth. Mid. Field. Amb. Appendix 11	11/05/1917	11/05/1917
Miscellaneous	2/2nd Nth. Mid. Field. Amb. Appendix 12	12/05/1917	12/05/1917
Miscellaneous	2/2nd Nth. Mid. Field. Amb. Appendix 13	13/05/1917	13/05/1917
Operation(al) Order(s)	Operation Order No. 3 by Officer Commanding 2/2nd nth Mid Fd Amb	15/05/1917	15/05/1917

Miscellaneous	2/2nd Nth. Mid. Field. Amb. Appendix 15	14/05/1917	14/05/1917
Miscellaneous	2/2nd Nth. Mid. Field. Amb. Appendix 16	15/05/1917	15/05/1917
Miscellaneous	2/2nd Nth. Mid. Field. Amb. Appendix 17	16/05/1917	16/05/1917
Miscellaneous	2/2nd Nth. Mid. Field. Amb. Appendix 18	17/05/1917	17/05/1917
Miscellaneous	2/2nd Nth. Mid. Field. Amb. Appendix 19	18/05/1917	18/05/1917
Miscellaneous	2/2nd Nth. Mid. Field. Amb. Appendix 20	19/05/1917	19/05/1917
Miscellaneous	2/2nd Nth. Mid. Field. Amb. Appendix 21	20/05/1917	20/05/1917
Miscellaneous	2/2nd Nth. Mid. Field. Amb. Appendix 22	21/05/1917	21/05/1917
Miscellaneous	2/2nd Nth. Mid. Fd. Amb. Appendix 23	22/05/1917	22/05/1917
Miscellaneous	Operation Orders 2/2nd. N.M.F. Amb.	24/05/1917	24/05/1917
Miscellaneous	2/2nd Nth. Mid. Fd. Amb. Appendix 25	23/05/1917	23/05/1917
Miscellaneous	2/2nd Nth. Mid. Fd. Amb. Appendix 26	24/05/1917	24/05/1917
Miscellaneous	2/2nd Nth. Mid. Fd. Amb. Appendix 27	25/05/1917	25/05/1917
Miscellaneous	2/2nd Nth. Mid. Fd. Amb. Appendix 28	26/05/1917	26/05/1917
Miscellaneous	2/2nd Nth. Mid. Fd. Amb. Appendix 29	27/05/1917	27/05/1917
Miscellaneous	2/2nd. North Mid. Fd. Ambulance	30/05/1917	30/05/1917
Miscellaneous	Operation Orders By Major F.W. Johnson Comdg. 2/2 Nth Mid Fd. Amb.	31/05/1917	31/05/1917
Heading	War Diary Of 2/2 N. Mid. Fd. Amb From 1-6-17 To 30-6-17 Volume 6		
Miscellaneous	To A.D.M.S 59th Division.	03/07/1917	03/07/1917
War Diary	Lechelle	01/06/1917	30/06/1917
Heading	War Diary Of 2/2 N. Mid. Fd. Amb From 1-7-17 To 31-7-17 Volume VII		
War Diary	Lechelle	01/07/1917	31/07/1917
Heading	War Diary Of 2/2 N. Mid. Fd. Amb. From 1-8-17 To 31-8-17 Volume 8		
War Diary	Lechelle	01/08/1917	24/08/1917
War Diary	Bouzincourt Aveluy Road	25/08/1917	31/08/1917
Operation(al) Order(s)	2/2nd North Midland Field Ambulance Operation Order No. 4		
Miscellaneous	March Table A		
Miscellaneous	March Table B First Stage		
Miscellaneous	Mechanical Transport		
Miscellaneous	Horse Transport		
Map	Map A		
Operation(al) Order(s)	Operation Order No. 5 By Lt Col F.W. Johnson Cmdg 2/2nd Nth Mid Fd Ambulance	29/08/1917	29/08/1917
Miscellaneous	Instruction For Officer In Charge Of Motor Ambulance Convoy	29/08/1917	29/08/1917
Operation(al) Order(s)	Operation Order No. 6 By Lieut Colonel F.W. Johnson Commanding 2/2nd N Mid Field Ambulance	31/08/1917	31/08/1917
Heading	War Diary Of 2/2 N. Mid Fd. Amb From 1-9-17 To 30.9.17 Volume 9		
War Diary	Bouzincourt Aveluy Road	01/09/1917	01/09/1917
War Diary	Watou	02/09/1917	15/09/1917
War Diary	Hillhoek	16/09/1917	30/09/1917
Heading	War Diary Of 2/2 N. Mid. Fd. Amb From 1.10.17 To 31.10.17 Volume 10		
War Diary	Watou	01/10/1917	01/10/1917
War Diary	Guarbecque	02/10/1917	06/10/1917
War Diary	Verchin	07/10/1917	09/10/1917
War Diary	Pernes	10/10/1917	11/10/1917
War Diary	Barlin	12/10/1917	12/10/1917
War Diary	Aix Noulette	13/10/1917	31/10/1917

Miscellaneous	War Diary Of 2/2nd North Midland Field Ambulance Vol X		
Diagram etc	Plan of Evacuation		
Heading	War Diary Of 2/2 N. Mid. Fd. Amb From 1/11/17 To 30/11/17 Volume 11		
War Diary	Aix-Noulette	01/11/1917	14/11/1917
War Diary	Duisans Camp No.3	15/11/1917	19/11/1917
War Diary	Hendecourt	20/11/1917	21/11/1917
War Diary	Gomiecourt	22/11/1917	23/11/1917
War Diary	Equancourt	24/11/1917	30/11/1917
Map	Map		
Heading	War Diary Of 2/2 N. Mid. Fd. Amb From 1-12-17 To 31-12-17 Volume 12		
War Diary	Near Metz Q.14.C.8.8. Sheet 57c France 1/40000	30/11/1917	02/12/1917
War Diary	Near Metz Q.14.C.8.8.	03/12/1917	21/12/1917
War Diary	Q.14.C.8.8. Metz (Sheet 57c)	22/11/1917	31/12/1917
Miscellaneous	Appendix I		
War Diary			
Heading	2/2nd North Midland F.A.		
War Diary	Buneville	01/01/1918	31/01/1918
Miscellaneous	Programme of Course of Lectures for Medical Officers, VIth Corps. Appendix I		
Miscellaneous	Programme of Training. Appendix II	30/12/1917	30/12/1917
Miscellaneous	Programme of Training. Appendix III	06/01/1918	06/01/1918
Miscellaneous	Programme of Training. Appendix IV	13/01/1918	13/01/1918
Miscellaneous	Programme of Training. Appendix V	20/01/1918	20/01/1918
Heading	War Diary Of 2/2 N. Mid. Fd. Amb Vol II From 1-2-18 To 28-2-18 Vol 13		
War Diary	Buneville	01/02/1918	08/02/1918
War Diary	Barly (P.IS.d.3.6 sheet & 51.c.	09/02/1918	09/02/1918
War Diary	Berles Au-Bois (W.IS.C.59 sheet & 51c)	09/02/1918	09/02/1918
War Diary	Bienvillers-Au-Bois (E8.A.9.2.sheet 57D)	10/02/1918	11/02/1918
War Diary	Ervillers B.13.d.27 sheet 57c)	12/02/1918	18/02/1918
War Diary	Ervillers	19/02/1918	28/02/1918
Heading	2/2nd Nth. Mid. Field Amb.		
War Diary	Ervillers B.13.d.2.7	01/03/1918	22/03/1918
War Diary	Douchy Les Ayette F.10.a.8.8. sheet 57D.	23/03/1918	23/03/1918
War Diary	Bouzincourt-Aveluy Road (W.15.A.sheet 57 D)	24/03/1918	25/03/1918
War Diary	Pont-Noyelles	26/03/1918	28/03/1918
War Diary	Frevillers (V.I.d-5-8 Sheet 36 B.1,40.000	29/03/1918	29/03/1918
War Diary	Bethencourt C.6 f. Sheet 51c.)	30/03/1918	31/03/1918
Heading	War Diary Of 2/2nd Nth. Mid. Field Amb. For The Month Of April, 1918 Vol. 4		
War Diary	Bethencourt [C.6.F. Sheet 51c	01/04/1918	01/04/1918
War Diary	Schools Camp Poperinghe Poperinghe L.3.f.2. Sheet 27 Bolgain near 1 to 40.000	02/04/1918	03/04/1918
War Diary	Brandhoek (G.12.b.6.8 Sheet 28 Belg)1/40000	04/04/1918	04/04/1918
War Diary	Brandhoek G12b.6.2 (Sheet 28)	05/04/1918	13/04/1918
War Diary	Godewaersvelde R.7.C.2.5. (Sheet 27)	14/04/1918	14/04/1918
War Diary	Kokereel Farm Near Westoutre [R.17.f.5.3 Sheet 27	15/04/1918	18/04/1918
War Diary	Terdeghem [P.10.a.7.3 Sheet 27	19/04/1918	19/04/1918
War Diary	Dozinghem [F.11.a.9.5. Sheet 27	20/04/1918	21/04/1918
War Diary	Herzeele (Road Camp) [D.11.C.2.5 Sheet 27	22/04/1918	26/04/1918
War Diary	Schools Camp St. Janter Biezen [L 3 b Central Sheet 27	27/04/1918	29/04/1918
War Diary	Remy Siding (L22.d.9.3. Sheet 27)	30/04/1918	30/04/1918

Heading	War Diary Of 2/2 N. Mid. Fd. Amb From 1-5-18 To 31-5-18 Volume V		
War Diary	Remy Siding [L.22 d.9.3 Sheet 27	01/05/1918	05/05/1918
War Diary	Houtkerque Area (E.8.C.2.8 Sheet 27) 1/40000	06/05/1918	06/05/1918
War Diary	Roubrouck Hogerhill (Hogenhill H.12.b.3.6 Sheet 27 1/40000)	07/05/1918	07/05/1918
War Diary	Nieurlet [M.8.f.b.3.6 Sheet 27 1/40000	08/05/1918	09/05/1918
War Diary	Ecques 4.D.30.10. Hazebrouck 5 A. 1/100,000	10/05/1918	10/05/1918
War Diary	Sains-Les-Pernes H.13.a.3.5 (Sheet36.B	11/05/1918	16/05/1918
War Diary	Les 4 Vents W.9.C.9.9 Sheet 36 B.	17/05/1918	31/05/1918
Map	Map		
War Diary			
Map	Plan Of Medical Arrangements For Defence Of The Bb Line, Southern Sector		
Heading	War Diary Of 2/2nd Nth. Mid. Fld. Amb Vol VI 1-6-18 To 30-6-18 Vol 17		
Miscellaneous	A Form. Messages And Signals. Appendix 2		
War Diary	Les 4 Vents [W.9 Central Sheet 44.6	01/06/1918	15/06/1918
War Diary	Estree Cauchie W.2.b.2.9.[Sheet 44b	16/06/1918	16/06/1918
War Diary	Divion I 2 4.d.10.9 (Sheet 44b)	17/06/1918	17/06/1918
War Diary	Herbeval G.33 a 7.2 [Sheet 44b	18/06/1918	22/06/1918
War Diary	Nouveauville [Q22.a.9.1 Sheet 3 6 D	23/06/1918	30/06/1918
Heading	War Diary Of 2/2 N. Mid. Fd. Amb. From 1-7-1918 To 31-7-1918 Volume VII		
War Diary	Nouveauville (Q.22.a.9.1)[Sheet 3 b D	01/07/1918	09/07/1918
War Diary	Maisnil-Les-Teneur [L. 32.A. Sheet44c	10/07/1918	24/07/1918
War Diary	Gouy-En-Artois [Q.19.a.7.7 Sheet 51c	25/07/1918	31/07/1918
Heading	War Diary Of 2/2 N. Mid. Fd. Amb From 1-8-1918 To 31-8-1918 Volume VIII		
War Diary	Gouy-En-Artois	01/08/1918	23/08/1918
War Diary	Saulty V.2-C [Sheet 51c.	24/08/1918	24/08/1918
War Diary	Witternesse [Q13b.8.8 Sheet 36 A.	25/08/1918	27/08/1918
War Diary	Berguette O.I.B.C.6 (Sheet 36 A)	27/08/1918	30/08/1918
War Diary	St. Venant Asylum [P.9.d.I.8 Sheet 36 A.	31/08/1918	31/08/1918
Diagram etc	War Diary 2/2nd N Midland Field Amb. Vol VIII. Appendix I		
Diagram etc	War Diary 2/2nd N Midland Field Amb. Vol VIII. Appendix 2		
Heading	War Diary Of 2/2 N. Mid. Fd. Amb From 1-9-1918 To 30-9-1918 Volume IX		
War Diary	St. Venant Asylum (P.9. d.I-8 Sheet 36 A)	01/09/1918	11/09/1918
War Diary	Lestrem (R.9.C.3.6. Sheet 36 A)	12/09/1918	30/09/1918
Diagram etc	Appendix I		
Diagram etc	Appendix 2		
Diagram etc	Appendix 3		
Diagram etc	Appendix 4		
Heading	War Diary Of 2/2 N. Mid. Fd. Amb From 1-10-1918 To 31-10-1918 Volume X		
War Diary	Lestrem Lestrem [R.9.c3.6.] (Sheet 36 A)	01/10/1918	03/10/1918
War Diary	Haverskerque (J. 27.d.Central Sheet 36 A.)	04/10/1918	08/10/1918
War Diary	Fort Rompu	09/10/1918	18/10/1918
War Diary	St. Andre Hospile Hospice (K.19. b.Central Sheet 36)	19/10/1918	19/10/1918
War Diary	Flers (L32.C.83 Sheet36)	20/10/1918	22/10/1918
War Diary	Hem (L.24.C.9.1 Sheet 36)	23/10/1918	31/10/1918
Map	Appendix 1		

Heading	War Diary Of 2/2 N. Mid. Fd. Amb From 1-11-18 To 30-11-18 Volume XI		
War Diary	Hem [L24.C.9.I. Sheet 36	01/11/1918	17/11/1918
War Diary	St. Andre (Lille)	18/11/1918	23/11/1918
War Diary	Emmerin (p.24.a.9.5 Sheet 36)	25/11/1918	30/11/1918
Heading	War Diary Of 2/2 N. Mid. Fd. Amb From 1-12-18 To 31-12-18 Volume XII		
War Diary	Emmerin (P 24 a.9.5 Sheet 36)	01/12/1918	04/12/1918
War Diary	Ruitz [K.19.C.3.3 Sheet 44b	05/12/1918	11/12/1918
War Diary	Dunkerque (St Pol-S-Mer)	12/12/1918	31/12/1918
Heading	59th Div 2/2nd North Mid. F.A.		
War Diary	Dunkerque (St. Pol-sur-Mer)	01/01/1919	31/01/1919
Heading	2/2nd North Mid. F.A.		
War Diary	Dunkerque (St Pol-Sur-Mer)	01/02/1919	28/02/1919
Heading	2/2nd Nth. Mid. F.A.		
War Diary	Dunkerque St Pol Sur Mer.	01/03/1919	31/03/1919
Heading	2/2nd Nth. Mid. F.A.		
War Diary	Dunkerque St Pol Sur Mer.	01/04/1919	16/04/1919
War Diary	Dunkerque	17/04/1919	30/04/1919
Heading	2/2nd Nth. Mid. F.A.		
War Diary	Dunkerque St Pol Sur Mer.	01/05/1919	23/05/1919
War Diary	Dunkirk	24/05/1919	31/05/1919
Heading	2/2nd Nth. Mid. F.A.		
War Diary	Dunkirk	01/06/1919	30/06/1919
Heading	2/2nd N. Mid. F.A. July 1919		
Miscellaneous	Cover For Documents. Nature Of Enclosures.		
War Diary	Dunkirk	01/07/1919	02/08/1919
Miscellaneous	Sgt. Henry R. Hill		

WOQS 3018/2

59TH DIVISION

2-2ND FLD. AMBULANCE

FEB 1917-~~DEC 1918~~

1919 JLY

also 1916 FEB

59th NM Division

CONFIDENTIAL.

War Diary

of

O.C. 2/2nd North Mid. Field. Ambulance.

From February 1st, 1916, to Feb 29th, 1916.

(Volume 2.)

WAR DIARY

Army Form C. 2118.

N.C.L. Reich

INTELLIGENCE SUMMARY. Major Comg 1/1 & N. H. Amb Range. (T)

(Erase heading not required.)

Hour, Date, Place	Summary of Events and Information	Remarks and references to Appendices
7 apr/11/xv Watford	Zeppelin reported over hospital, inner funnel rescued and except solanin filtered out, lamp dimmed 10pm.	
14/11/xv	Muster Parade 1st check by C.O.	
17/11/xv	Muster Parade 2nd — Inspection R.C.	
21/11/xv	Inspection of shoes. 18 men 1st line reinforcements.	
	5 and 16 3rd line.	

Feb 1917

59ᵃ Div

2/2 N. Mid. F.A.

(6414) Wt. W3906/P1607 2,500,000 7/18 McA & W Ltd (E 3591) Forms W3091/4.   Army Form W.3091.

Cover for Documents.

Nature of Enclosures.

Notes, or Letters written.

Confidential

War Diary

of 2/2nd North Midland F.A. Amb.

From 23.2.17   To 28/2/17

Volume II

2/2th Midland Field Ambulance

Confidential

Page 1.

Army Form C. 2118.

WAR DIARY
or
INTELLIGENCE SUMMARY.

(Erase heading not required.)

Instructions regarding War Diaries and Intelligence Summaries are contained in F. S. Regs., Part II. and the Staff Manual respectively. Title pages will be prepared in manuscript.

Place	Date	Hour	Summary of Events and Information	Remarks and references to Appendices
GILLINGHAM	23.2.17	a.m.	Entrained for SOUTHAMPTON in route for B.E.F. and embarked at 6 p.m. (A.D.M.S. 59th Div. wire DMS 191/1/22.2.17) 12.P.M6.	
HAVRE	24.2.17	9.30 a.m.	Disembarked from South Western Miller and proceeded to "Rest Camp" for the night. 24.P.M6.	
HAVRE	25.2.17	11 a.m.	Proceeded to GARE DES MARCHANDISES and entrained. 24.P.M6.	
GLISY	26.2.17	8.30 a.m.	Arrived from HAVRE 24.P.M6.	Appendix 1.
GLISY	27.2.17	7.30 a.m.	Marched to BAYONVILLERS, arriving at 3.30 p.m. One H.D. Rowe no.992 accidentally drowned 24.P.M6.	
BAYONVILLERS	28.2.17	10.30 a.m.	at BAYONVILLERS. Established a temporary hospital in Lunch huts at POINT W.3.a. (Sheet 62.D) 24.P.M6.	Appendix 2.

Holley Ren Pitt
LT. COL.
COMMANDING 2nd Fd. AMB. 69th DIV.

Appendix I.

15203

Officer Commanding 2/2 N.M. Field Ambulance.

1. The Field Ambulance

under your command will entrain as detailed in paragraph 4.

2. O's. C. units must be very careful that every man in their units is told the station and "Point of Entrainment" before marching off. Most of the numerous cases of men left behind have occured through neglect of this precaution.

3. The entrance to Points Nos. 1, 2 and 4 is at No. 70, Cours de la Republique, and to Point 3 at the Boulevard d'Harfleur.

4. Entrain at { **Gare des Marchandises** / ~~Gare Maritime~~ } Point No. 1

   Time 10.30 a.m. Date 25 February 1917

   Ration party (Strength, 1 Officer, 20 men)* to report to the Officer i/c Detail Issue Store:—

   { **Gare des Marchandises** / ~~Gare Maritime~~ } Point No. 4

   Time 10.30 a.m. Date 25 February 1917

5. Attention is directed to the "Special Orders for Units passing through Havre Base," especially paragraph 6, and to "Notes for Entrainment."

   Any further imformation regarding entrainment can be obtained from the D.A.D.R.T., **rue Jules-Lecesne**.

   The Orderly Room Sergeants, if any, should report to this office, as under, ready in all respects for immediate entrainment on being posted to the D.A.G., 3rd Echelon, for duty.

   Time Date

   The times given are the hours of arrival at the specified place.

Issued at ...., Captain.
                                                D.A.Q.M.G., Havre Base.

Date 24 February 1917

59th Div.

1/1st N.M. Field Ambulance

140/2042

Mar. 1917 / 5

COMMITTEE FOR THE
MEDICAL HISTORY OF THE WAR
Date 11 MAY 1917

2/2 North Midland Field Amb.
March 1917. France.

Army Form C. 2118.

WAR DIARY or INTELLIGENCE SUMMARY

(Erase heading not required.)

Instructions regarding War Diaries and Intelligence Summaries are contained in F.S. Regs., Part II. and the Staff Manual respectively. Title pages will be prepared in manuscript.

Place	Date	Hour	Summary of Events and Information	Remarks and references to Appendices
BAYONVILLERS	1.3.17		Nothing of note. RDMC.	
"	2.3.17		RDMC.	
"	3.3.17		RDMC.	
"	4.3.17		RDMC.	
"	5.3.17		RDMC.	
"	6.3.17		One second class nursing orderly evacuated to C.C.S., suffering from cut and Schwann line RDMC.	
"	7.3.17		Nothing of note. RDMC.	
"	8.3.17	1.30 p.m.	Marched to PROYART by order of A.D.M.S. 59th Div. RDMC.	Appendix 1
PROYART	8.3.17	4 p.m.	Arrived at PROYART from BAYONVILLERS and took over Divisional Main Dressing Station and Divisional Rest Station (Map reference – France ROSIERES R.20.6.5.8.) from 1/3rd Northumbrian Fd Amb. RDMC	Appendix 1.
PROYART	9.3.17	8 a.m.	Despatched bearer subdivision – 1 officer + 33 other ranks – to report for duty to O.C. 2/1st Mtd Fd Amb at KASINO M.29.c. (Map. ROSIERES) by order of A.D.M.S. 59th Div. RDMC.	Appendix 1.
PROYART	10.3.17		Received from A.D.M.S. 59th Div., information as to position of Regimental Aid posts, advanced Dressing Stations. Bearer posts. Advanced Dressing Station and Divisional cycling Station. During 3rd 9th March, 97 patients were admitted, 4 discharged to duty and 34 evacuated. RDMC.	Appendix 2
PROYART	11.3.17		Instructions as to whether a case admitted on 10.3.17 was cholera - spinal meningitis or typhus. Patient was evacuated to No 38 C.C.S. The ward was smoked and patients bathed and isolated. RDMC.	Appendix 3
PROYART	12.3.17		1 officer and 19 other ranks of 1/4/5th Northumbrian Fd Amb. reported and were attached for duty. RDMC	
PROYART	13.3.17		Report received from A.D.M.S. 59th Div. (D.M.S. 62 of 13.3.17) that case mentioned under date 11.3.17 was found to be cerebro-spinal meningitis. RDMC.	
PROYART	14.3.17		Received from A.D.M.S. 59th Div. Copy of A.D.M.S. 11th Corps send letter No 1757/17 dated 12.3.17 ordering 50 ties to be kept in readiness to receive gassed cases. Copies were distributed to Medical Officers RDMC	

2/2 North Midland Fld. Amb.

France. March 1917.

Army Form C. 2118.

WAR DIARY
or
INTELLIGENCE SUMMARY.
(Erase heading not required.)

Instructions regarding War Diaries and Intelligence Summaries are contained in F. S. Regs., Part II. and the Staff Manual respectively. Title pages will be prepared in manuscript.

Place	Date	Hour	Summary of Events and Information	Remarks and references to Appendices
PROYART.	16.3.17		One Officer, Capt. W.P. TINDAL ATKINSON and one private were sent for duty to 2/3rd Lincolns Regt.	
PROYART.	17.3.17		Summary of admissions, discharges and transfers from 10.3.17 to 14.3.17, attended. 2776.	Appendix 4
" "	" "		Leaving the west extension of accommodation have been made. This is now 7 Bivouac huts, 2 hors., 1 store tent, 2 N.P. marquee tent, 2 Indian tents, total accommodation 650 bed places, 1800 patients would be accommodated temporarily if sufficient personnel were available. 2776.	
" "	" "	12.30 p.m	Notification of expected advance received from A.D.M.S. 59 Div., accordingly preparations were made to deal with a large number of casualties. 2776.	Appendix 5
PROYART.	18.3.17		1 Offr. and 19. O.R. of 1/3rd North Midland F. Amb., returned to their Unit. 2776. Stretchers to being experienced in clipping the Divisional Rest Station. 2776.	
PROYART.	19.3.17		Nothing of note. 2776.	
PROYART.	20.3.17		Two motor ambulances were sent for duty to O.C. 2/1st 9th Midd. F. Amb. 2776.	
PROYART.	21.3.17		Nothing of note. 2776.	
PROYART.	22.3.17		Capt. W.P. TINDAL ATKINSON returned from duty with 2/5th Lincolns and was replaced by Capt. E.D. ELLIS 2776.	
PROYART.	23.3.17		From 15.3.17 to 22.3.17, 476 casualties (sick & wounded) were admitted, 149 discharged to duty and 347 transferred 2776.	Appendix 6.
PROYART.	24.3.17.		Five Indian personnel arrived from Lucknow Cavalry F. Amb., for purpose of attending Indian casualties 2776.	
PROYART.	25.3.17.		Sen. Lewin (Dentist) reported for duty from 5th Div. Sanitary Section 2776.	
PROYART.	26.3.17.		Nothing of note. 2776.	
PROYART.	27.3.17.		One Officer Capt. F.H.C. WATSON was sent for duty to 2/6th Sherwoods. 2776.	

2/2. N.d. Fd. Amb.
France.
March 1917.

WAR DIARY
or
~~INTELLIGENCE SUMMARY~~

(Erase heading not required.)

Army Form C. 2118.

Instructions regarding War Diaries and Intelligence Summaries are contained in F. S. Regs., Part II. and the Staff Manual respectively. Title pages will be prepared in manuscript.

Place	Date	Hour	Summary of Events and Information	Remarks and references to Appendices
PROYART.	28.3.17.		One officer unit detachment took over hospital hut at ST MARTINS WOOD from 2/1st Wx Mid F.d. Amb. RAMC. Entire Personnel and two Horse were transferred to 1/1st South Midland Fd Amb at PERONNE (DDMS iii Corp No 193/17 17.3.17. 30/4)	
PROYART.	29.3.17		One motorcar (fully equipped) and personal hit sent to FOUCACOURT (D.D.M.S. iii Cps.) One Clerk sent to Corp Rest Station CERISY (ADMS 59 Div) 30/6 1 NCO + 3 men attached to Commandant Div Training School VAIRE for duty on 22nd (PRO 19.3.59 Div.) 30/6	
PROYART.	30.3.17.		One officer (Capt Young) out for Duty to 2/5 Lincolns From 23.3.17 to 29.3.17. 468 casualties (Sick + wounded) were admitted. 136 Diselsonged. 6 Duty	Appendix 7. 203
			334 transferred.	
PROYART	31/3/17.		Capt R Ellis RAMC. returned from Duty with 2/5 Lincolns.	203.
			Motor Cars to and returned from FOUCACOURT.	

Holley Run Hitt
Lt. Col.
O.C. 2/2ND N. MID. Fd AMB. R.A.M.C.

2/2 N. Mid. Fd. Amb.
War Diary.
March 1917.

Appendix 1.

COPY.

OPERATION ORDERS
BY
COLONEL H. H. C. DENT A.D.M.S. 59th DIVISION

Map reference – FRANCE ROSIERES.

Para. 2. The Officer Commanding 2nd/2nd North Midland Field Ambulance will send the bearer sub-division of one section to report to Officer Commanding 2/1st North Midland Field Ambulance at the Kasino.M.29.C. Central by 9-30 a.m. 9th March 1917.

The remainder of the 2nd/2nd North Midland Field Ambulance will relieve 1st/3rd Northumbrian Field Ambulance and take over the Divisional Main Dressing Station and the Divisional Rest Station at PROYART on March 8th 1917.

In the Field
3/3/1917

(Signed) H.H.C. Dent Col.
A.D.M.S. 59th Division

2/2 Nth Mid. Fd. Amb.
War Diary.
March 1917.

Appendix 2.

Copy of Appendix 2

Scheme for the evacuation of wounded in event of heavy casualties.

1. The following scheme for evacuation makes provision for the reception of 1000 lying and 2000 sitting cases.

2. **Positions of Regimental Aid Posts**

Left Battalion	N.28.c.2.3
Left Support Battalion	Belloy N.21.c.1.5.
Centre Battalion	M.33.d.7.5
Right Battalions	T.9.A.9.7.
Right Battalion	T.9.a.2.2

    In each of these posts 1 N.C.O. and 6 men R.A.M.C. are posted.
    These posts are in deep dug-outs and are capable of accomodating a few lying and 12 sitting cases on an average - it is not easy to lower lying cases into the dug-outs.

3. **Positions of Advanced Dressing Posts**

For left sector	N.27.c.3.3.
For right sector	Berny T.2.b.7.3

    These posts receive the wounded from the Regimental Aid Posts. They are situated in deep dug-outs and have a normal personnel of 2 Medical Officers and 14 other ranks R.A.M.C. This personnel can be increased as regards stretcher bearers.

4. **Positions of Relay Posts**

On the Estrees-Villers-Carbonnel Road	(1)	N.26.d.3.3.
	(2)	N.25.d.8.2
ESTREES E.	(3)	N.25.c.8.3
ESTREES W.	(4)	N.30.c.8.2
Bois Bulow	(5)	N.25.b.5.0.
	(6)	T.2.b.1.8

    At each of these posts 1 N.C.O. and 6 stretcher bearers are posted. In the event of heavy fighting this personnel can be increased by an equal number at least.

5. **Advanced Dressing Station**

    Casino in the Bois de Satyre. M.29.c.9.2

    2 Medical Officers and 32 other ranks remain here - this establishment in the event of heavy fighting would be increased by four or five Medical Officers and three bearer sub-divisions.

6. **Divisional Collecting Station**

    Four huts, each capable of accomodating 100 walking cases will be taken over as a Divisional Collecting Station. They are situated at the West end of Foucaucourt, North of the Road. Map reference M.27.c.1.0.

7. **Main Dressing Station**

    The main dressing station at Proyart can at short notice be made ready to receive 250 lying down cases. Normally it can receive 100 lying down cases. A small DECAUVILLE Railway on which trolleys for wounded can be used, runs from near these huts to the Main road to Foucaucourt at R.29.c.5.5.

2/2. n.a. Mid. Fd. Amb.
War Diary.
March 1917.

Appendix 3.

	Admitted.	Discharged.	Evacuated.
Wounded.	13.	,	11.
Gassed.	.	,	,
Trench feet.	24.	,	,
Diarrhoea.	3.	,	,
Scabies.	11.	,	11.
Frost Bite	.	,	,
Venereal.	.	,	,
Infectious.	1.	,	,
Other diseases	45.	4.	11.
Admitted Total.	97.		
Discharged "	4.		
Evacuated "	34.		
	135		

March 8th/9th/1917.

Appendix 3. (signed)

March 10 & 14th.

Remained   318
Admitted   289
Discharged   14
Transferred   136
Remaining   457.
    March 11th/17.

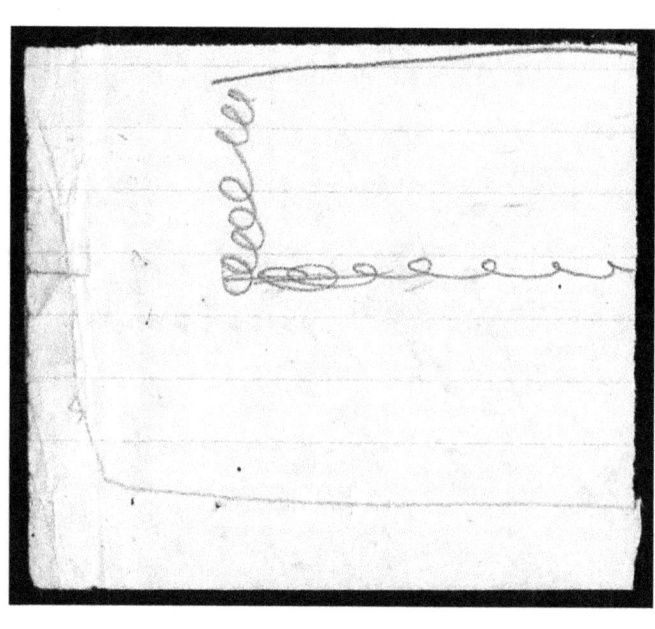

Division	Wounded			Shell Shock			Sickness - Infectious			Trench feet			Diarrhoea			Venereal			Other Sick		
	Admitted	Discharged	Transferred	Admitted	Discharged	Transferred	Admitted	Discharged	Transferred	Admitted	Discharged	Transferred	Admitted	Discharged	Transferred	Admitted	Discharged	Transferred	Admitted	Discharged	Transferred
59th Division	28	-	23	1	-	21	-	21	-	-	-	48	-	-	24	-	-	-	133	3	19
50th							10	-	10										8	9	28
1st								1	-	1									1	-	1
48th										1	-	1									
other Divisions										4	1	1							9	2	6
other Divisions total	28	-	23	1	-	36	1	-	36	1	-	50	-	24	21	-	1	-	151	14	51

2/1. H₂ M.S. F.C.
War Diary
March 1917

2/2. N'th Mid. F. Amb.
War Diary.
March, 1917.

Appendix - 5.

"A" Form.
MESSAGES AND SIGNALS.

Army Form C.2121
(in pads of 100).
No. of Message

Copy

This message is on a/c of:
O.H.M. Service
H.H.C. Dent

TO: O.C. 2nd Field Ambulance

Sender's Number.	Day of Month.	In reply to Number.	A A A
A.D.M.S. 2	March 17. 17.		

Two Brigades advancing aaa Make arrangements for Casualties

From Place: A.D.M.S. 59 Division
Time: 11.55 a.m.

(sd) H.H.C. Dent

MARCH 23/17 to MARCH 29/17. Appendix 7

	59th Division			1st Div			42nd Div			III Corps		
	adm	dis	trans	adm	dis	trans	adm	dis	trans	adm	dis	trans
Wounded	7	1	7	2	-	2				6		6
Gassed	-	1	-									
Scabies	52	-	52				12		12	2		2
Infectious	16	-	16							3		3
Diarrhoea	84	34	52									
Trench feet	3	32	21							1		1
Venereal	2	-	2									
Other Sick	231	59	130	4		1	4		2	39	9	25
	395	127	280	6	-	3	16	-	14	51	9	37

Remained 437
Admitted 468
Discharged 136
Transferred 334
Remaining 435

March 15th to 22nd /1917 — Appendix 6

	59th Div.			50th Div.			1st Div.			48th Div			3rd Corps.			
	ADMITTED	DISCHARGED	TRANS.	ADMITTED	DISCHARGED	TRANS.	ADMITTED	TRANS.	DISCHARGED	ADMITTED	DISCHARGED	TRANS.	ADMITTED	DISCHARGED	TRANSFERRED	212. No. Mid. F.D. Cur. War Diary. March 1917
WOUNDED.	27.	5.	25				1.	1.					3.	3		
GASSED.	3.	4														
SCABIES	40.	40		19	19								1.	1.		
INFECTIOUS	15.	15														
TRENCH FEET.	41.	3.	4										1.			
DIARRHOEA.	96.	31.	19	1.		3.							1.	1.		
VENEREAL	4.	4														
OTHERS SICK	137.	39.	86.	27/42.	65	105.		1.	2.	2.			15	5	15	
	363.	78	197.	89.	65	127	1	1	3	2	-	-	21	5	20	

Remaining 457.
Admitted 476.
Discharged 149.
Transferred 347
Remaining 437.

40/2086

59th Div.

2/1st North Midland F.A.

COMMITTEE FOR THE
MEDICAL HISTORY OF THE WAR
Date −6 JUN.1917

2/2 Wx. Mid. F.A. Amb.

April 1917.

Vol. 4. Page 1.

Army Form C. 2118.

WAR DIARY
or
INTELLIGENCE SUMMARY.
(Erase heading not required.)

Instructions regarding War Diaries and Intelligence Summaries are contained in F. S. Regs., Part II. and the Staff Manual respectively. Title pages will be prepared in manuscript.

Vol 3

Place	Date	Hour	Summary of Events and Information	Remarks and references to Appendices
PROYART	1.4.17		Nothing of note. RAMC.	
"	2.4.17		Nothing of note. RAMC.	
"	3.4.17		One man arrived from base - 19.7. Lucas F.H. RAMC.	
"	4.4.17		Nothing of note. RAMC.	
"	5.4.17		One Officer Capt. P.G. Phillips evacuated to C.C.S. suffering from Pea Fever, and struck off strength of Unit. RAMC.	
"	6.4.17		Pte S.T. MARTIN (Whist 620 - R292) was evacuated and the detachment returned to the Unit. RAMC. From 30.3.17 to 5.4.17. 588 patients were admitted, 111 discharged and 567 transferred RAMC.	App. 1.
"	7.4.17		Nothing of note. RAMC.	
"	8.4.17		One section reported to 2/1st Wx. Mid. Ft. Amb. for duty in the Line. RAMC. One Officer Capt. R. Cox R.A.M.C. was attached for duty. Authority R.A.M.S. 59 2 Dec RAMC.	
"	9.4.17		Nothing of note. RAMC.	
BOUZINCOURT	10.4.17		Heavy action took over the Advanced Dressing Station from 2/1st Wx. Mid. Ft. Amb., in the Church Bouzincourt RAMC. One section was left at PROYART - to remain until relieved or all patients evacuated - Authority R.A.M.S. Operation Order No 9 dated 7.4.17. RAMC. Advanced Dressing Posts were taken over at HANCOURT v ROISEL. RAMC.	
"	11.4.17		Nothing of note. RAMC.	
"	12.4.17		Nothing of note. RAMC.	
"	13.4.17		Nothing of note. RAMC.	
"	14.4.17		The right Advanced Dressing Post was advanced from HANCOURT to BERNES. RAMC.	
"	15.4.17		Nothing of note. RAMC.	
"	16.4.17		Nothing of note. RAMC.	
"	17.4.17		Nothing of note. RAMC.	
"	18.4.17		Nothing of note. RAMC.	
"	19.4.17		Nothing of note. RAMC.	
"	20.4.17		Nothing of note. RAMC.	
"	21.4.17		Nothing of note. RAMC.	

2/2 N^d Mid. F^d Amb. Vol 2 Page 2

April 1917. Army Form C. 2118.

WAR DIARY
or
INTELLIGENCE SUMMARY
(Erase heading not required.)

Place	Date	Hour	Summary of Events and Information	Remarks and references to Appendices
BOUVINCOURT	22.4.17		The Dressing station was inspected by D.M.S. 4th Army 22/4/16.	
"	23.4.17		Gas Officer. Capt W.P. TINDAL ATKINSON, was transferred for 10 days duty 63 C.C.S. Authority A.D.M.S. 59 Div. D.M.S. 197/1/24.17 22/4/16. The Dressing Station at PROYART was evacuated and the actions which had been left there reported to M.H.Q at BOUVINCOURT for duty 24/7/16.	
"	24.4.17		Nothing of note. 22/7/16.	
"	25.4.17		Nothing of note. 22/7/16.	
"	26.4.17		Nothing of note. 22/7/16.	
"	27.4.17		Nothing of note. 22/7/16.	
"	28.4.17		On 27th inst an attack was made by the Left Brigade of the Division, 176 wounded were passed through the A.D.S. on the 27th inst and during the night 27/28.	
"	29.4.17		Nothing of note. 22/7/16.	
"	30.4.17		Nothing of note. 22/7/16.	

O.C. 2/2ND N. MID. F^d AMB. R.A.M.C.

30/3/17 to 5/4/17.

DISEASE	59TH DIV.			48TH DIV.			42ND DIV.			1ST DIV.			III CORPS			INDIAN TROOPS		
	ADM	DIS	TRANS	ADM	DIS	TRANS	ADM	DIS	TRANS	ADM	DIS	TRANS	ADM	DIS	TRANS	ADM	DIS	TRANS
WOUNDED	211		211	10		10							4		4			
GASSED	1																	
SCABIES	29		29	14		14							1		1			
INFECTIOUS	8		8										1		1			
DIARRHOEA	45	16	58										1		1			
TRENCH FEET	9	27	27															
VENEREAL	3		3															
OTHER SICK	189	57	150	2		20		5	2	1			39	9	32	1		1
	495	100	486	10	-	2	-	10	34	-	-	-	19	2	-	-	1	46	-	9	-	39	1	-	1

REMAINED   435
ADMITTED   588
DISCHARGED   111
TRANSFERRED 567
REMAINING   345

C O N F I D E N T I A L.

WAR DIARY

OF

2ND/2ND. NORTH MIDLAND FIELD AMBULANCE.
- - - - - - - - - - - - - -

From :- 1/5/17.   To 31/5/17.

(Volume 5.).

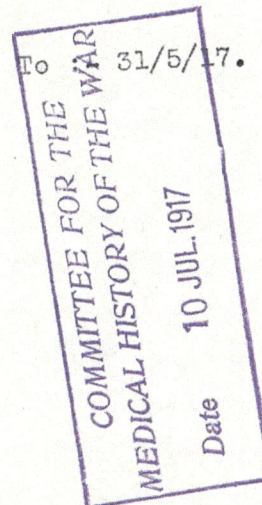
COMMITTEE FOR THE
MEDICAL HISTORY OF THE WAR
Date 10 JUL.1917

Title Page

2/2 N. Midland Ft. Amb.
May 1917.

WAR DIARY
or
INTELLIGENCE SUMMARY.
(Erase heading not required.)

Army Form C. 2118.

Instructions regarding War Diaries and Intelligence Summaries are contained in F.S. Regs., Part II. and the Staff Manual respectively. Title pages will be prepared in manuscript.

Place	Date	Hour	Summary of Events and Information	Remarks and references to Appendices
BOUVINCOURT P.23.b.4.9 (Sheet 62c)	1.5.17		One Officer, Capt. R.J. McCONNELL, was attached to 2/5 North Staffords in relief of an Officer of the 2/3rd West Mid. F.d Amb. RAMC.	
"	2.5.17		Luthers from A.D.G. RAMC. Reinforcements:— 1 expert and 3 men were received for Amb. (Authority ADMS 57/Da) RAMC. Instructions received from Div. Hqrs. that an Office of the Unit, Capt. F.H.C. WATSON had been noted for mention in Dispatch (57/Da. Letter 57/47/11 87/5/17. RAMC.) Operation Order No 1 received from A.D.M.S. RAMC. " " Special Order No. 1 based upon this was issued.	Appendix 1. Appendix 2.
"	3.5.17			
"	4.5.17		During the 4th April 97 wounded were passed through ADMS. from 10 a.m. to 4.5.17. 2032 cases were sick.	
"	5.5.17		559 of these were wounded, the remainder sick. RAMC. history for C. RAMC.	
"	6.5.17		From 8 p.m. 5.6.17 to 8 p.m. 6.5.17. Four wounded and forty six sick were received at the Advanced Dressing Station and passed on to the M.D.S. RAMC. The numbers of sick wounded by Units are given in Appendix 3. RAMC.	appendix 3.
"	7.5.17		As the description of the Unit and the method used to evacuate casualties while the Unit has been in the collecting area, has been too brief, and appendix No 4 giving a general account of these particulars has been made out. RAMC. — — appendix 4 The medical situation of Units on the 7.5.17 is as follows:— Map Ref. France 62c. 1/40000. RAMC. Regtl. Sector of Line.	

Left Sector of Line.
Units
176th Inf. Bde. { 2/5 North Staffs
                  2/6 "   "
                  2/5 South "
                  2/6 "   "

R.A.P.
L.10.a.2.5
L.10.a.2.5
HERVILLY
ROISELLE

In Reserve
Units
178th Inf. Bde. { 2/5 Sherwoods
                  2/6   "
                  2/7   "
                  2/8   "

R.A.P.
VRAIGNES.
HANCOURT.
Q.4.a.
HAMELET.

Regtl. Sector of Line.
Units
177th Inf. Bde. { 2/4th Lincolns
                  2/5   "
                  2/4th Leicesters
                  2/5   "

R.A.P.
L.33.a.2.5.
L.26.c.6.5.
L.28.a.4.5.
L.22.c.6.0.

72 N.d. Mid. Ft. Amb.

May 1917.

Vol I   Page. 2.

Army Form C. 2118.

WAR DIARY
or
INTELLIGENCE SUMMARY.
(Erase heading not required.)

Place	Date	Hour	Summary of Events and Information	Remarks and references to Appendices
BOUVINCOURT	7-5-17		Left A.D.P. — ROISEL K.16.d. Right A.D.P. BERNES Q.4.b.2.9. MMG Advanced Dressing Station — BOUVINCOURT CHURCH P.23.b.4.9. MMG	
			From 8.p.m. 6.5.17 to 8.p.m. 7.5.17. Six wounded and thirty sick were passed through the A.D.S. MMG	Appendix 5
BOUVINCOURT	8-5-17		From 8.p.m. 7.5.17 to 8.p.m. 8.5.17. Four wounded and thirty seven sick were passed through. The A.D.S. MMG	Appendix 6
BOUVINCOURT	9-5-17		From 8.p.m. 8.5.17 to 8.p.m. 9.5.17. Thirty eight wounded and fifty seven sick were passed through the A.D.S.	Appendix 7
"	10.5.17		From 8.p.m. 9.5.17 to 8.p.m. 10.5.17. Sixteen wounded and forty one sick were passed through the A.D.S. MMG Reinforcements from other ranks were received from the Base, authority A.D.M.S. 59th Div. MMG	Appendix 8
"	11.5.17		Lieut. Col. J. Colley Burkitt, proceeded to England:- Authority 2 A.g.M.S.(B). 1496/38 and No 5/5/17. 59 TDes Hagn. 289/77 and Ca 10/5/17. A.D.ml 59th Division 36/5/34 and Cd 11/5/17 — and was struck off the strength of the Unit. MMG Received Operation Order No.12 by A.O.M.S. 59th Division 2 MMG Operation Order No.2, based on M.M.S. Operation Order No.12 transmitted 2 MMG. From 8.p.m. 10.5.17 to 8.p.m. 11.5.17. Nine wounded and forty-six sick were passed through 2 A.D.S. MMG.	Appendix 9 Appendix 10 Appendix 11
"	12.5.17		From 8.p.m. 11.5.17 to 8.p.m. 12.5.17. Seven wounded and fifty four sick passed through the A.D.S. MMG	
"	13.5.17		Positions of Units and Regimental Aid Pos.G on 13.5.17:- Mch, France 62.c. 1/40000. 2MMG. A.D.S (Hayn. +/A F/Mid F. Amb.) — Church P.23 b.4.9. Left Sector A.D.P. — ROISEL K.16.d. Regt. Aid. Pos.b. 176th Bde. 2/5 North Staffs. — HEAVILLY 2/6 " " — K.16.d.2.2. 2/5 South " — L.10.a.5.5. 2/6 " " — L.10.a.8.5. Right Sector A.D.P. — {BERNES Q.4.b.2.9. {JEANCOURT L.26.d.2.2. Regt. Aus. Pos.b. 177th Bde. 2/4 Leicesters:- L.28.a.4.5. 2/5 " — L.28.a.5.b. 2/4 " Lincolns — K.23.d.2.5. 2/5 " " — L.26.b.6.5. Regt. Aid. Pos.b. Reserve Bde. 178th 2nd Bde. 2/5 "Sherwoods:- Q.19.d.9.0. 2/6 " " — Q.8.d.1.9. 2/7 " " — Q.4.a.2.2. 2/8 " " — K.20.6.65. L.MMG.	

2/2 N.M. Mid. 7th Amb.

May 1917.

WAR DIARY
or
INTELLIGENCE SUMMARY.
(Erase heading not required.)

Army Form C. 2118.
Vol. II Page 3.

Place	Date	Hour	Summary of Events and Information	Remarks and references to Appendices
BOUVINCOURT	13/5/17	From 8. P.M. 12.5.17 to 8. P.M. 13.5.17	five wounded and fifty sick passed through A.D.S. RZMG. Copy of D.R.O. No 320 of 13.5.17. BZMG. * 320 Strength.	Appendix 12
BOUVINCOURT	14.5.17	From 8.P.M. 13.5.17 to 8.P.M. 14.5.17.	Lieut-Colonel J. COLLEY BURNITT, R.A.M.C. (T.F.) Commanding 2/2 N.M. Mid. 7th Amb., having proceed to England on 11.5.17, is struck off the strength of the Division accordingly. (Authority: Fourth Army No. P.2/112 dated 8.5.17)" RZMG. Three wounded and forty eight sick passed through A.D.S. RZMG.	Appendix 13
BOUVINCOURT	15.5.17	From 8.P.M. 14.5.17 to 8.P.M. 15.5.17.	Operation Order No 15 by R.P.M. 5th Div. received. Opealin No. 5 based on this, was issued. R2MG. A.D.P. JEANCOURT. (House 62.C.1/4000) unmarked over to 141 Secunderabad (Indian Cavalry) 7th Amb. RZMG. Three wounded and fifty Sick were passed through the A.D.S. RZMG. The main dressing station at ST CREW (Map 62.C.1/4 0000) was taken over by 141 Mid. 7th Cav.L. by the 141 Secunderabad (Indian Cavalry) 7th Amb., the latter unit continue to take casualties 8 5th Division. RZMG.	Appendix 14. Appendix 14. Appendix 15
BOUVINCOURT	16.5.17	From 8.P.M. 15.5.17 to 8.P.M. 16.5.17.	The A.D.P. BERNES was used and the personnel returned to Hegra. BOUVINCOURT. RZMG. seven wounded (five of whom were wounded Lt. S.) and thirty seven sick passed through A.D.S.RZMG. One Officer and thirty seven other ranks were sent to 141 Secunderabad (Indian Cavalry) 7 Amb. M.D.S. ST CREW to attend to and supervise needs of casualties admitted from 5th Division: Authority MDMS 5th Div. RZMG.	Appendix 16
BOUVINCOURT	17.5.17	From 8.P.M. 16.5.17 to 8.P.M. 17.5.17	five wounded twenty seven sick were passed through MDS. RZMG.	Appendix 17
BOUVINCOURT	18.5.17	From 8.P.M. 17.5.17 to 8.P.M. 18.5.17	two wounded forty eight sick passed through MDS. RZMG.	Appendix 18
BOUVINCOURT	19.5.17	From 8.P.M. 18.5.17 to 8.P.M. 19.5.17.	three wounded and forty three sick passed through RZMG. MDS.	Appendix 19
BOUVINCOURT	20.5.17		During this week the 177th Inf. Bde. was relieved by 5 Cavalry Division. The 176th Inf. Bde remains in this line. Medical disposition 20.5.17:— A.D.S (Hosp. 2/2 N. Mid. 7th Amb) — Church P.23.6.4.9. (Map 62.c./10000) A.D.P. — Roisel. K.16.a. 2/5 N. Staffs — L.10.a.5.5. 2/6 " — L.10.a.5.5. 2/5 " S. F.O.m/C.1113.1/3 — Hervilly 2/6 " — Roisel.	

R.A.P.s. 176th Inf. Bde.

A5534 Wt.W4973/M657 750,000 8/16 D.T.

2/2nd Mid. F'd Amb.
May 1917.

Vol v. Page 4.

Army Form C. 2118

WAR DIARY
or
INTELLIGENCE SUMMARY.
(Erase heading not required.)

Instructions regarding War Diaries and Intelligence Summaries are contained in F. S. Regs., Part II. and the Staff Manual respectively. Title pages will be prepared in manuscript.

Place	Date	Hour	Summary of Events and Information	Remarks and references to Appendices
BOUVINCOURT	20/5/17		From 8 A.M. 19-5-17 to 8 P.M. 20-5-17. 6 wounded and 20 sick passed through A.D.S. 2276.	Appendix 20.
"	21/5/17		Major F.W. JOHNSON R.A.M.C.(T) took over command of unit. From 8pm 20-5-17 to 8 P.m. 21-5-17. 1 wounded and 32 sick passed Through A.D.S. One officer of 2/10 N.M.F. Amb. doing duty at A.D.S. ROISEL returned to 2/11 N.M.F. Amb. Visited A.D.S. at Roisel. One officer and 4 men reported there from Ambulance Car. Field Amb. as a preliminary to taking over the post on 23rd inst.	Appendix 21.
"	22/5/17		Capt. H.P. Malcolm temporarily detached as 2/A.D.M.S. 59th Div. From 8 pm 20-5-17 to 8 pm 22-5-17, 2 wounded & 36 sick passed through A.D.S.	Appendix 22.
"	23/5/17		From 8pm 22-5-17 to 8pm 23-5-17. 2 wounded & 33 sick passed through A.D.S. Handed over A.D.S. ROISEL to section of Ambala Indian Cav. F. Amb., and withdrew Capt. R. Cox and all men of this unit, under instructions from A.D.M.S.	Nil/app'dix 23
"	24/5/17		Received instructions from A.D.M.S. to prepare to move the Field Ambulance in a few days from BOUVINCOURT to LECHELLE at LE MESNIL when the Division will move into the XV Corps area. Accompanied the A.D.M.S. to the new area and selected a site for one section Divisional Rest Station at LECHELLE. Orders received this evening to proceed tomorrow morning, by route march to EQUANCOURT with the 177th Infantry Brigade tomorrow, by route march to proceed tomorrow on this duty. Issued orders for Capt. Young and B section to proceed tomorrow through Field Ambulance. From 8pm 23-5-17 to 8pm 24-5-17. 3 wounded and 44 sick passed through Field Ambulance.	Appendix 24 Appendix 25
"	25/5/17		Capt. Young, with B section marched at 7.30 a.m. in rear of 177th Infantry Brigade to Rest Camp near EQUANCOURT. The section bivouacked there for the night. I proceeded to LECHELLE, with Capt. Young later and made arrangements for him to march those tomorrow with B section and commence the erection of West Station. From 8pm 24-5-17 to 8pm 25-5-17. no wounded, 22 sick passed through Field Amb. Sent 2 horse ambulances and 2 motor ambulances to collect men of the 177 I.B. falling out on the line of march to LECHELLE. B section under Capt. Young marched	Appendix 26
"	26/5/17		Proceeded this morning with the Quartermaster to LECHELLE and commenced work on the new camp. From EQUANCOURT to LECHELLE 25/5/17. From 8pm 25/5/17 to 8pm 26/5/17. 12 sick passed through Field Amb.	Appendix 27

Vol. V Page 5 Army Form C. 2118.

WAR DIARY
INTELLIGENCE SUMMARY.
(Erase heading not required.)

Place	Date	Hour	Summary of Events and Information	Remarks and references to Appendices
BOUVINCOURT	27/5/17		Work of preparing Field Ambulance site at LECHELLE continued today. Ground cleared - marquees erected - cook-house improved etc. Capt. Watson returned from leave to England. From 8pm 26-5-17 to 8pm. 27-5-17, 4 sick were passed through Field Amb.	Appendix 28
"	28/5/17		Detailed Capt. Young to proceed on temporary duty with 2/5 Lincolns, in relief of M.O. who is sick. Saw Staff Officer of 178th Inf. Brigade today and made arrangements to supply horsed-ambulances to pick up men falling out on line of march into rest area, on 30th, 31st and ... June. Places through Field Ambulance from 8pm 27-5-17 to 8pm 28-5-17. —	Appendix 29
"	29/5/17		Only Notify of route.	
"	30/5/17		178 Inf. Brigade moved into XV Corps area today. Sent 'C' Section under Capt. Ellis to march with the Brigade, and horsed ambulances to follow & pick up men falling out. Transferred Headquarters the ambulance to LECHELLE (P.25.C.5.5, Sheet 57C, 40,000) today leaving A section behind at Bouvincourt to accompany the 176. Inf. Brigade on 31st.	Appendix 30
LECHELLE	31/5/17		176. Inf. Brigade marched to XV Corps area today. Sent horsed ambulances to carry their men unable to march, and without all remaining personnel & equipment from Bouvincourt today. Capt. Watson marched with A section through to LECHELLE.	Appendix 31

J.W. Johnson
Major Remount
Comdg 2/2 N. Midland Field Amb.

Appendix 1.   War Diary.
Copy.   2/2 Nth. Mid. Fd. Amb.
May 1917.

Confidential.

"A"
Subject: Honours and Rewards.   51/47/11

A.D.M.S. 59th Div.

    The following extract from 4th Army letter No. H/N/AMS dated 27/4/17 is to be communicated to Captain Watson:-

    "With regard to the recommendation of Capt. F.H.C. Watson R.A.M.C. (TF) attached 5th Bn. North Staffs Regt., this Officer's name has been noted for a "Mention in Despatch" in a future Honours Gazette

                              (Signed) E.U. Bradbridge Lt.Col.
1st May 1917   A.A. & Q.M.G. 59th Division

                                                462/20/181

To O.C.
    2/2nd Nth. Mid. Fd. Amb

    Forwarded. Please communicate to Captain Watson R.A.M.C. T.

                              (Signed) H.H.C. Dent Col.
2/5/17   A.D.M.S. 59th Division

Appendix 2.
2/2ⁿᵈ Mid. F⁰ Amb
War diary
May 1917.

Secret.   Special Orders No. 1.   Copy. No 4

by

Lt. Col. J. Colley Burkitt Commg. 2/2nd N.M. Fd. Amb.

Map Ref. 62 c N.E.)
          62 b N.W.) 1/20000

3rd. May 1917

(1) 178th Infantry Brigade will on the 3rd/4th May attack and capture Cologne and Malakoff Farms.

(2) Ambulance Cars:-
    a. Four cars will be stationed on the Roisel-Templeux Road 500 yards S.E. of Templeux under cover of the Hill.
    b. Four cars will be stationed at Roisel.
    c. Three cars will be stationed at Bouvincourt.
These cars are to be in position by 12 midnight on 3rd/4th May. Their positions will be maintained by the system of exchange i.e. when a car arrives at A.D.P. from Templeux if it cannot be immediately returned another car will be sent forward to replace it at once. The same system will be adopted at the A.D.S.

(3) Bearers:-
    (a) Twelve bearers will be sent to R.A.P. at Templeux
    (b) Twelve additional bearers will be sent to A.D.P. Roisel.
        These bearers will be withdrawn and returned to the A.D.S. when collection of wounded is completed.

(4) Acknowledge

Copy No. 1 A.D.M.S.
"   2 A.D.P. Roisel
"   3 War Diary
"   4 War Diary
"   5 File.

2/2nd Nth. Mid. Field Amb.   Appendix 3.

WAR DIARY.   MAY 1917.

Passed through A.D.S.

Unit.	Wounded	Sick. Inf.	Sick. Other Disease.	Diarr.	Septic Sores	Tr. Feet.	Regtl. Totals
2/5 N. Staffs			5	3	5	—	13
2/6 "			4		1		5
2/5 S. Staffs			1		1		2
2/6 "			1		1		2
2/5 Sher. For.	1						1
2/6 "			1	1	2		4
2/7 "			1				1
2/8 "			2				2
2/4 Leicester			2				2
2/5 "	1		2				3
2/4 Lincolns			1				1
T.M.B.	1		1				2
174 M.G.C.				1			1
296 Bde. R.F.A		1	1				2
R.E.		2					2
40 Bde. R.G.A.			1				1
1/7 Lancs. Fus.			2	2			4
1/9 Manchester	1						1
111 Corps Cyclist Co.				1			1
Day Totals	4	3	25	8	10	—	50

From 8 p.m. 5/5/17
To. 8 p.m. 6/5/17.

2/2nd Nth. Mid. Fd. Amb.   Appendix 5

War Diary

May 1917.

	Wd.	Sick. Other Infec. Diseases	Diarr.	Septic Sores	T. Feet	Totals
200 M.G.C.	1					1
37 R.G.A.		1				1
2/5 Sher For.	1	1		1		3
1/7 Lancs. Fus.		1		1		2
2/4th Leics.	2	1				3
1/5 Lancs Fus.		2				2
2/6 S. Staffs		3	1			4
2/6 Sher. For.		1				1
2/4 Lincolns		5				5
2/5 "		2				2
59 Div Sig Co. RE			1			1
III Corps Cav. D.L.O.Y.		1				1
III Corps Cycls.		1				1
1/5th Sussex			1	2		3
2/5 N. Staffs		1				1
2/6 "	1					1
34 Squad. R.F.C				1		1
59 Div. T.M.B.		1				1
2/5 S. Staffs				1		1
175 M.G.C.	1					1
	6	1 20	3	6	—	36

From 8 pm. 6/5/17
To. 8 pm. 7/5/17

2/2nd Nth. Mid. Fd. Amb.　　　　　　Appendix 6

War Diary

May 1917

Unit	Wd.	Sick. Other Inf. Diseases.	Diarr.	Septic Sores	Tr. Feet.	Total.
2/5 Leicesters		1				1
2/6 Sher. For.		1				1
2/4 Leicesters	1	4		1		6
2/5 Sher. For.		2				2
2/8 "		1		1		2
59 T.M.B.	1		1			2
2/6 N. Staffs	1	1	2			4
2/6 S. Staffs	1	2				3
1/7 Lan. Fus.		2				2
2/5 S. Staffs		3	1			4
59 Sig. Co. R.E		1				1
III Corps Cyl. Bn		2				2
296 Bde. R.F.A.		1	1			2
469 Fd. Co. R.E.		1	1			2
Seige Baty. R.G.A		1				1
2/5 N. Staffs		2	3			5
180 Tun. Co. R.E		1				1
	4	26	9	2		41

Passed through A.D.S
From 8 pm. 7/5/17
To   8 p.m. 8/5/17

2/2nd Nth. Mid. Fd. Amb.   Appendix 7

War Diary

May 1917

Unit.	Wd.	Sick. Inf.	Other Diseases.	Diarr.	Septic Sores	Tr. Feet.	Totals
2/7 Sher For.			9	1	1		11
M.G.C.			6				6
3 Co. R.E. Wireless			1				1
K.R.R.			1				1
180 Co. R.E					1		1
4 Fd. Co. R.E.			1				1
59 D.A.C.			1				1
2/6 N. Staffs	33		6		1		40
2/5 "	4		2	1	2		9
2/5 Sher For.	1		1				2
2/6 "				1			1
K.LR. att. A.A.			1				1
2/5 Lincolns			1				1
295 Bde. R.F.A.			1				1
5 Royal Sussex			1		1		2
279 Co. A.S.C			1				1
2/4 Lincolns			1		2		3
2/2 N.M.F.A.			1				1
2/4 Leicesters			1				1
59 T.M.B.			1				1
R.W. Kents att. 59			1				1
469 Fd. Co. R.E			2				2
2/5 S. Staffs			6				6
	38		46	3	8		95

Passed through A.D.S.

From 8 p.m. 8/5/17
To 8 p.m. 9/5/17

2/2nd Nth. Mid. Fd. Amb.　　　　　　　　Appendix 8.

War Diary

May 1917.

Units	Wd.	Sick. Inf.	Other Diseases.	Diarr.	Septic.	Tr. Feet	Totals
177 M.G.C.			1		1		2
295 Bde. R.F.A			1				1
2/5 N.Staffs	2		3	1	1		7
2/6 "	11		1				12
2/6 S.Staffs			2				2
Roy.Can.H.Arty			2				2
2/5 S.Staffs			3				3
296 Bde. R.F.A.			1				1
2/5 Leicesters	2				1		3
2/5 Sher. For.			5				5
2/5 Lincolns			1		2		3
175 M.G.C.			1				1
RAMC att. 2/7 S.For			1				1
2/6 Sher For.				2			2
5 Sussex Regt.					1		1
1/7 Lancs.Fus.			2				2
174 M.G.C			1				1
No.1 Can Rly.Trps.			1				1
No.1 Co.A.S.C.			1				1
2/4 Leicesters			2	1			3
176 T.M.B.	1						1
177 "			1				1
208 S.Bty.R.G.A			1				1
	16		31	4	6		57

Passed Through A.D.S.
From 8 p.m. 9/5/17
To　　8 p.m. 10/5/17

2/2nd Nth. Mid. Fd. Amb.
War Diary
May 1917.

Appendix 9

Secret

Copy No. 3

OPERATION ORDERS NO. 2.

by

Officer Commanding 2/2nd Nth. Mid. Fd. Amb.

Reference France 62 c 1/40000   11/5/17

(1) The Field Ambulance will take over the elephant huts at JEANCOURT for the purpose of forming an A.D.P. on the morning of the 12th inst. The A.D.P. will be staffed by one Officer and twelve other ranks from the A.D.P. BERNES. The Officer in charge will report to Headquarters 177th Infantry Brigade when post is ready to receive wounded.

(2) One Officer and the remainder of the personnel already at A.D.P BERNES will remain at BERNES and the A.D.P. will function until further orders are issued.

(3) Acknowledge.

Copy No. 1   A.D.M.S. 59th Division
"   " 2   M.O. i/c A.D.P. Bernes
"   " 3   War Diary
"   " 4   War Diary
"   " 5   File.

E.M.Calder Capt.
for O.C. 2/2nd Nth. Mid. Fd. Amb.

2/2nd Nth. Mid. Fd Amb. Appendix /0

War Diary

May 1917

Unit.	Wd.	Sick Inf.	Other Diseases.	Diarr.	Septic Sores	Tr. Feet.	Totals
2/5 Leicesters	1						1
2/5 N.Staffs	1		1	1	6		9
2/2 Nth.Mid.Fd.Am.			2				2
2/5 S.Staffs			5		1		6
2/4 Lincolns	1						1
2/6 N.Staffs	3		2	1			6
2/6 S.Staffs	2		3		1		6
2/8 Sher. For.			1				1
2/5 "			2		1		3
2/4 Leicesters	1				1		2
A.S.C.att.2/2nd N.M.Fd. Amb.					1		1
R.A. att.T.M.B.			1				1
1/7 Worsters					1		1
295 Bde.R.F.A.			1				1
2/7 Sher For.			3		1		4
467 Co. R.E.			1				1
12 H.B. R.G.A.			1				1
1 Can.Rly.Tps.			2				2
2/6 Sher For.			2				2
174 M.G.C.			1				1
1/7 Lancs.Fus.					1		1
180 Tun.Co. R.E				1			1
208 Baty.R.G.A.			1				1
	9	—	29	3	14	—	55

Passed through A.D.S.

From 8 p.m. 10/5/17
To   8 p.m. 11/5/17

2/2nd Nth. Mid. Fd. Amb.					Appendix //

War Diary

May 1917.

Unit.	Wd.	Sick. Inf.	Other Diseases.	Diarr.	Septic Sores	Tr. Feet.	Totals
2/4 Leicesters			1		2		3
2/5 "			5		2		7
2/4 Lincolns	2		2				4
126 M.G.C.	1						1
120 R.G.A.			3				3
2/6 S.Staffs	3		2		2		7
174 M.G.C.			1		1		2
2/5 S.Staffs			2	1			3
2/7 Sher For.			4	2	2		8
R.N.A.S.	1						1
176 T.M.B.			1				1
177 M.G.C.			1				1
2/5 Sher For.			2				2
2/6 "			1	1			2
178 T.M.B.			1				1
2/5 Loncolns			4				4
175 M.G.C.			1				1
34 Squad. R.F.C.				1			1
12 H.B. R.G.A.			1				1
2/5 N.Staffs			1				1
R.A.M.C.att.							
2/6 S.Staffs			1				1
2/6 N. Staffs		1	2				3
469 Co. R.E.			2				2
West Lancs.R.F.A.			1				1
	7	1	39	5	9	--	61

Passed through A.D.S.
From 8 pm. 11/5/17
To   8 p.m. 12/5/17

2/2nd Nth. Mid. Fd. Amb.   Appendix 12

War Diary

May 1917

Unit.	Wd.	Sick. Inf.	Other Diseases.	Diarr.	Septic sores	Tr Feet.	Totals
2/8 Sher For.	1	1	2	1			5
2/6 N. Staffs			1		1		2
2/6 S. Staffs	1		3	1			5
120 H.B. R.G.A.			1				1
2/5 N. Staffs			2		1		3
2/4 Leicesters	1		1		1		3
2/4 Lincolns	1		3	1			5
2/5 "		1	1	1	2		5
2/7 Sher For.			1		1		2
2/5 S. Staffs	1						1
2/6 Sher For.				1			1
2/5 "			4				4
470 Co. R.E.			2				2
296 Bde. R.F.A.		1	1				2
1 Can. Rly. Tps.		1	1				2
4 Fd. Sur. Co. R.E			1				1
514 Co. A.S.C.			1				1
1/5 Lancs. Fus.			1				1
K.L.R. Lab. Bn.			1		1		2
2/5 Leicesters			2				2
59 D.A.C.			1				1
180 Tun. Co. R.E			1				1
469 Co. R.E.				1			1
2/3 N.M. Fd. Amb.				1			1
295 Bde. R.F.A.			1				1
	5	4	32	7	7	-	55

Passed through A.D.S.
From 8 p.m. 12/5/17
To   8 p.m. 13/5/17

2/2nd Nth. Mid. Fd. Amb.   Appendix /3

War Diary

May 1917.

Unit.	Wd.	Sick Inf.	Other Diseases.	Diarr.	Septic Sores	Tr. Feet.	Totals
2/5 Sher. For.			5		1		6
2nd K.R. Rifles		2					2
2/5 S. Staffs	1		1				2
120 H.B. R.G.A.	1						1
2/6 S. Staffs			1		1		2
III Corps Cy. Bn			2				2
2/6 Sher For.			2	1			3
101 A.A. Batty.			1				1
177 M.G.C.			1				1
2/7 Sher For.				1	6		7
1 Can. Rly. Tps			1				1
Air Line R.E.			2				2
12 H.B. R.G.A.			1	1			2
2/4 Leicesters				1			1
1/7 Manchesters			1				1
R.E. Wireless			1				1
176 T.M.B.	1						1
2/6 N. Staffs			2				2
2/2nd Nth. M. Fd. Am.			1				1
2/5 Leicesters			2		2		4
59 T.M.B.			1				1
2/5 N. Staffs			1	1	1		3
125 M.G.C.			1				1
175 M.G.C.					1		1
5 Manchester			1				1
A.S.C. E.F. Canteen			1				1
	3	2	29	5	12	–	51

From 8 p.m. 13/5/17
To 8 p.m. 14/5/17

Secret   2/2 Nth. Md. Fd. Amb.   Appendix No 14.
War Diary.
May 1917.   Copy No. 4

OPERATION ORDER No. 3

by

Officer Commanding 2/2nd Nth. Mid. Fd. Amb.

(1) The M.O.i/c A.D.P.s. JEANCOURT and BERNES will hand over the A.D.P. JEANCOURT to the 5th Cavalry Division on 15/5/17 and will withdraw his personnel.

(2) He will close the A.D.P. BERNES on 16/5/17, hand over the Nissen hut to the Town Major and will return with personnel and Mob. Equipment to Headquarters

(3) *Acknowledge.*

W Malcolm Capt.

15/5/17   for O.C. 2/2nd Nth. Mid. Fd. Amb.

Copy.
No. 1   A.D.M.S. 59th Div.
" 2   M.O.i/c A.D.P. Jeancourt & Bernes
" 3   War Diary
" 4   War Diary
" 5   File.

2/2nd Nth. Mid. Fd. Amb.   Appendix 15

War Diary

May 1917.

Unit.	Wd.	Sick Inf.	Other Diseases.	Diarr.	Septics. (Sores)	Tr. Feet.	Totals
2/5 Sher For.	1						1
2/8 "		1	5		2		8
295 Bde. R.F.A.			2				2
120 H.B. R.G.A.			1				1
175 M.G.C.			1				1
2/4 Leicesters	1		1				2
2/5 S.Staffs			1				1
4 Cav. Div. R.H.A. Amm. Col.			1				1
2/6 Sher For.			1		1		2
2/7 "			4				4
2/6 N.Staffs	1		4	1	1		7
174 M.G.C.					1		1
59 T.M.B.			2				2
Kings R. Rifles		1	3		1		5
2/5 N.Staffs			4	1	12		17
2/4 Lincolns			1		1		2
2/6 S. Staffs			2				2
	3	2	33	2	19	—	59

Passed through A.D.S.

From 8 p.m. 14/5/17
To   8 p.m. 15/5/17

2/2nd Nth. Mid. Fd. Amb.   Appendix 18

War Diary

May 1917

Unit.	Wd.	Sick. Inf.	Other Diseases	Diarr.	Septic.	Tr. Feet.	Total.
2/5 Sher For			1				1
2/6 "			6		1		7
2/7 "					1		1
2/5 S.Staffs		1-Ven	7		2		10
2/6 "			3		1		4
2/5 N.Staffs	1		1		1		3
2/6 "	1		3				4
2/4 Leicesters			2				2
2/5 Leicesters			3				3
59 T.M.B.			1				1
2/5 Lincolns			4		1		5
D.L.O. Yeo.			1				1
1/7 Lancs			1				1
90 Lab. Bn. K.LR.			1				1
1 Can. Rly Tps.			1				1
120 H.B. R G.A			2				2
40 Siege Bat.R.G.A			2				2
180 Fd. Co.R.E			1				1
	2	1	40	–	7		50

Passed through A.D.S.

From 8 p.m. 17/5/17
To   8 p.m. 18/5/17

2/2nd. Nth.Mid.Fld.Amb.   Appendix. 19

War Diary

May 1917.

Unit.	Wd.	Sick Inf.	Sick Other	Diar.	Septic Sores	Tr. Feet.	Total.
2/5 N.Staffs.	1		3	1	2		7
2/6 "	1		1				2
2/6 S.Staffs.			1	1			2
2/4 Lesters			3		1		4
2/5 "	1		1				2
2/5 Lincolns.			2				2
2/7 S.Foresters.			2	1	4		7
2/8 "			4		2		6
2/5 S.Staffs.			2				2
295 Bde.R.F.A.					1		1
296 "			1				1
No.3 Coy.A.S.C.			1				1
21 Sec.A.A. Bty.			1				1
1 Can.Rly Troops.			3				3
177 M.G.C.					1		1
469 Fd.Coy.R.E.					1		1
90 Lab.Batt.K.L.Pool.			1				1
120.Hy.R.G.A.			1				1
59 T.M.B.			1				1
	3	—	28	3	12	—	46.

Passed Through A.D.S.

From. 8p.m. 18/5/17.
To   8p.m. 19/5/17.

2/2nd.Nth.Mid.Fd.Amb.   Appendix. 20.

War Diary.

May, 1917.

Unit.	Wd.	Inf. Sick.	Other	Diar.	Septic Sores	Tr. Feet.	Total.
2/5.S.Foresters.			1.				1
2/5.N.Staffs.			1.		1.		2.
2/6.S.Staffs.	2				3.		5.
2/4.Lesters			3.		1.		4.
2/5. "			1.		1.		2.
2/4.Lincolns.			3.				3.
2/5. "			1.		1.		2.
296.Bde.R.F.A.			1.				1.
295. "					1.		1.
2/6.N.Staffs.	3.				2.		5.
180.T.Coy.R.E.	1.		1.				2.
210.R.F.A.			1.				1.
	6.	-	13.	-	9.	-	26.

Passed Through A.D.S.

From. 8 p.m. 19/5/17.
To.   8 p.m. 20/5/17.

2/2nd. Nth. Mid. Fd. Ambce.   Appendix. 21

War Diary.

May. 1917.

Unit.	Wd.	Inf. Screen Disease	Other Disease	Diar.	Septics. Sores	Tr. Feet.	Total.
2/5. S. Staffs.			5.		2.		7.
2/6. "					9.		9.
2/5. N. Staffs.		1.					1.
2/6. "			3.		1.		4.
2/4. Lesters.			1.				1.
2/4. Lincolns.					1.		1.
2/5. "			1.				1.
295 Bde. R.F.A.			3.				3.
174. M.G.C.	1.		1.		1.		3.
1??. "			2.				2.
1. Lester. Yeo.					1.		1.
1. Can. Rly. Troops.				1.			1.
2/8. S. Foresters.			1.				1.
59. Div. Train. A.S.C.			1.				1.
513. Coy. A.S.C.			1.				1.
A.S.C. att. 2/2.N.M.F.A.			1.				1.
	1.	1.	20.	1.	15.	—	38.

Passed Through A.D.S.

From. 8 p.m. 20/5/17.

To.   8 p.m. 21/5/17.

2/2nd. Nth. Mid. Fd. Amb. Appendix. 22

War Diary.

May 1917.

Unit.	Wd.	Sick.	Diar.	Septics. Sores	Total.
2/5 N. Staffs.		4.		2.	6.
2/6. "	1.	4.			5.
2/5. S. Staffs.	1.	1.			2.
2/6. "		3.			3.
2/7. S. Foresters.		2.	1.	1.	4.
2/8. "		1.		1.	2.
2/4. Lesters.		2.		1.	3.
2/5. "				1.	1.
2/4. Lincs.		3.			3.
2/5. "		2.			2.
177. M.G.C.		1.			1.
No. 3. G.R.U.		1.			1.
90 Lab. K.L. Pool.		1.			1.
469 Fd. Coy. R.E.		1.			1.
10 Res. Park.		1.			1.
2/2. N.M.F.Ambce.		1.			1.
1st. Can. Rly. Tro.		1.			1.
	2.	29.	1.	6.	38.

Passed through A.D.S.

From. 8 p.m. 21/5/17.

To. 8 p.m. 22/5/17.

2/2nd. Nth.Mid.Fd.Amb. Appendix. 23

War Diary.

May 1917.

Unit.	Wd.	Sick.	Diar.	Septic. Sore.	Total
2/5. N.Staffs.		5.			5.
2/6. "		6.			6.
2/6. S.Staffs.		2.			2.
2/4. Lincolns.		3.	1.	1.	4.
2/5. "		1.		1.	2.
2/7. S.Foresters.		1.			1.
2/8. "		1.		1.	2.
2/5. Lesters.		1.			1.
11 M.G.C.	1.				1.
469 Fd.Coy.R.E.			1.		1.
174. M.G.C.				1.	1.
59 Div. Supply Col.		1.			1.
59 T.M.B.	1.				1.
10 Res. Pk. A.S.C.		1.			1.
R.E. ?		1.			1.
120 R.G.A.		1.			1.
37 Siege R.G.A.		1.			1.
R.A.M.C. att. 2/5.Lesters.		1.			1.
1st. Can.Rly. Troops.		2.			2.
	2.	28.	1.	4.	35.

Passed through A.D.S.

From. 8.pm. 22/5/17.
So. 8.p.m. 23/5/17.

Appendix 2v

OPERATION ORDERS 2/2nd. N.M.F.Amb.

"B" Section, under Capt. Young, with transport and two horsed ambulances will parade at 6.45. a.m. in marching order ready to move off at 7.0. a.m.

    Reveille.   5.0. a.m.
    Roll Call.   5.15. a.m.
    Breakfast.   5.45. a.m.

Route. - via Beaumetz and Hancourt.

The section will follow in rear of the 177th. Infantry Brigade from Hancourt.

Route. - Boucly, Tincourt, Templeux - la -Fosse, Aizecourt, Nurlu, to Rest Camp South of Equancourt.

The Section will billet there for the night.

H.W. Johnson

In the Field.
24/5/17.
                        Major Commanding,
            2/2nd. N.Mid. Field Ambulances.

2/2nd. Nth.Mid.Fd.Amb.   Appendix. 25

War Diary.

May 1917.

Unit.	Wd.	Sick.	Diar.	Septic sores.	Total.
No. 3 G.R.U.		1.			1.
2/5. N.Staffs.		6.		1.	7.
2/8. S.Foresters.		2.	1.		3.
2/6. S.Staffs.	2.	3.	1.	3.	9.
2/2 N.M.F.Amb.		1.			1.
177 M.G.C.		2.		1.	3.
2/5. Lesters.		5.		2.	7.
2/1. N & D.Mtd.F.Amb.		1.			1.
2/5. Lincs.		1.			1.
1st. Can.Rly.Troops.		1.			1.
2/4. Lincs.		1.			1.
469. Fd.Coy.R.E.		1.			1.
4th.Cav.10.M.G.Sq.		1.			1.
4th.In.Cav.10.Res.A.S.C.		1.	(Gonorrhea.)		1.
90th. Labour Coy.		1.			1.
2/5. S.Foresters.	1.				1.
1st.Ind.Cav.R.H.A.		1.			1.
2/7. S.Foresters.		1.		3.	4.
59th.R.G.A.12 H.Bat.		2.			2.
	3.	32.	2.	10.	47.

(In addition 45 Dental Cases have passed through.)

Passed through A.D.S.

From. 8.p.m. 23/5/17.
To.   8.p.m. 24/5/17.

2/2nd. Nth.Mid.Fd.Amb.   Appendix. 26

War Diary.

May 1917.

Unit.	Wd.	Sick.	Diar.	Septic.	Total.
2/4th. Lesters.		3.			3.
2/6th. S.Staffs.		3.			3.
2/5th. N.Staffs.			1.		1.
2/5.th. Lincs.		2.		3.	5.
2/4.th. "		5.			5.
2/5.th.Lesters.		2.		1.	3.
513. Coy. A.S.C.		1.			1.
2/7.th.S.Foresters.		1.			1.
	–	17.	1.	1.	22.

Passed through A.D.S.

From. 8.p.m. 24/5/17.

To.   8.p.m. 25/5/17.

2/2nd. Nth.Mid.Fd.Amb.   Appendix. 27

War Diary.

May 1917.

Unit.	Wd.	Sick. Inf.	Sick. Other.	Diar.	Septics.	Total
2/2nd.N.M.F.A. (att) 513 Coy.A.S.C.			1.			1.
470. Fd.Coy.R.E.			1.			1.
No.4 Sec.Sigs.R.E.	1.		1.			2.
296. Bde.R.F.A.				1.		1.
2/6. S.Staffs.			1.			1.
175. M.G.Corps.					1.	1.
2/7. S.Foresters.			1.			1.
R.G.A. 12 How.Battery.			1.			1.
59th. D.A.C.			1.			1.
59th. A.O.C.			1.			1.
	—	1.	9.	1.	1.	12.

Passed through A.D.S.

From. 8.p.m. 25/5/17.
To.   8.p.m. 26/5/17.

2/2nd. Nth. Mid. Fd. Ambce.　　　　Appendix. 28

War Diary.

May 1917.

Unit.	Wd.	Sick.	Diar.	Total.
2/8th. S.Foresters.		1.		1.
4th. Div. R.H.A.			1.	1.
2/4th. Lesters.		1.		1.
2/5th. S.Foresters.		1.		1.
-		3.	1.	4.

Passed through A.D.S.

From 8p.m. 26/5/17.
To. 8.p.m. 27/5/17.

2/2nd. Nth.Mid. Fd.Ambce.   Appendix. 29

                    War Diary.

                    May 1917.

Unit.	Wd.	Sick.	Septic.	Diar.	Total.
174 M.G.Coy.		3.			3.
2/6th. N.Staffs.		1.			1.
—	—	4.	—	—	4.

Passed through A.D.S.

From. 8p.m. 27/5/17.

To.   8.p.m. 28/5/17.

Appendix 30

OPERATIONS ORDERS.

2/2nd. North Mid. Fd. Ambulance.

1. On 29/5/17. two horsed ambulances will leave BOUVINCOURT at 6. p.m. and proceed to HAMELET, where they will report to M.O., 2/7th. Sherwood Foresters, and billet there for the night. Route- BOUVINCOURT, HANCOURT, HAMELET.
   Rations for 30th. inst. to be carried.

2. On 30th. inst. the two horsed ambulances at HAMELET will march at 5.30.a.m. in rear of 2/7th. Sherwood Foresters to camp south of EQUANCOURT, picking up any men of the brigade falling out on the march. On arrival at EQUANCOURT, they will report to Capt. Ellis, fresh horses will be obtained and they will return to BOUVINCOURT.

3. Another horsed ambulance will leave BOUVINCOURT at 4.45am 30/5/17. and proceed via HANCOURT and ROISEL to VILLERS FAUCON. It will go through the village and wait just outside, on the road leading to SAULCOURT, until the 2/8th. Sherwood Foresters pass, and will follow them to camp east of EQUANCOURT. After completion of duty, it will go on to the camp south of EQUANCOURT and report to Capt. Ellis.

4. C. Section (as detailed) will parade under Capt. Ellis at 3.45.a.m., and march at 4.0.a.m., via. HANCOURT, TEMPLEUX BOUCLY, TINCOURT, TEMPLEUX - LA - FOSSE to AIZECOURT - LE - BAS.
   They will not enter the village before 6.30.a.m. and will wait until the 2/7th. Sherwood Foresters have passed through. They will then follow the 2/7th. Sherwood Foresters to camp south of EQUANCOURT, billeting there for the night.
   An Officer will ride forward from NURLU and make arrangements for billeting with STAFF CAPTAIN and be ready to direct the section to its lines on arrival.

30/5/1917.

Comdg 2/2 N. Mid. Fd. Amb.

Appendix 31

OPERATION ORDERS.

BY

MAJOR F.W. JOHNSON COMDG. 2/2 N.M. FD. AMB.

31. 5. 17.

1. All personnel remaining with the exception of Sgt. Oakley and 4 men will parade at 3.45 p.m. in full marching order, ready to move off at 4.0 p.m. under Capt. Watson, march via HANCOURT, BOUCLY, TINCOURT, TEMPLEUX-LA-FOSSE, and AIZE-COURT-LE-BAS.
They will arrive at AIZECOURT-LE-BAS by 7 p.m. and wait there until the 2/5th. North Staffords pass through.
They will then follow that Battalion to camp South of EQUANCOURT ~~and billet there for the night~~, proceeding to LECHELLE ~~next morning~~. after a halt.
"A" section transport will accompany this party.

2. Two horsed ambulances will leave BOUVINCOURT at 4.30 p.m. and proceed to HAMELET, and will follow in rear of the 2/5th. North Staffords who leave there at 6 p.m.
They will follow the Battalion to camp South of EQUANCOURT and then report to Capt. Watson.

F W Johnson
Major,
O.C. 2/2nd. Nth. Mid. Fd. Ambulce.

Original

Confidential

War Diary
of
2/2 H. C. F. A.
R. A. M. C.

From 1-6-17.
To 30-6-17

Volume 6

COMMITTEE FOR THE
MEDICAL HISTORY OF THE WAR
Date -7 AUG. 1917

To A.D.M.S.,
    59th. Division.

War Diary for June returned herewith, please.

                                                    Major.
3.7.17.   O.C. 2/2nd. N. Mid. Fd. Ambulance.

WAR DIARY

2/2. 20th Midland Field Ambulance

INTELLIGENCE SUMMARY

Army Form C. 2118.

Vol VI Page 1

Place	Date	Hour	Summary of Events and Information	Remarks and references to Appendices
LECHELLE	1/6/17		The Field Ambulance is now fulfilling the function of a Detention Hospital for sick. No wounded are admitted (all are sent to Corps main Dressing Station at Fins). Only slight cases likely to be fit for duty in a few days are being retained here. Hospital accommodation consisting of marquees & belltents has now been erected on a good site about 5 miles from the front line. Sanitary arrangements satisfactory. 13 sick admitted to-day.	JFJ
"	2/6/17		Cpl R. Cox detailed for temporary duty with 59 D.A.C. 26 sick admitted to-day. Working parties from the unit detailed for road repairs in neighbourhood of the camp. Rest detailed for divisional baths etc.	JFJ
"	3/6/17		21 sick admitted. Church of England Service for C.E. Non-C of E & R.C. held in camp during the day. Details training under A.D.M.S. instructions for divisional baths etc. Construction work at Corps Main Dressing Station & 20, 21 C.C.S. etc.	JFJ
"	4/6/17		A.D.M.S. visited the camp to-day. Nothing of note to report today. 28 sick admitted.	JFJ
"	5/6/17		34 sick admitted today. Very hot weather. Comparatively large number of sick is no doubt due to weather conditions.	JFJ
"	6/6/17		26 sick admitted today. Everything is being done to reduce the number of flies. Manure heaps covered or burnt & ground cleaned up about the village. Capt E.D. Ellis admitted to hospital & transferred to Cas.	JFJ
"	7/6/17		26 sick admitted to-day. Sent 25 men to assist in construction of a new 3 Corps Rest Sta: Main Dressing Station at Moislains, which is being established by 2/1 N. Mid. F. Amb.	JFJ
"	8/6/17		Nothing of note. 20 sick admitted during the day.	
"	9/6/17		Today I received information that the ambulance will probably be moved from LECHELLE to LE MESNIL in the near future. I therefore visited LE MESNIL this morning to see what ground was available. Found very bare ground everywhere. 35 sick admitted today.	JFJ
"	10/6/17		Usual work today. C.E. service in camp this afternoon. 31 sick admitted.	JFJ
"	11/6/17		Severe thunderstorm during night lasting 5 hours. Camp flooded this morning. All available men & all types in drainage. Wrote to O.C. 5 admission tray-incase accounted for by fact that 176 Bde. goes into the line today.	JFJ

Army Form C. 2118.

2/2nd North Midland or Field Ambulance

Vol VI Part 2

WAR DIARY INTELLIGENCE SUMMARY

(Erase heading not required.)

Place	Date	Hour	Summary of Events and Information	Remarks and references to Appendices
LECHELLE	12/6/17		Evacuated over 50 men today. 6 either highly diseased states or temp/ront states. Admitted 31. D.D.M.S. 32nd Corps visiting the hospital today with A.D.M.S. He gave instructions & more hospital accommodation is to be delayed near Dressing Station. Prepared with rest bivouaced. Capt. L. Lazarus R.A.M.C. (Temp) joined for duty today from the Base. F.J.J.	
"	13/6/17		Erected another large tarpaulin bivouac to accommodate personnel in it. This provides room for 50 more patients. Admitted 36 today. F.J.J.	
"	14/6/17		Two more Medical Officers, Lieuts. J.C. Marshall R.A.M.C. (Temp) & C.J.D. Bergin R.A.M.C (Temp) joined for duty today from the Base. Admitted 36 today. F.J.J.	
"	15/6/17		Nothing of note — Admitted 32 sick. F.J.J.	
"	16/6/17		Visited A.D.M.S. this morning. A.A.Q.M.G. 59th Div. visited the hospital today. Admitted 48 sick. F.J.J.	
"	17/6/17		Capt. Lazarus sent 6 3rd Corps Convalescent Depot. Going today for temp. duty (D.D.M.S. letter.) Admitted 36 F.J.J.	
"	18/6/17		Nothing of note — Thunderstorm & heavy rain. Admitted 34. F.J.J.	
"	19/6/17		Visited LE MESNIL with A.D.M.S. & finally selected site for Field Ambulance in case of a move into that district. Admitted today 34. F.J.J.	
"	20/6/17		Nothing of note. Sick admissions today 42. Total patients in hospital now 160. Our accommodation being now fully taken up. There are an slight pyrexia cases well in indoors in bivs & infection. Burden of sick is chiefly due to the exceptionally hot weather, the temp. being 10 sq F.J.J.	
"	21/6/17		A.D.M.S. & A.D.V.S. visited us today & inspected the hospital. Evacuated 15, admitted 14. 6 Corps Reg. St. & C.C.S. One Prussian prisoner (wagon) 631st I.R. admitted slightly wounded. Transport to 137 F.A. by order of A.D.M.S attached to Cav. G.O.C. 59th Div. who inspected the hospital & camp this afternoon. F.J.J.	
"	22/6/17		Visited British Red Cross stores at Ságnicourt this afternoon with a view to obtaining some comforts for the inmates of the hospital. 37 sick admitted. F.J.J.	
"	23/6/17		Nothing of note. Capt. F.H.C. Walton detailed for temporary duty with 2/6 N. Staffs. Batty. 36 sick admitted. F.J.J.	

Army Form C. 2118.

Vol VI Page 3

WAR DIARY
or
INTELLIGENCE SUMMARY

2/2nd North Midland Field Ambulance

Place	Date	Hour	Summary of Events and Information	Remarks and references to Appendices
LECHELLE	24/6/17		Nothing of note. Daily admissions of sick, 24th 21; 25th 22, 26th 32. JW.	
"	25/6/17			
"	26/6/17			
"	27/6/17		Various improvements carried out. The last foot-trap in the hospital - enlarged the pack-store. Improved the bathing & ablution arrangements, & further Knockdown walk. Sick admitted 42. JW.	
"	28/6/17		Visited Sanitary Exhibition at PERONNE today, with the Q.M. & Capt. Young, 1st/1st service. Much useful information. July 18 sick admitted today. JW.	
"	29/6/17		Usual routine. 25 sick admitted. JW.	
"	30/6/17		38 sick admitted. Attended lecture at French Military hospital Amiens with A.D.M.S. & other officers on the subject of Carrel's method of treatment of wounds. The health of the troops has been on the whole good during the month, and the proportion of number of sick admitted has not been excessive and serious cases have not been any, I serious case is very small. Diarrhoea has not been serious. JW.	

J W Stevenson
Major
O.C. 2/2ND N. MID. FD. AMB. R.A.M.C.

30 JUN 1917

Confidential War Diary of 2/2 N. Mid. Fd. Amb.

FROM. 1-7-17   To 31-7-17

VOLUME

Committee for the Medical History of the War — 10 SEP 1917

Army Form C. 2118.

2/2nd North Midland Field Ambulance Vol VII Pages

WAR DIARY

~~INTELLIGENCE SUMMARY~~

(Erase heading not required.)

Place	Date	Hour	Summary of Events and Information	Remarks and references to Appendices
MESNIL (P.2.5.C.Central) Sheet 57C FRANCE 20000	1/7/17		22 sick admitted today. Services held in hospital wards this afternoon. F.W.	
"	2/7/17		35 sick admitted. Ordinary routine of work. (Authority A.D.M.S. letter A.D.M.S.M.1467) F.W.	
"	3/7/17		Despatched Lt. J. Cole Marshall to 44th Army of Kitchener Centre, PERONNE for Temporary duty. Increase in number of sick due to Infantry Brigade going into Line from Reserve Camp. 45 sick admitted. F.W.	
"	4/7/17		36 sick admitted. Nothing of note today. F.W.	
"	5/7/17		A.D.M.S. visited hospital this morning. 34 Sick admitted. Transferred 20 cases to new Corps Rest Station at MOISLAINS. (2/1st N.M.D.F.Amb.) who are now ready for patients. F.W.	
"	6/7/17		Reduced number of patients in hospital by sending another 30 to Corps Rest Station Moislains this evening. Of the large store tent to be used as a dining tent. 34 admitted. F.W.	
"	7/7/17		One Infantry Brigade (176") moved this morning from EQUANCOURT to the new Divisional area, near BARASTRE (O.9.d. q 10c. Sheet 57C). Made arrangements for collecting sick from them until 2/3 N.M.D. F.Amb. moved to the new area. 17 Sick admitted. F.W. Brigade pertains to the 58th Division, our Brigade pertains to Equancourt.	
"	8/7/17		58 sick admitted today - a large number belong to the 2/3 Home Counties F. Amb. at BUS now at Equancourt.	
"	9/7/17		Visited A.D.M.S. office this morning. Arranged to transfer sick of 58th Division to the Equancourt Hosp. Admitted 42 during today, including a large proportion of 58 Div. This relieved the congestion here. Lieut F.W. JOHNSON to be acting Adjutant Col whilst Commanding 2/2 N. mid. F. Mad. (May 25") Extract from 59 Div R.O. "Capt (Temp Major) F.W. → M." 2/3 → 1/3 Corps. The Infantry Brigade are now all in Camps in the ROCQUIGNY area. Visiting the 178 (Sherwood Foresters) Brigade near LE MESNIL Huts arrangements for collecting their sick. Also arrangd to collect the sick of the 177 (Lincoln & Leicester) Brigade, near BARASTRE.	
"	10/7/17		22 sick admitted during the day. F.W.	

WAR DIARY

2/2ⁿᵈ North Midland or Field Ambulance Vol VII. Page 2

Army Form C. 2118.

INTELLIGENCE SUMMARY.

(Erase heading not required.)

Instructions regarding War Diaries and Intelligence Summaries are contained in F.S. Regs., Part II. and the Staff Manual respectively. Title pages will be prepared in manuscript.

Place	Date	Hour	Summary of Events and Information	Remarks and references to Appendices
ECHELLE	10/7/17		A.D.M.S. visited us this morning. 22 sick admitted during the day.	F.o.g.
"	12/7/17		D.D.M.S. II Corps inspected the hospital & camp this morning. 40 patients admitted today.	F.o.g.
"	13/7/17		nothing of note. 27 admissions.	F.o.g.
"	14/7/17		nothing of note. 33 admissions today. Full.	
"	15/7/17		Athletic & other competitions are being held during the Divisional Rest – arrangements made today to select representatives from the R.A.M.C. of the Division. Only 13 sick admitted to-day.	Full.
"	16/7/17		Nothing of note. July 17 sick admitted.	J.P.
"	17/7/17		Capt. R. Cox rejoined from duty with DAC. details, and was posted for temporary duty with 59 Div. Train. 17 sick admitted during the day.	F.o.g.
"	18/7/17		20 sick admitted. Capt. R. Cox rejoined for duty, an M.O. having been appointed to the 59 Div. Train Fy.	
"	19/7/17		19 sick admitted. A Divisional Transport Competition was held today. This unit entered 14 competitions & won 1st prize for G.S. Wagon turn out & 2nd prize for water cart.	F.o.g.
"	20/7/17		24 sick admitted today. Divisional holiday observed – 11 am. Conf. on occasion of Divisional Sports.	F.o.g.
"	21/7/17		23 sick admitted. About 60 in hospital now. Lt. J. Cole Marshall posted to 2ⁿᵈ Army for Orl.[?] taking work. Lt. Keay (authority Admin. 59 Div. & D.R. M.S. 9 H.Q.) F.o.g.	
"	23/7/17		23 sick admitted. No.1 F.E. & C.F.E. services held us during last today.	F.o.g.
"	24/7/17		19 sick admitted. Nothing of note to [report?].	F.o.g.
"			The Division is carrying out a Tactical Scheme on the 27ᵗʰ inst. comprising an attack on "enemy" trenches in the training area near SAILLY-SAILLISEL. Instructions received from A.D.M.S. to prepare a scheme for the collection & evacuation of sick and 1600 casualties from the 177ᵗʰ & 178ᵗʰ Inf. try. Brigades who will attack on the left. I went over the ground today with Capt. Mitchell, an A.D.S./A divisional dressing Sta.) Bearer Posts & C I drew up a plan for the right brigade in the Tactical Scheme & Fw.f.	
"	25/7/17		Met O.C. 2/3 N. Mid. F. Amb., who is responsible for the Casualties in the movements of this F. Amb. & transferred with him as to arrangements.	F.S.J.

2/2 North Midland Field Ambulance   Vol VII Page 3

WAR DIARY or INTELLIGENCE SUMMARY

Army Form C. 2118.

Place	Date	Hour	Summary of Events and Information	Remarks and references to Appendices
LECHELLE	26/7/17		Number of cases in hospital now averages 70 - from the two brigades collected from. 20 admitted today. ADM.S. visited the hospital today.	J.W.J.
"	27/7/17		Divisional Tactical Scheme carried out this morning. Two M.O.'s, the Sergt Major & 3 N.C.O.'s attended with myself, & the forming of advanced Dressing Stations &c. (inc. the evacuation routes) & stretcher cases brought by. 19 sick admitted today.	J.W.J.
"	28/7/17		Instructions received to be prepared to detail 1 M.O. & Tent Sub division to 21 C.C.S. Capt. C.J.D. Bequin & 15 other ranks proceeded there during the day. 30 sick admitted during the day.	J.W.J.
"	29/7/17		Orders received to despatch party to 21 C.C.S. 13 admissions today. Severe thunderstorm during the afternoon.	J.W.J.
"	30/7/17		Nothing of note. 20 sick admitted.	J.W.J.
"	31/7/17		20 sick admitted today. A.D.M.S. inspected the hospital camp. Also visited by B.D.M.S. IV Corps. Advising Officer in Horse management IV Corps visited the horse lines today. Total number of patients in hospital averages about 75 (70) daily. About half this number are cases of "P.U.O." most of which show definite signs of "Trench Fever." The greater number are fit for duty again after about 7 days in the Field Ambulance, a further 7-10 days in the Corps Rest Station. Except for these cases of "P.U.O." the sickness of the two Brigades this Ambulance collects from has been very small in amount - instructors have been carried out during the month while the Division was in Training, and anti-gas protection. Re-work of the Ambulance in the Field.	

J W Munro Lt Col RAMC
Comdg 2/2 N Midland F Amb

Confidential
War Diary
of
2/2 N. Mid. Fd. Amb

From 1-8-17   To 31-8-17

Volume 8

WAR DIARY

2/2nd North Midland Field Ambulance

INTELLIGENCE SUMMARY

Army Form C. 2118.

Vol: VIII. Page 1.

Place	Date	Hour	Summary of Events and Information	Remarks and references to Appendices
LECHELLE P.25.c.central Sheet 57c FRANCE 1/40,000	1.8.17		Detachment of 25 men who have been attached to the 2/1st N. Midland Field Amb Troops, the Cavalry Section of III Corps Rest Station, MOISLAINS, were relieved today. (Authority D.D.M.S. III Corps. J.W.) No admissions during today. 24.	
"	2.8.17		Capt. W.J. Nicholl returned from temporary duty with 2/4 Lincoln Regt. (Authority ADMS 57 Div. J.W.) 21 sick admitted today.	
"	3.8.17		D.M.S. 3rd Army, with D.D.M.S. III Corps inspected the hospital camp today & expressed himself all arrangements. He suggested that a commencement might be made in making out a hutting scheme for the Field Ambulance site, & the provision of drying rooms etc. Capt F.H.C. Watson returned from temporary duty with 2/6 North Staff.d Regt. (Authority ADMS 59 Div. J.W.) 13 sick admitted during the day. Standing for the motor Ambulances, and also for the Horse lines - the Latter having only a temporary arrangement. 30 sick admitted J.W. Commenced making a formed wood standing for the construction of a drying room. Completed wood	
"	4.8.17		Made preliminary arrangements for the construction of a temporary summary drying room. 21 sick admitted. J.W.	
"	5.8.17		Made preliminary arrangements of hot air standing for hot air ambulances. 25 sick admitted. J.W.	
"	6.8.17		Nothing of note. 32 sick admitted. J.W.	
"	7.8.17		Nothing of note.	
"	8.8.17		D.D.M.S. IV Corps visited us today & enquired as to the class of cases sent to hospital by R.M.O.s of Treatment. It was shown that no cases or very few which could be treated regimentally while in reserve, are being sent to hospital here. J.W. 18 sick admitted. J.W. Commenced construction of Drying Room, which will consist of an iron "elephant house" type about concrete with tin indiarubber. Heavy rain prevented much work being done.	
"	9.8.17		24 sick admitted.	
"	10.8.17		Drying room construction continued. Scheme prepared & submitted to A.D.M.S. for the provision of hut accommodation for this Field Ambulance site. No replacement canvas in use at present. J.W.	

J.W.

Vol VIII Page 2

Army Form C. 2118.

WAR DIARY
2/2nd North Midland Field Ambulance
INTELLIGENCE SUMMARY

(Erase heading not required.)

Place	Date	Hour	Summary of Events and Information	Remarks and references to Appendices
LECHELLE	11/8/17		D.D.M.S. IV. Corps. inspected the hospitals and camp. He expressed his approval of present conditions and gave instructions that the making of walkways &c to render the camp suitable for winter use should be proceeded with. 2/2NMFA. Lieut. Col. Johnson proceeded on 10 days leave to England. 2/2NMFA.	
"	12.8.17		Lieut C.J.D. Bergin proceeded on 15 days contact leave to England. 2/2NMFA.	
"	13.8.17		Capt. F.H.C. Watson was evacuated to 48 C.C.S. suffering from P.U.O. 2/2NMFA.	
"	14.8.17		Nothing of note. 2/2NMFA.	
"	15.8.17		" " " " 2/2NMFA.	
"	16.8.17		" " " " 2/2NMFA.	
"	17.8.17		" " " " 2/2NMFA.	
"	18.8.17		Nothing of note 2/2NMFA. Capt. F.H.C. Watson returned to duty from hospital. 2/2NMFA.	
"	19.8.17		Nothing of note 2/2NMFA.	
"	20.8.17		Received A.D.M.S. 7th Div. Order No 20 containing instructions to move until 178 Inf. Bde on 24.8.17, by bus & route march to camp between BOUZINCOURT & AVELUY. 2/2NMFA.	
"	21.8.17		Evacuated 94 patients 6.28.7 D. Amb. and 64 patients to C.C.S. in accordance with D.M.S. line. D.M.S. 645 of 20.8.17. 2/2NMFA.	
"	22.8.17		Made preparations for packing etc incidental to movement. 2/2NMFA.	
"	23.8.17		131 Inf.Bde. Order No10 + March Table received, with instructions to proceed to camp between AVELUY + BOUZINCOURT (Shut. 57.D). 2/2NMFA.	
"	24.8.17		Field Ambulance left LECHELLE this morning according to Bde orders, a portion proceeding to march to points S.W. of Bapaume en route there to entrain for the destination — a camp between Aveluy + Bouzincourt. The shut. arrived at destination about 4 p.m. ... [illegible details]... reported to 17 & 8 Inf.Bde ... before leaving LECHELLE Capt. McBeath handed over 2 nco 5 men & 9 hrs of the 158 F.Amb. (36.Div.) Fy. [see Appendix 3]	Appendix 3

Vol VIII Page 3

2/2 North Midland Field Ambulance

Army Form C. 2118.

WAR DIARY or INTELLIGENCE SUMMARY.
(Erase heading not required.)

Place	Date	Hour	Summary of Events and Information	Remarks and references to Appendices
BOUZINCOURT - AVELUY Road 57.b.0.9 Sheet 57D	25/8/17		The morning was occupied in cleaning up the camp which consists of a number of huts of different types & the preparing of tomas hospital in Bettenune. Wire from the 178 Brigade group (2 cards admitted today) Brigade commands 178 Bue visits the camp this morning. Arrangements made for a daily collection truck from the 1st R.A.P.s, at the hy. & which we all situated between the camp and AVELUY. FnT	
"	26.8.17		Church parade (C.of E.) held at 10 a.m. with the 1/470 F'd G. RE. Box respirator practice after. FnT	
"	27.8.17		Inspection by G.O.C. 59 Div. at BOUZINCOURT at 11 a.m. FnT. Orders received to send an advance party & the new area - minimum 28 a/n. & to be preferred to arrive the unit at BEAUCOURT on the 30 inst. Reconnoitre the road out & return with Capt. Malcolm this morning. FnT	
"	28.8.17		Col Lindsay O.M.S. for newly appointed ADMS 57 Div. visits the camp this morning. Despatched Capt. Cox, 1 Sgt. 1 man by motor ambulance to repair & fixed (connected St. POL LILLERS HAZEBROUCK) to meet the WINNEZEELE (the advance Division STRL billeting from at F.D.) FnT. Brigade artillery party on arrival (around 1st 178 Bde between 30-31st until moved to be loan received for most 5 sections up to 178 Bde again from Visiting 178 Bde H.Q. & nine nurse. Capt. C.J.D. Boyce joined the unit.	
"	29/8/17		Orders received to complete march & by nearly finishing. Visit the stations. Route march & from them until the 30th. (Lebeau an ambulance /this div. Received orders while on march to fire days tour by motor at the location for commanding units until the 30th. Lebeau 3rd day. FnT. The Divisional vent for 24 hours were warned to offer lorries to convey travel personnel W.A.3 appx six 2.	
"	30/8/17		Loaded Capt. Began to offload ambulance wagons & stores there to C. W.A.3 today. FnT. admitted 15 sick.	
"	31/8/17		Capt. Begin proceeded to 1 a.m. on site to his unloaded ammo convoy to BEAUCOURT station. appendix 3. Leaved Lt. Hansen, lies No.6 & 10 nurses for the march to close the station hospital. FnT peaked up the remainder of equipment of the unit.	

H.H. Johnson Lt. Col.
Comdg 2/2 N. Midland Field Ambulance

SECRET.   Appendix 1   Copy No. 3

2/2nd. North Midland Field Ambulance.

OPERATION ORDER No. 4.

Map Reference: LENS 11. 1/100000

(1).   The unit will move with the 178th. Infantry Brigade on 24th. inst. to R.E. Camp South of road AVELUY-BOUZINCOURT about south of first O in BOUZINCOURT.

(2). GENERAL INSTRUCTIONS...
Stores. Tents, bivouacs, trench covers etc. and all surplus stores will be handed over to incoming Division.

Supplies. The day's rations will be carried on the man. Rations for the 25th. inst. will be carried in the Supply Wagon which will move with the Divisional Train.

Accommodation. On arrival a Detention Hospital of 20 beds will be opened. The Transport will be accommodated in the Camp. No covered horse sheds will be used unless thoroughly disinfected.

Water Point. Water Duty men will report to O.C. 250th. Labour Coy. at 9 a.m. on 24th. inst.

March Discipline. Strict March and Water Discipline will be enforced. No man will be allowed to fall out without permission of an Officer, in writing.

(3) MARCH ORDERS.
R.A.M.C. Personnel. The R.A.M.C. will be divided into two parties. First party, consisting of Capt. Malcolm, Lieut. Sidwell, and 103 Other Ranks will proceed as in Table A..
Second Party, consisting of Capt. Cox and 60 Other Ranks will proceed as in Table B.

Horse Transport. Will proceed under Capt. Watson as in Table C.

MECHANICAL TRANSPORT. Motor Ambulances, less one Daimler which will accompany Capt. Malcolm's Party, will proceed under the instructions of Sgt. Cooper.

MARCH TABLE A.

PERSONNEL.
The Q.M., the Sgt. Major, and 103 R.A.M.C. under Capt. Malcolm, with three Horse Ambulances and one Daimler.

FIRST STAGE.

Parade: 4.50 a.m. marching off at 5.15 a.m.

Starting Point. Junction of BUS and LE MESNIL road at ROCQUIGNY at 6.5 a.m.

Order of March.
    200 M.G.C.
    2/7th. Sherwood Foresters.
    2/8th.   do.   do.
    2/2nd. N.M.Fld. Ambulance.
    470 Field Coy. R.E.

Intervals. 200 yards behind preceding unit.

Route. ROCQUIGNY - Rd. Junction on BAPAUME-PERONNE Road S.E. of LE TRANSLOY - Road Junction North of b in Fbg. de PERONNE - THILLOY.

Destination. Cross Roads on BAPAUME-ALBERT Road ½ mile N.E. of T. in WARLENCOURT.

Halts. At the hour less 10 minutes - starting at the hour again.

SECOND STAGE.

The Second Stage will be completed by bus.

Bus Numbers 73 - 77.
25 are allotted to each bus or lorry; not more than 13 men will travel on the top.

Start. At 10 a.m. details will be formed up in groups of 25, at 10 paces interval, on the right hand side of, and off the road: head of column being at a point 200 yards south-west of the Cross Roads on ALBERT-BAPAUME Road, ½ mile N.E. of T. in WARLENCOURT.
    Capt. Cox will now take charge of this party.
    Capt. Cox and the first 24 men will mount Bus No. 73.
    The second 25 men will mount   Bus No. 74.
    The third   "   "   "   Bus No. 75.
    The fourth   "   "   "   Bus No. 76.
    The remaining 3 men "   Bus No. 77.
There will therefore be 22 vacancies in the buses allotted, and it is essential that these vacancies be in Bus No. 77.
    The Commander of each group will have in writing the number of the bus he has to mount.

Destination. R.E. Camp AVELUY - BOUZINCOURT Road.

---o---

    Copy No. 1.   Capt. Malcolm.
    Copy No. 2.   Capt. Watson.
    Copy No. 3.   Capt. Cox.
    Copy No. 4.   Lieut. Sidwell.

These Operation Orders to be returned to Orderly Room when the journey is completed.

MARCH TABLE B.

First Stage.

1. Cpt. Cox and 60 other ranks will proceed by motor bus and lorry to Cross Roads on ALBERT-BAPAUME Road, ½ mile N.E. of T in WARLENCOURT.

2. Bus. Numbers allotted are 75, 76, & 77.
   Buses will be drawn up on the LE MESNIL-ROCQUIGNY Road. Units will leave their camps and will be formed up in front of buses and lorries, 25 to each bus or lorry, in the following order:-

2/5th. Sherwood Foresters at	8.15 a.m.
2/6th. do. do.	8.22 a.m.
175 M.G.C.	8.29 a.m.
178 T.M.B.	8.32 a.m.
2/2nd.N.Mid.Fld.Amb.	8.35 a.m.

   Not more than 13 men will travel on top of a bus.

3. Start. This party will parade at 7.40 a.m. marching off at 8 a.m.

4. Buses Nos.75 and 76 are to have their full complement of 25. Bus No.77 will therefore have 14 vacancies.

SECOND STAGE.
(By March Route.)

1. On arrival at rendezvous details will dismount and will form up off the left hand side of the road. Capt.Cox will take charge of party in Table A. Capt.Malcolm and Q.M. will proceed with party in Table B.

2. They will march to R.E. Camp AVELUY - BOUZINCOURT Road.

3. Starting Point. Cross Roads LE SARS.

4. Time. Zero plus 55.

5. Order of March.

   2/5th. Sherwood Foresters.
   2/6th.   do.   do.
   175   M.G.C.
   178   T.M.B.
   2/2nd.N.Mid.Fld.Amb.
   470 Field Coy.R.E.

6. Route. BAPAUME-ALBERT Road to Road Junction N.of C in CONTAL-MAISON. (FRITZ-WELL) - Ovillers - AVELUY.

7. The Horse Ambulances and 1 Motor Ambulance will complete the march with this party, following 470 Fld.Coy. R.E.

MECHANICAL TRANSPORT.

1. One Motor Ambulance will follow Capt. Malcolm's party, starting off at 5.15 a.m. This car will follow the column in jumps of one mile.

    Route. BUS - ROCQUIGNY - BAPAUME-PERONNE Road - South end of BAPAUME - THIEPVAL - BAPAUME-ALBERT Road - OVILLERS (Road junction marked FRITZ-WELL - AVELUY.

    Destination. R.E. Camp on South Side of AVELUY-BOUZINCOURT Road, near BOUZINCOURT.

2. The remaining ambulances will proceed at hourly intervals by the same route as above, the first car starting at 7.30 a.m. and will pick up any sick they find on the way.

3. Sgt. Cooper will proceed in the last car.

HORSE TRANSPORT.

1. The Transport, less three Horse Ambulances, will march under Capt. Watson.

2. <u>Starting Point.</u>   Junction of ROCQUIGNY Road with BAPAUME – PERONNE Road at 5.30 a.m.

3. <u>Order of March.</u>
   - 200   M.G.C.
   - Brigade Headquarters.
   - 2/5th. Sherwood Foresters.
   - 2/6th. Sherwood Foresters.
   - 2/7th.   do.   do.
   - 2/8th.   do.   do.
   - 175 M.G.C.
   - 2/2nd. N. Mid. Fld. Ambulance.

4. <u>Route.</u>
   <u>First Stage:</u> Cross Roads ½ mile S. of CHAU in SAILLEY– SAILLISEL – COMBLES – GUILLEMONT – MONTAUBON – FRICOURT – ALBERT.

   <u>Second Stage.</u> Church in ALBERT – AVELUY.

5. <u>Destination.</u> R.E. Camp on AVELUY – BOUZINCOURT Road.

6. <u>Parade.</u>   Transport will be paraded and ready to march off at 4.10 a.m.

7. The three Horse Ambulances will parade under Sgt. Spencer at 5 a.m. and march off with Capt. Malcolm's Party.

8. All petrol tins will be filled with water; the day's forage will be carried.   Water Carts will be filled.

---o---

MAP A.

Road 1st Class
Road Unmetalled
Railway
Mineral

ALBERT.
AVELUY
MARTINSART
BOUZINCOURT

Victoria Huts
Salamanca Huts
Talavere Huts
Dead Leg Midland Huts
175 M.G. 118 T.M.B. 2/9
Trafalgar Tents 4,8. 2/9
Cabstand Huts
Recreation Huts
E H.Q
2,5 Bn Bruges Huts
Fusilier Camp
122 H.B. Camp
270 Field Coy
R.E Camp
2/2 Field A.M.C
210 Field Coy R.E
122 Battery Camp

Appendix 2

COPY 3

OPERATION ORDER NO. 5.

BY LT.COL. F. W. JOHNSON.

CMDG. 2/2nd. NTH. MID. FD. AMBULCE.

1. All motor ambulances except one will be ready to proceed by convoy to the new area at 9 a.m. on 30th. inst., in charge of Capt. Bergin.

2. The motor ambulances of the 2/1st. N. Mid. Fd. Ambce. will be picked up at BOUZINCOURT, and those of the 2/3rd. N. Mid. Fd. Ambce. at the road junction ¼ mile West of BOUZINCOURT.

3. The whole convoy under the charge of Capt. Bergin will proceed by the following route :—
   DOULLENS, ST. POL, LILLERS, HAZEBROUCK, STEENVOORDE, to WINNEZEELE.

4. The convoy will not pass through HAZEBROUCK before 12 noon.

5. On arrival at WINNEZEELE the O.C. convoy will report to the Town Major, and also to the A.D.M.S., 39th. Div.

F W Johnson
Lt. Col.
29. 8. 1917.   Cmdg. 2/2nd. Nth. Mid. Fd. Ambulance.

Copy No. 1.   Capt. Bergin.
  "   " 2.   War Diary.
  "   " 3.   War Diary.
  4   " 4.   File.

~~Instructions for Officer in charge of Motor Ambulance~~

Instructions for Officer in Charge of

Motor Ambulance Convoy.

1. On arrival at WINNEZEELE the O.C. Convoy will obtain information from A.D.M.S. as to the position of the three Field Ambulances. He will then send the motor ambulances to report to the advance parties of thier respective Field Ambulances.

2. After unloading any stores carried one motor ambulance from the 2/1st. Field Ambulance will be instructed to proceed to HOPOUTRE Station and await the arrival of the first train conveying the 176th. Brigade.
One car of the 2/2nd. Field Ambulance will proceed to GODVAERSVELDE Station to meet the first train of the 178th. Brigade.
One car of the 2/3rd. Field Ambulance will proceed to PROVEN Station to meet the first train of the 177th. Brigade.

F W Johnson
Lt. Col.
20. 8. 1917. Cmdg. 2/2nd. N. Mid. Fd. Ambulance.

Appendix 3

Copy No. 2.

OPERATION ORDER No. 6.

By Lieut.Colonel F.W. Johnson, Commanding,
2/2nd.N.Mid.Field Ambulance.
Sept.1st.1917.

-----o-----

1. The Transport Section, including wagon orderlies, will parade at 2.0 am, and will move off at 2.20 am, under the command of Capt. Watson.

2. On arrival at Beaucourt Station, the wagons will be formed up in the appointed place, clear of the road. Capt. Watson will report to the Brigade Entraining Officer at the station, who will entrain the Section.

3. The remainder of the personnel will parade at 3.0 am. and will march off at 3.30 am. to BEAUCOURT Station for entraining.

4. Haversack rations for the journey will be carried by all ranks.

5. On arrival at GODVAERSVELDE Station the unit will march to billets at WATOU.

F.W. Johnson
Lt.Colonel Commanding,
2/2nd.N.Mid.Field Ambulance.

31/8/1917.

Copy No. 1. Capt. Watson.
"   No. 2. War Diary.
"   No. 3. - do.-
"   No. 4. File.

Confidential

War Diary
of
2/2 N. Mid. Fd. Amb.

From 1-9-17.   To 30-9-17

Volume 9

Vol. IX Page 1.

Army Form C. 2118.

Instructions regarding War Diaries and Intelligence Summaries are contained in F.S. Regs., Part II. and the Staff Manual respectively. Title pages will be prepared in manuscript.

WAR DIARY of 2/2-d North Midland Field Ambulance
INTELLIGENCE SUMMARY.
(Erase heading not required.)

Place	Date	Hour	Summary of Events and Information	Remarks and references to Appendices
BOUZINCOURT-AVELUY ROAD W.14.b.6.9 Sheet 57D France 1 in 40,000	1/9/17		The unit left camp this morning, the transport at 2.20 am, remainder at 3.30 am, and marched to BEAUCOURT STATION where it entrained the last train) the 178th Brigade Group. After travelling all day, detrained at GODVAERSVELDE STATION (R.18.b.2.9. sheet 27, B gun. France 40,000) marched to WATOU and took over hospital & billets at the Hospice, WATOU (K.4.b. medal sheet 27) from the 1/1st E. Lancs F.A. Hrs., 42nd Div.) F.W.)	
WATOU K.4.b. alt 1/20 Sheet 27. Belgium and France 40,000	2/9/17		Opened detention hospital in the Hospice with accommodation for 25 patients. The premises are in good but sanitary condition very unsatisfactory. Had parties at work all day cleaning up the place. Reported arrival to A.D.M.S. at WINNEZEELE this morning, and also called at 176th Brigade Headquarters WINNEZEELE. Quite a number of sick men arrived. Stretcher bearer party to collect sick from units not attached. F.W.) Capt. W.G. Knight reported for leave to Ireland. F.W.) 13 patients admitted.	
"	3/9/17		Met the R.M.O.'s of the 176th Brigade at Bde.H.Q. this morning and conferred with them on various medical subjects. F.W.) Capt. C.J.B. 13? gun for temporary duty at XIX Corps Reinforcement Camp. M.O. on inoculation pro A.D.M.S. despatched Capt. J. Bosley sick (authority A.D.M.S. S.9.B.4.) depot, MERCEGHEM this evening F.W.	
"	4/9/17		Capt. Nicolet proceeded to 2/1 N. Staffords for temporary duty in relief of Capt. Bosley sick. Officers, N.C.O.'s and privates inspected (latrines & cookhouses &c) A.D.M.S. visited the hospital this evening F.W.)	
"	5/9/17		D.D.M.S. XIX Corps inspected the hospital & Field Ambulance Selt Generally. F.W.) Daily average number admitted remains about 10 to 12. F.W.	
"	6/9/17		Nothing special. F.W.	
"	7/9/17		The sanitary condition of the Field Ambulance Self is now much improved. Incineration of excreta is carried out daily. Manure heaps are being removed & the camp cleaned up generally. Visited the 76 N. Staffs Camp & A.D.M.S. this morning. F.W.	
"	8/9/17		Capt. H.P. Mahoh proceeded on ten days leave to Ireland. F.W.)	
"	9/9/17		Rather more sick admitted to last ten days. Diarrhoea cases are increased, chiefly due to the camp being near mountainous depots. It is caused not including a satisfactory meat safe. Parties of persons to the Field Ambulance F.W.	

Vol. IX Page 2

2/2 North Midland WAR DIARY OF Field Ambulance

INTELLIGENCE SUMMARY.

(Erase heading not required.)

Place	Date	Hour	Summary of Events and Information	Remarks and references to Appendices
WATOU K.4.b central Sheet 27.	10/9/17		D.D.M.S. 5th Corps visited the hospital & inspected the Field Ambulance site. A.D.M.S. also had a visit to the ambulance. F.V.	
"	11/9/17		Continued work improving cookhouse. (R.M. attended a conference at A.D.M.S. Office on the subject) the welfare of the troops, as regards clothing, washing & feeding. F.V.	
"	12/9/17		A.D.M.S. called. By his instructions, 1 D.D.M.O.V.Corps (a hospital that which is used as a Signal Office) until he has been erected in Field Ambulance site was occupied today in the Department of 11th Div H.Qrs. and used as award for (2 tents) (12 tents) for D.T.J. Th.T. in the Belgian & despatch VAN de CAPELLE was for to this unit (Surgery for D.T.) Th.T.	
"	13/9/17		Orders received for this unit to take over the 5th Corps Rest Station at HILL HOCK, the move to be completed by 15th inst. (authority A.D.M.O. 57 Div. & DDMOV Corps) 5 This morning, with the Q.M. & arranged with OC 2/2 South Midland a Field Ambulance to move to the 5th Corps Rest Station to relieve his unit on the 15th inst. I went over the ground & arranged for 5 lorries (14 cwt.) & a ground (18 cwt.) today F.V. F. Amb. & tend an advance party tomorrow. Saw Cap. Rest Sta. + OC today F.V. Evacuated all sick for water either to Cap. Pleas. Sta. (tent) (Ambulance	
"	14/9/17		Capt. Watson, Lt. & QM Sidwell and 20 Other ranks proceeded to the 2/2 South Midland M.C. Ambulance closed the this morning, & while attached to that unit, they collect sick & disposed of them. The remainder of the unit efs & packs of all equipment. 176 Brigade, F.V. detached to Hospital at WATOU & remained for 2/1 N. Midland field amb. carried on general duty F.V. Capt. Fordyce & Lt. Kennedy from 2/1 N.Midland Field Amb. attached for 14 days contract labor & gale. Capt. R. Cox proceeded to Col. Pleat. Sta. Ruthock (NC) (Ambulance by instruction of A.D.M.S.	
"	15/9/17		The hospital hut taken over from 11th Div. Signal on the 12th inst. was occupied by 61 Div. Signals this morning by order of the Town Major of WATOU & Area Commandant. 1 NCO & 4 men in charge At 11 am. the unit marched off, leaving a holding party 1 NCO & 4 men in charge 1 officer, 27 NCO & Privates 4 ors moved out at 12.46 p.m. and arrived at the 5th Corps Rest Station HILHOCK (L.20.b.6.4.sheet 27 Belg.) The 2/2 South Midland F. Amb. moved out at 2pm. & took over the command of the Rest Stat. F.V.	

Vol IX page 3

Army Form C. 2118.

2/2nd North Midland Field Ambulance

WAR DIARY
INTELLIGENCE SUMMARY

(Erase heading not required.)

Place	Date	Hour	Summary of Events and Information	Remarks and references to Appendices
HILLHOEK [Capt Regt Station] 2.20.C.6.4 Map 27 Belg: 1F. Sheet 20.A.	16/9/17		There were 570 patients on the books of the hospital, on taking over. This number was increased to 795 by admissions up to 6.30 p.m. today. Today nightly staffs & various departmts. Detailed all N.C.O.s to respective duties & posted day & night staffs on the Camp & various dispy. All day today fatigue parties were employed in cleaning up the camp & general extensions. Made plans for repair & roads already existing, and for extension of the existing cooking arrangts. The Q.M.S. acted as Reg. Statff. The Senior acceptance not already existing, and for extension of the existing cooking arrangts. A.D.M.S. 56 Div. visited the hospital. JW.	
"	17/9/17		Many acc. admitted today. Total number in hospital at 6 p.m. 998. Evacuated about 30 to CCs & 40 to 60 trucks during the day. 3 Dns. V Carps night to the R.S. Sta: and 7 ac instructed for the evacn. tom. 7.am. 8 Dns. V Carps tomorrow + 6 duty. 117 more marquees arrived this afternoon, & CCS tomorrow + 6 duty. Erected 8 this afternoon & several arrivals of CCS - tomorrow + 6 duty. brought in economical team up to 1000. Bulk of hospital	
"	18/9/17		13 more bigames arrived from the Depot mt. 50 bigames were put up. Base were about 1 am. Rearranged the marquees. So as to economize space & at the same time increase accom. to CCS. & economic personnel. Admissions today numbered about 780, 150 were admitted, & about 50 to duty, leaving about 80 in hospital evacuated to CCS. JW.	
"	19/9/17		Capt. Fordyce & Nesbitt Lieut Kennedy with 35 O.R. of the unit were sent this morning to Cap Main Dressing Station, Red Farm. Capt. Watson was transferred for temporary duty from No.5 as N.O. to 2/6 N. Staffords. Capt. J Howard (2/1 N.M.F.A) who was posted (untilly A.D.M.S. 57 Div.) this afternoon to D.M.S. Capt wrote the hospital in the afternoon, inspected (& was altered) suggestions at the new increasing of mound, cooking accom & latrine accom made - all of which were acted upon at short intervals for the following (authority D.M.S. 58 Carps) 50 light duty patients were sent to Cap Main Dressing Station to accommodate this large party for fatigues Includg 2 bearer sqds. of 3 Division. 200 & 300 cases this morning - 9th 57 Div. In support near Pratt top. The attack by 9, 45 & 55 Div, which is due tonight. One bigame of the C.O.S. arrived this morning about 5 a.m.	
"	20/9/17		Attack on the Cap front was successful, all wounded casualties were arriving at the C.C.S. about to the slight degree. Arrived them very ill in Cap 58, Div. Capt. P. Malcolm (our liner Field Ambulance.) Capt. O'Dea & Lt. brittan Hardwig, with 2 Regt. Stations. Capt. H. Malcolm (our liner Field Ambulance. Com lum; B Dins V Carps, arriving from 7th Field Amb. (3 Div) for temporary duty. JW.	

Vol IX Page 4

Army Form C. 2118.

2/2nd North Midland Field Ambulance

WAR DIARY / INTELLIGENCE SUMMARY

(Erase heading not required.)

Instructions regarding War Diaries and Intelligence Summaries are contained in F.S. Regs., Part II. and the Staff Manual respectively. Title pages will be prepared in manuscript.

Place	Date	Hour	Summary of Events and Information	Remarks and references to Appendices
HALLHOEK Corps Rest Station L.20.b.6.4 Sheet 27	21/9/17		DDMS inspected the Rest Station & Bearer Relay Post today. Patients arriving all day, till our accommodation was nearly all taken up by evening. F.O.	
"	22/9/17		I went with the Q.M. this morning to the RE (Workshops) to try to obtain our requirements for latrines etc. but everything required. The DDMS appointed first Capt. H.P. Malcolm, via Lieut. Watson (RAMC) to be this Rest Station i/c (authority of Dns. 59 Div.) F.O. All M.O.'s personnel of the 9th Field Ambulance (33rd Div.) were here (with Capt. McGrath & Capt. Cruickshanks 28th Regts.) for advice and instruction. Lieut. Forbes 1st S. African H.A.C. reported for duty and was sent as for transfer charge of MO's vaccinated me to the Canebury Rest Station, to enable me to get as all advance from... many features carried as possible & duty. F.O.	
"	23/9/17		The 59th Division moves up to the front area today – Collected back from the 178 Bde Rgt. who are near & took over others from the 2/1 N.M.F.A. who move up to after Advanced Dressing Station today. Sent Capt. Howard to relieve Capt. Nicholl at the Cafe Main Dressing Station, and detailed Capt. Leonard and 65 N.C.O.s men to proceed to join the 2/1 N.M.F.A. as Field Amb. This party proceeded to join the 2/1 N.M.F.A. as Field Amb. Bearers & went attached for duty with the ADMS 59th Div. F.O. at an appointed rendezvous near Ypres. The Amb. Cars ran as usual for evacuation. F.O. DDMS paid us visit this morning – visit were reported. At six p.m. 25 cwts. Rpts. to Bearers to all possible cases to duty as 6 CCS today – 6 this unit were reported to be Brandhoek before then. F.O.	
"	24/9/17		Sent out one 200 cases to duty this morning – more being sent by the personnel of this unit – Heavy Casualties amongst HM officers, also Res: Lieut. Brigham & Capt. Barrass (Beecres) had room for 500 – The pay from F. Amb. today – Pte Rayworth W. (wounded shell fire) OC 2/1 N.M.F. Amb. reports 20-6 MAS: at Men Dressing Station, also my ambulance was to report to today to operate today was 1149. F.O. All motor ambulances assisted as late as the afternoon today for loading 8 hours together, also Capt. Watson was motorcyclist and sidecar proceeded on leave England today. Pte Nt. I N.Co. 4 were returned from Paris Hill A, Karachi H.H. (gassed) N. & Benn EE (wounds) admissions amount to about 160. Casualties in unit today: F.O. Wounded Priv. F.S. unit 2/1 N.M.F. Amb. as Bearers, not returning over 100 men to duty today. F.O.	
"	25.9.17		Attack by the 5th & 2nd Armies was resumed this morning the 5th Division taking all their objective successfully & collecting them. Casualties light enough for Bearers have began to arrive about 2 am, 246 were admitted (slightly gassed). (Mustard gas). They it contained night shell-stop cases. Chiefly had today. Casualties in the unit today were White + Smart killed, & several officers wounded & passed. Pte Harvey, plus. White was entered this evening by our ADms v. 9th Div. Capt. Forbes of the Out-patient Deps of the 1st S. African F. Amb. attached to the 9th Div. visited me to have conference the of the visit of said that the Wilde, the personnel of the 9th Dw. attached unit is having. F.O.	

WAR DIARY / INTELLIGENCE SUMMARY

Vol IX Page 5
Army Form C. 2118.

Place	Date	Hour	Summary of Events and Information	Remarks and references to Appendices
WILLHOEK Corps Rest Station 20.J.b.4 Sheet 27 1/40,000	27.9.17		A very busy day again. 172 rank admissions. Capt. McGrath & the Rev Sabin & the 2/82 Field Ambulance were withdrawn this morning by orders A.D.M.S. 9th Div. I retained the 2 M.O.'s until tomorrow as I had no other M.O. to carry on with. Several men came in among our bearers who had been wounded - two or three of the Divisional front were also killed. Several more came in among our bearers today, but this morning's front was also hard. Several men were reported today, including Pte J. L. Houblett & three killed. German aeroplanes bombed the area where we & the Rest Station - during the evening - two or three bombs fell fairly near. J.W.	
"	28.9.17		No two M.O.'s of the 28th Field Ambulance came up for this morning so I was obliged to carry on with the Rest Station above. S/B. Inhabitants admitted, about 60 & 70 returned to duty. Major J.W. V. Corps handed over to this IX Corps today; we are now under them administratively. A/D Divs II Anzac Corps took them over. This afternoon I went round the hospital. He promised to send 2 M.O.'s tomorrow morning & a Field Ambulance to take over the Rest Station later. There are now about 600 in hospital. J.W.	
"	29.9.17		Saw sick parade at 9.0. admitted about 60. Heavy firing this morning. Two M.O.'s arrived from the 10th Australian Field Ambulance at noon. Tf the party & ambulance arrived about 1 p.m. with orders to take over the Rest Station by 6 p.m. I went to the A.D.M.S. 69 Div. for instructions & received orders I was to hand over but remain here tonight. Capt Kirby of the unit was admitted to C.C.S. today. Guns (W) & two of these men also. This afternoon all our equipment was packed & and the patients & hospital with all stores handed over to the 10th Australian Field Amb. J.W. Another two big raids this evening, many bombs falling. Opening up, and three fell with 200 yards of the Rest Station. During our camp Boopes knocking down trees & telephone. Capt M. Cox returned from leave this evening. J.W.	

Vol IX Page 6

Army Form C. 2118.

WAR DIARY
INTELLIGENCE SUMMARY.
(Erase heading not required.)

Place	Date	Hour	Summary of Events and Information	Remarks and references to Appendices
HILL 40 E14 c/s (Belgium)	30/9/17		Instructions received this morning to proceed to WATOU, & open a detention hospital in the Hospice. Capt. H.P. McColm rejoined from duty with 2/5 South Staffordshire Regt early this morning. The unit marched from HILHOEK at 11 a.m., reached WATOU about 1.0 p.m. and found the Hospice still occupied by a unit of a New Zealand Division. Obtained billets for officers guard for the night later, instructions received from A.D.M.S. to be prepared to move early tomorrow, morning, by two lorries. This Division is now being relieved by a New Zealand Division. Our bearers the 59th Division is now being relieved to us today, M/O's a very arduous weeks work under fairly constant shell fire & gas shell bombardment. Casualties for the whole week in this unit have been heavy, 8 being killed (9 wounded, and one officer, & 16 N.C.O's & men gassed (battle casualties).	

H. J. Hanson Ravie (TF)
Lt Col Commdg Field Amb
OC 2/2nd North Midland Fd Ambce

Original

19

Confidential

War Diary

of

[illegible] H. Mid. Fd. Amb.

From 1 X 17 To 31 X 17

Volume X

Vol 9

Vol. X Page 1

Army Form C. 2118.

2/2nd North Midland Field Ambulance

WAR DIARY / INTELLIGENCE SUMMARY

(Erase heading not required.)

Instructions regarding War Diaries and Intelligence Summaries are contained in F.S. Regs., Part II. and the Staff Manual respectively. Title pages will be prepared in manuscript.

Place	Date	Hour	Summary of Events and Information	Remarks and references to Appendices
WATOU K.4.6. central	1/10/17		Received orders at 2 a.m. to march to an embarking point to be transported at 5.30 a.m. Marched off with all transport by 6.30 a.m. attached to 2/1st N. Mid. 3rd Amb. having rejoined to-day from WATOU. Travelled by motor lorries to the Steenbecque area nearly sixteen miles. (Toulouse Aire) about 2 p.m., the transport marched & rejoined Guernes at 6 p.m. Received instructions from A.D.M.S. to open a hospital for the receipt of 176th Brigade sick also a separate ward for the treatment of sickness cases. The building and furnishing of an exhaustive search though the billeting area as no suitable building existed. A/Lt. an exhaustive canvas one pitched and decisions to pickets work. So as to avoid the necessity of any sanitary arrangement, neither latrines, incinerators. The men is absolutely without any means of acceptance accommodation. An ablution place being in existence. After much trouble the tents for the sick not no decanses being available. Some of the wounded of the patients of the camp were received. & 312 N Mid 3 Amb. Company latrine this evening. Lieut. C. Watson rejoined for temporary duty & 2/6 N. Stafford. was relieved by Captain F/Lt. C. Watson rejoined E.S. Edie.	
GUARBECQUE (Toulouse SE AIRE)	2/10/17		Capt F/Lt. C. Watson rejoined for temporary duty, also went to 176 Brigade Headqrs. Reported to the A.D.M.S. arrangements and also to the suite of duty, & the hospital. Arranged for the collection of sick & the hospital. F/L.	
"	3/10/17		Visited Bde. H.Q. & also the R.M.O.'s of the 4 battalions. Visited No. 3/9 Stationary Hospital Aire and arranged for dental cases to attend.	
"	4/10/17		Capt. R. Cox left for temporary duty with 2/6 North Staffords the majority in relief of Lieut. Ellis who is attached to this unit for instruction (authority for D.S. 5 Div.) the Field Ambulance attended a special parade with parts of the 176 Bde. Bn. relieving 15 sick men to hospital today. F/L.	
"	5/10/17		Nothing of importance. F/L.	
"	6/10/17		Orders received to move to new tomorrow by march of lorry. Jenny now with the helpers thoroughly accordingly accommodation except a barn evacuated all sick who were unfit to rejoin their trenches today, & passed all group not fit to travel. F/L.	

Vol X Page 2

2/2nd North Midland Field Ambulance

Army Form C. 2118.

WAR DIARY
INTELLIGENCE SUMMARY.
(Erase heading not required.)

Place	Date	Hour	Summary of Events and Information	Remarks and references to Appendices
VERCHIN K.5.R.9	7/10/17		Marched with 176 Fd. Brigade from GUARBECQUE at 8 a.m., reaching the Entraining point about 12.30 p.m. & reached destination at VERCHIN by lorry at 2.30 p.m. Established hospital accommodation for 18 patients in a ghost house at VERCHIN Chateau. Headquarters in Chateau. Personnel billeted in the village in barns. Also erected tents for extra accommodation. All the men arrived without throwing his movements & got their watery ration in the farm houses at which they are billeted. F.D.	
Near BERGUENEUSE in 40,000				
"	8/10/17		Arranged collection of sick from the 176th Brigade groups by horse ambulances. Weather conditions still very bad. No sanitary arrangements of any kind are available here. Through their representations places are disinfected. Pte. Sidwell rejoined for duty from hospital F.D.	
"	9/10/17		Capt. A. Mearns joined for duty from hospital. Orders received to move with 176 Brigade tomorrow. F.D.	
PERNES H.M. in centre Sheet 36 B (40,000)	10/10/17		Evacuated the few remaining sick & marched from VERCHIN at 7.30 a.m. to PERNES where the unit was billetted. No hospital requirements at AIX-NOULETTE with Advanced Dressing station at LIEVIN on the Division taking over the LIEVIN Sector on the 14th inst. F.D.	
"	11/10/17		Proceeded with Capt. Malcolm this morning to AIX NOULETTE (R.22.a.2.7, sheet 36 B) and were shown over the Advanced Dressing Station also visited the Field Ambulance State over this first tomorrow. Field Ambulance site to be O.C 2 Canadian Field Ambulance & arranged to take over a new party at LIEVIN (M.28.b.7.1 sheet 36 c). Arranged to letter over the Advanced Dressing Station & the rest of the unit marched to LIEVIN this morning from 23 Canadian Field Ambulance.	
BARLIN FOSSE 9 Q.2.4.5.3 Q (sheet 36 B)	12/10/17		Sent Capt. Malcolm & 15 other ranks as an advanced party & west billetties the Field Ambulance site at "Fosse 9" for the night at 7 p.m. BARLIN, and west billetties in the Field Ambulance with the 2 Canadian Field Ambulance by 6 pm this evening.	
AIX-NOULETTE R.22.a.2.7. sheet 36 B	13/10/17		Marched to AIX-NOULETTE this morning and billetted with the orderly ambulance. Capt. Malcolm LIEVIN. Relieved all the personnel of the advanced Dressing Station arrangements for the nursing of the personnel & for the staffing of both at the 4 dressing station and the main Dressing Station is estimated in the attached. and 25 other ranks forming the Nest of the 8 orderly staff. heard report on the arrived at M.28.b.7.1 (Sheet 36c) Château LIEVIN at M.28.b.7.1 (Sheet 36c)	

Army Form C. 2118.

WAR DIARY

2/2nd North Midland Field Ambulance

INTELLIGENCE SUMMARY.

Vol. X Pag. 3

(Erase heading not required.)

Place	Date	Hour	Summary of Events and Information	Remarks and references to Appendices
AIX NOULETTE R.22.a.2.7 (Sheet 36 B)	14/10/17		2nd Canadian Field Ambulance left at 9.30 am. and took over the administration. The hospital and the few patients handed over. Details parade at 10.30 to clear up the surroundings and also reported at the Stables & appliances at 11.10 am. The OC & Officers and Church Parade. This afternoon arrangements reported to B. Bryde. Response for sick parade at the field & bivouac for all Volunteers sick & for Leaving line details: to the headquarters of the Ambulance & inspected the site A.D.M.S. paid a visit to the heads quarters there.	
"	15/10/17		Visited & viewed during state visit the Q.M. Inspected the way parts & found all satisfactory. This two improvements suggested. B.D.M.S. Capt. went with the H.q.rs. at AIX NOULETTE this afternoon. Inspected the premises. There is a large R.A.M.C. cellar and in the building, at present used as billets but her under RAMC at present not suitable for a hospital or the only available place being a ground attic above the main room which is too low to be over-night. Accommodation there for 20 patients, also beds, an 8 beds be ??? Zig.	
"	16/10/17		Went to A.D.M.S. Office this morning & reported preparations arrival at LIEVIN and I was asked A.D.M.S. accompanied the ??? after to take over all the arrangements with the Jale of the regiment and fort; became by now to an instruction with the regiment there is description in an building - the arrangement reported but to day and was at once for to be for infantry duty Capt. C9. Thomas joined fr. duty (arising from A.D.M. of 59th Div. Zig) at 2/3 N. Middx 2nd Amb.	Appendix l
"	17/10/17		This morning was spent in planning improvements at the place. Less ???than responsible for the approaches to the right battalion line and to the Capt ??? arrival at cellars and reserve attend to our right became fully under ??? army ??? by the main LENS-LIEVIN road is unpassable in daylight. Water the main B. notes Red Cross Store and at Ches were kept & store both Ambulance ???	

Army Form C. 2118.

2/2nd North Midland Field Ambulance

WAR DIARY
INTELLIGENCE SUMMARY
Vol X Page 4

(Erase heading not required.)

Place	Date	Hour	Summary of Events and Information	Remarks and references to Appendices
VIX-NOULETTE R.2.2.a.2.7 C 36 B	18/10/17		Small working party from 2/1 N Mid Field Amb. carry out work assigned during night. Latrine ground forts & by approx reported to the Div on some conditions & improvement of the forts. Our J. Capt. E. Cox posted on the tackles W/9 to M.O. (temporarily to) 63rd Heavy Artillery As S.M.O. the 176th Infantry Brigade, the responsibility for the sanitary conduct of the brigade area devolves upon me (A.D.M.S. letter 1/10/17). J also visited This visited the lines of the 2/6 S.Staffords (NOULETTE K.9 (R.27.b. sheet 36B) that morning + inspected all arrangements — found all satisfactory except one spot where moss was ensuring & to be cleared. This afternoon I visited LEVIN and inspected the sanitary arrangements (the division J camp is subsidiary to the A.D.S. It seems the [?] are not set enough & [?] with fly proof lattices. Saw the R.M.O's on the subject) & completes inspection. There was a little fire the heat too — Great carnelian for the A.D.S. shelter for men very small — they are very rudimentary the night land the A.D.S. was shelled [?]. [?] was damaged & must be towed Two lite to an ambulance standing there [?] were advised giving the two J. 2nd the unit left later. It would be advised the this.	
"	19/10/17		Attended a lecture in the J.O.C. 67th Div at the Mairie Drancy Cliche this afternoon to all busted officers on the subject of Trench + a Pierre Trench Forts.	
"	20/10/17		Capt. A. Weaver [?] for the Company Left Lieut 2/3 N. Midsex Field Amb. Lieut J.S. Ellis accepted to the Colonels. Leaving [?] & 55 Days. Lieut 2/3 S. Ellis accepted to tear yearbook learn Dressing Station and Caps at the C.D.G. 14 wounded passed through today. Lieut J. Dean is in charge at the C.D.G. toking his B.C. & Capt J.23 reinforcements arrive today. Col. [?] in pulled up unlisted trade newly built purpose forts hopes in this week. [?]	

WAR DIARY

Army Form C. 2118.

2/2nd North Midland Field Ambulance
Vol X Page 5

INTELLIGENCE SUMMARY

Place	Date	Hour	Summary of Events and Information	Remarks and references to Appendices
AIX NOULETTE R.22.a.27	21.10.17		Visited the advanced dressing stations at LIÉVIN and all the Regimental Aid Posts of the support & right relay posts. Inspects the work at the latter. There is just food accommodation there for about 18 to 20 stretcher cases, & good shelter for bearers in dug outs. This post it is contemplated using as an advanced Dressing Station. Inspected more hospital, the sanitary by team in the area. Two of bearers were inspected at headquarters at 2.30 pm. Church services held at headquarters.	F.A.Q.
"	22/10/17		Made a tour of inspection of the sanitary arrangements at the Transport Lines 1 the 2/5 N. Staffs, 2/5 S. Staffs & 2/6 S. Staffs & 2/6 S. Staffs & 174 M.G. Co. at BOUVIGNY–BOYEFFLES. Found very imperfect arrangements and gave instructions requiring consideration. Two units were well kept, two indifferent and one the others require considerable improvement. Called at F. Amb. headquarters and also at the A.D.S. 2½q. A.D.M.S.	F.A.Q.
"	23/10/17		Inspected sanitary conditions of Marguffle Farm & Forue (Transport Lines of 2/6 N Staffs) and suggested improvements wanted. Advanced Dressing Station. D.Q.D.mo visited the G.O.C. 176 Inf. Bde. visited the Left Brigade. Inspected bearer posts & front line system of the Left Brigade. J.Y.Q.	
"	24/10/17		Visited the advanced dressing station, LIÉVIN & noted the progress made in construction. 1 dying room in the Chapel and extra shelter accommodation in the cellars. Bearer posts visited by the Secs. F.Q.	
"	25/10/17		Nothing to note. F.Q.	

Army Form C. 2118.

WAR DIARY 2/2nd North Midland Field Ambulance

INTELLIGENCE SUMMARY.

Vol X Page 6

(Erase heading not required.)

Place	Date	Hour	Summary of Events and Information	Remarks and references to Appendices
AIX NOULETTE R.22.a.2.7 (Sheet 36B)	26/10/17		Capt. F.N.C. Watson proceeded on special leave to England. Capt. H.P. Malcolm took charge of A.D.S. A.D.M.S. called at F.Ad. Headquarters (Bois de Noulette) Fw.9.	
"	27/10/17		Capt. Malcolm visited all posts & Regimental aid posts. Lieut. A. Bostock, 2/1st North Mid. Field amb. arrived for temporary duty. Sanitary reports attended to and sanitary arrangements of the Brigade area carried out by A.D.M.S. of the Head Quarter state Fw.9.	
"	28/10/17		Visited A.D.S. LIEVIN. The morning and part a second visit to Bouvigny this afternoon. I found all sanitary arrangements was satisfactory & all seen to from a to open.	
"	29/10/17		Nothing of note Fw.9.	
"	30/10/17		The final "trench foot" cases of this season were admitted today from the 2/6th South Staffs. Precautions are being taken by all units, but these cases appear to have resulted from too long a period in the front line without a relief. Lieut. (15 & 6 days) 176 Inf. Bde. was relieved in the left Brigade sector by the 177 Inf. Bde. Fw.9.	
"	31/10/17		Main notice boards & directing posts were placed along the lines of evacuation today. The work of the right relay post is almost completed now & the working party of the 2/1st Nmidland Fd Amb. was withdrawn today, to be replaced by men of this Unit. Is complete. The Spa-hotel Hasluck & the remainder of the billeting area generally without the communication trenches and the main lorries movement through by this unit had escaped. Unit is being done on the main lorries movement through by this right battalion scheme & soon it will be possible to bring stretcher cases out by these Hacheo. Fw.9.	F.B. Johnston Lt. Col. Cmdg 2/2 North Mid F.A.

War diary - 2/2nd North Midland Field Ambulance
Vol. X

Appendix. 1.

System of evacuation of casualties in left Brigade area as taken over from the 2nd Canadian Field Ambulance.

Advanced Dressing Station. This is established in the cellars of the "White Chateau" on the south side of LIÈVIN (Map reference M.28.b.7.1, Sheet 36 C. FRANCE 1/40,000)

Two Brigades are in the line, the third being in reserve. The Left Brigade area is cleared by 2/2nd North Midland Field Ambulance. In this area two battalions are in the line, one in support in LIÈVIN & the 4th in reserve in ROLLENCOURT.

The two battalions in the line use one Regimental Aid Post which is situated in cellars of a house on the south side of the LIÈVIN - LENS road at M.23.d.2.8 (Sheet 36C, S.W. 1 in 10,000.)

As this is a long "carry" from the front line, each battalion has a Field Ambulance Relay Post between the front line and the Reg. Aid post, that for the left battalion being on the north side of the LENS-LIÈVIN road at M.24.a.8.2, & that for the right in the east side of the railway embankment at M.24.c.6.6 (Sheet 36.C.)

At each of these posts 4 R.A.M.C. bearers are stationed.

The Regimental Aid Post for the Battalion in support is the cellar of a house on the south side of the LENS road at M.23.C.4.5.

A Field Ambulance Relay Post is established near this, in a dug-out at M.22.d.90.25, with 4 bearers.

Wounded are carried from the front line by regimental stretcher-bearers after dusk (except in urgent cases) to the Right or Left Field Amb. Relay Post.

Field Amb. bearers then carry them by wheeled stretcher to the Reg. Aid. Post common to both Battalions. Four R.A.M.C. bearers are attached here & carry from this point to the support relay post. Here more R.A.M.C. bearers carry to the Advanced Dressing Station.

Evacuation from the Advanced Dressing Station is by motor ambulance to the Main Dressing Station at JENKS' SIDING, near Souchez.

A light railway can also be used from the A.D.S. to the main dressing station, but this is not in use at present, as the numbers are not too large to be dealt with by motor ambulance. A sketch plan is attached.

F.W. Johnson Lt. Col. R.A.M.C.

Plan of Evacuation

Confidential
War Diary
of
2/2 N. Mid. Fd. Amb

From 1/11/17   To 30/11/17

Volume 11

Army Form C. 2118.

Vol. XI Page 1

WAR DIARY 2/2nd North Midland Field Ambulance
INTELLIGENCE SUMMARY

Place	Date	Summary of Events and Information	Remarks and references to Appendices
AIX-NOULETTE	1.11.17	Continue to work & improvement at headqrs, AIX NOULETTE. During room complete, and improved latrines. Visited Advanced Dressing Station, LIEVIN this morning. Work of increasing accommodation for stretcher cases in the cellars, by fixing racks to support them, is proceeding. Visited all the Regimental Aid Posts & Reg'l Medical Officers of the 177 Inf Brigade, which has relieved the 176 Inf Bde. in the left Brigade sector. Also inspected our bearer relay posts. A.D.M.S. visits M.D.S. & also the communication trenches in front of the bearer relay posts - with a view to suggesting alterations further forward - which are at present 2500 yards from the fond line, for the Reg. Aid Posts. Capt. R. Cox returned from Temp. duty with 63rd H.A.G.	
"	2.11.17	Capt. R. Cox relieves Capt. S. Walsh at the Advanced Dressing Station. Attended conference of Field Amb. Commanders at A.D.M.S. Office this morning, at which various subjects were discussed & improvements suggested. Proceeded to LIEVIN this afternoon to make arrangements for moving the R.A.P's. Interviewed the 177 Inf Bde. Staff & also inspected scheme. Lieut. A. Bostock left for duty at No. 22 C.C.S. (authorised A.Thos 67 Div) + Thos M.Army W).	
"	3.11.17	Proceeded to LIEVIN this morning. Met the O.C. 2/5 Leicesters & staff Capt. at the 177 Battalion Hedqrs & accompanied them up to the front trenches - we select a site about 100 yards short of the tram known as the "Blue line". We select a site about 100 yards short of the front trenches will have to be constructed in the communication trench called "Arcade Trench". There is nothing here at present & dug-outs & small trench. The Brigade pioneers to put the work into hands of the 12th Bn B.R.E.	

Vol XI. Page 2

2/2nd North Midland WAR DIARY Field Ambulance

Army Form C. 2118.

INTELLIGENCE SUMMARY.
(Erase heading not required.)

Place	Date	Hour	Summary of Events and Information	Remarks and references to Appendices
AIX-NOULETTE	3.11.17 (continued)		The Commandant No trench is at present in such a bad condition that it will be impossible to put wounded down it; work is being done on it; trench boards being put down; it will be a very good evacuation route for the Tan & walking cases when completed. F.W.J. Visited some of our Bearer posts in the course of the morning.	
"	4.11.17		Parade at headqrs at 11.0 a.m. at which the A.D.M.S. presented the G.O.C.'s Card of acknowledgement of bravery in action & gallant conduct to the following N.C.O. & men of this unit. No. 419313 L-Cpl. I.O. Thompson No. 419142 Pte. R.N. Johnson No. 419392 Pte. J.A. Cartwright. During the recent operations to the east of YPRES. Lieut. E.S. Ellis posted for temporary duty with 2/5 North Staffs Regt (walking wounded Capt. J.A. Young M.O.(i/c) 2/5 Lincs Regt. posted for temporary duty with this unit. Several cases of gas-shell poisoning admitted to Adv. Dr. Sta. this evening — all (28 and 59 Dn.) apparently of a bogue character.	F.W.J.
"	5.11.17		Went to L.I.E. VIN this morning — took the Cafe Young this day at Advance Dressing Sta. Called at Bde. Headqrs. went round into Staff Capt. & see a new of general Brigade Rest House near the Regtl. aid posts. There is accommodation about 25 men, and cases of exhaustion & slight wounds can be sent there by R.M.O.'s. The Brigade is on at Kitchen is not of door, and a new bath-house is under construction near by. A.D.M.S. inspected the Field Amb. Headquarters this morning & made several inspections for the improving of the accommodation for patients — F.W.J.	

Vol. XI Page 3

Army Form C. 2118.

2/2nd North Midland WAR DIARY Field Ambulance

INTELLIGENCE SUMMARY.

(Erase heading not required.)

Place	Date	Hour	Summary of Events and Information	Remarks and references to Appendices
AIX NOULETTE	6.11.17		Commenced the erection of a new ablution house at Hd.Qrs. the morning. Stokes the fitting up of a drying room. This afternoon the G.O.C. 59th Division accompanied by the A.A.& D.M.G. + A.D.M.S. inspected the field ambulance headquarters, hospital, billets, transport lines. The G.O.C. appeared himself satisfied with all arrangements. A.D.M.S. & D.A.D.M.S. also visited the F.Amb. this afternoon. J.W.	
"	7.11.17		Capt. Malcolm visited the Adv. Dr. Sta. & the bearer-posts this morning. J.W.	
"	8.11.17		Nothing of note. J.W.	
"	9.11.17		Attended conference of F.Amb. Commdg. at A.D.M.S. Office. Gas also continued. Put-up canvas screen round the tarpaulins today. walk on the ablution-house. J.W.	
"	10.11.17		Visited A.D.S. & all bearer-posts this morning. The provision of brackets totally stretcher-cars at the A.D.S. is now almost completed. There is now accommodation for storing from 36 to 40 stretcher cars. Inspected the brigade drying-room, gun-footstore + sanitary arrangements generally in Liévin. Everything now working satisfactorily. J.W.	
"	11.11.17		Church parade at 11 a.m. at headqrs. J.W.	
"	12.11.17		Nothing of note. J.W.	
"	13.11.17		A.D.M.S. visited headquarters. Orders received to recall the personnel from the A.D.S. & bearer-posts today on relief by personnel from 2/3 N.M.F.Amb. to be prepared to move tomorrow with the 178 Inf. Brigade. Proceed to LIÉVIN this afternoon & arrange for Capt. Horne and all personnel required, report at headqrs this evening, Lieut. Osman in charge. J.W.	

Vol. XI Page 4

2/2nd North Midland Field Ambulance

Army Form C. 2118.

WAR DIARY / INTELLIGENCE SUMMARY

(Erase heading not required.)

Place	Date	Hour	Summary of Events and Information	Remarks and references to Appendices
AIX NOULETTE	14.11.17		Marched from AIX NOULETTE under orders received for 178th Inf. Bde. at 9.15 a.m. via SOUCHEZ & LA TARGETTE to DUISANS (L.8.c.6.2. Sheet 51.C.) The transport marched independently via BOUVIGNY & GOUY SERVINS to ST. ELOY. Rec'd rats under Lieut R.A.M. Sidwell. Remained on foot until we heard this evening by the 2 3 Canadian Field Ambulance, who took over the Folld. site at AIX NOULETTE. F.W.	
DUISANS Camp No. 3 L.8.c.5.2. Sheet 51.C. [France 1"= 40,000]	15.11.17		The Unit occupies a row of Nissen huts in Camp No. 3, adjoining the 2/6 Sherwood Foresters. The day was spent in cleaning up the camp and equipping a hut as hospital. Capt Young detailed for temporary duty with 2/8th Sherwood Foresters Inf.	
"	16.11.17		All kit overhauled and re-packed on the waggons. F.W.	
"	17.11.17		Capt Cox rejoined from its Adv. Dressing Sta. LIEVIN, having been relieved by the 2/3 Canadian F. Amb. F.W. A.D.M.S. visited the camp. F.W.	
"	18.11.17		A.D.M.S. visited hospital accommodation provided by way of Record Nissen Hut, increased by one more bivouac & a Church painted at 10.a.m. Condensed to Rome tents & into the 178th Inf. Bde. Experienced to the Rome tents & his office at HERMAVILLE this evening. Received his instructions. And Lieut R.A. BOSTOCK re-posted to the unit for duty. Visited A.D.M.S. at his office at HERMAVILLE. Fw. Lieut R.A. BOSTOCK re-posted to the unit for duty. F.W. Marched with 2/4 Lincolns to C.C.S. F.W.	
"	19.11.17		Packed up all equipment & stores. Cleared all sick to HENDECOURT (X.17.b Sheet 51.C. 178th Inf. Bde. at 4.15 pm, via Danville & Wailly, the rest of the Brigade being at 1 occupied billets (huts) in the village, France 1/40,000) HENDECOURT & BLAIREVILLE (X.4.a.) in the two villages. F.W.	

Vol. XIV Page 5

Army Form C. 2118.

2/2nd North Midland WAR DIARY Field Ambulance

INTELLIGENCE SUMMARY.

(Erase heading not required.)

Instructions regarding War Diaries and Intelligence Summaries are contained in F.S. Regs., Part II. and the Staff Manual respectively. Title pages will be prepared in manuscript.

Place	Date	Hour	Summary of Events and Information	Remarks and references to Appendices
HENDECOURT X.17.b.8 Sheet 51C [France 1:40,000]	20-11-17		Remained at HENDECOURT today - overhauled equipment, separating stores not required for advanced dressing station work from those required. The attack on Cambrai began this morning and we are in reserve and are to be prepared to move "light" with only receiving stores. Capt. Cox posted to temporary duty to No. 48 C.C.S. & Lt. Bostock to No. 21 C.C.S. today. Capt. B. Whitehead, Capt. H. More & Capt. J.J. Meenan posted to this Unit for duty. Capt. Meenan went for temporary duty to No.1 & 1/1 North Mid Fd Ambs. (by order of 88th D.D.M.S. VIth Corps). One horse and ambulance detached in duty at office of D.D.M.S. VIth Corps. Called at Brigade Headquarters this morning. J.W.J.	
"	21-11-17		Attended conference Field Amb. Commanders at A.D.M.S. Office, Barastre (Q.34.b. sheet 51C) this morning. Received instructions as to the duties of this field ambulance in the event of the division going into action. Orders received at 5:30pm to dump all surplus kit stores at Brigade Dump to be prepared to turn out at 6pm. Surplus of three lorry loads of stores & kits unloaded at 9pm with the Brigade. Occupied billets vacated by 4/1 Field Amb. (Naval D.W.). The battalions are under canvas in the immediate neighbourhood of the village. J.W.J.	
GOMIECOURT A.29.b.1.9 Sheet 57C [France 1:40,000]	22-11-17		Weather very bad. Visited all battalion camps today. The M.O.s arranged to collect sick & transferred all to C.C.S. or battn Rest stations. The front occupied by the 56th Division. Visited their main dressing station at BEUGNY (J.21.b. Sheet 57C). A.D.M.S. called & I accompanied him with Capt. Waters to the sector to be prepared to move to train for BIHUCOURT WEST station near BOURSIES at J.11.b.10.9 (All sheet 57C). Advanced dressing stations at J.9.d.5.3 & near.	
"	23-11-17		Orders received 1am to be prepared to move to Yerwick, remaining & after several Evacuated to the aft school marched at 11.15am to BIHUCOURT WEST (Q.16.b. sheet 57C) & near ACHIET-LE-GRAND at noon. Cancelling orders as well. Marched at 9.30am via transport of 178th Inf. Brigade entrained at half past transport detained at FINS (V.12.C.) Batteries and ammunition EQUANCOURT (V.10.b.) & turned in billets there. Marched to EQUANCOURT [(V.10.b.) Sheet 57C.]	J.W.J.

Vol. XI Page 6

Army Form C. 2118.

2/2nd North Midland WAR DIARY Field Ambulance

INTELLIGENCE SUMMARY

(Erase heading not required.)

Place	Date	Summary of Events and Information	Remarks and references to Appendices
EQUANCOURT V.10.a.9.9. Sheet 57c France 1:40,000	24.11.17	No further news of any move today. Capt. Meenan returned from temporary duty with N. Mid. Horse to do the motor ambt. work (Lieut. Davis 2nd i/c). A.D.M.S. called this afternoon.	
	25.11.17	Weather very cold & wet. The spare kit & horse blankets left at Brigade dump GONIECOURT (?) were brought on today by lorry. A Nissen hut is used as hospital ward, men being billeted in Nissen huts, but some men under canvas. (J.W.)	
"	26.11.17	Nothing of note. (J.W.)	
"	27.11.17	Orders received to be prepared to move with 178 Inf. Bde. early tomorrow. Division was transferred to 4th Corps today - (J.W.)	
"	28.11.17	Move orders cancelled. Dump & surplus hut stores formed in Equancourt, and wagons loaded with necessary equipment only. (J.W.)	
"	29.11.17	Orders received to move with the A.D.M.S Divnl Stretcher Bearers tonight, to take over the Fontaine-les-Croisilles advanced dressing station & ... bearers & relief bearers to Hesquières (K.24 & 6.) Sheet 57c Division in with Capt Watson. Meenan & the rest arriving at 1 am. of the 30th. (J.W.)	
"	30.11.17	At 5 am. I posted Capt Watson, 6 Meenan, & 12 other ranks at the advanced dressing station at La frotte (L.1.d.8.8 Sheet 57c), & also posted bearers at the Relay posts & appointed advd posts relieving the personnel of the 4th I./ad. there. Orders received to establish our headquarters at Neuville (Q.4.c Sheet 57c) & later, I proceeded there with the rear ½ the personnel, & Capt. Meehan brought the remainder of the unit & transport on from Equancourt, arriving late in the evening, & encamped for the night. A sick collecting station was taken over from the 3.F.Amb. consisting of 2 dug out accommodating 14, & one tent.	

Fred (?) Fitzsimon
Lieut. Col. Ramsay
OC 2/2 N. Mid. F. Ambl

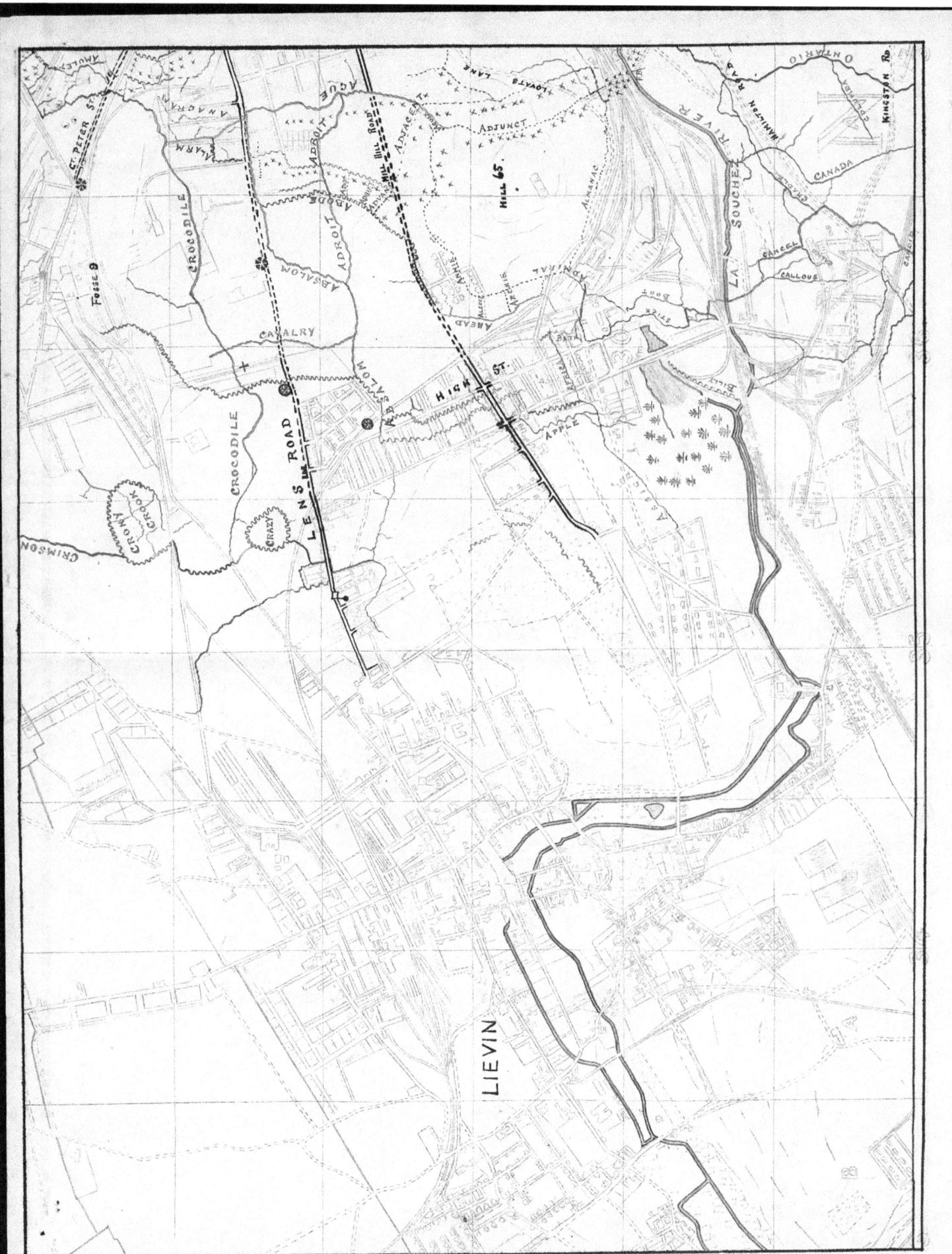

Confidential
War Diary
of
2/2 N. Mid. Fd. Amb

From 1-12-17.   To 31-12-17.

Volume 12

Vol. XII Page 1

2/2nd North Midland Field Ambulance

Army Form C. 2118.

WAR DIARY

INTELLIGENCE SUMMARY.

(Erase heading not required.)

Place	Date	Summary of Events and Information	Remarks and references to Appendices
METZ Q.14.c.8.8. Sheet 57C France	30.11.17	The Advanced Dressing Station at LA JUSTICE and Bearer-posts in the BOURLON–FONTAINE sector having been taken over by this unit yesterday, the evacuation of casualties from the 59th Divisional front is now proceeding satisfactorily. Visits & inspections of the 59th Divisional front led us this morning to the Advanced Dressing Station. Visits & inspections on this Divisional front as well as opening commenced early this morning at other points. Casualties commenced to arrive about 8 a.m. at the Advanced Dressing Station. Many gassed patients were coming from the battalions in Bourlon Wood, and a request for more bearers was met by the dispatching Capt. MacDonald & 20 extra bearers to the R.A.P. in the Quarry, in 2/1st N. Mid. Fd. Ambe. (F.18.c.7.5 Sheet 57c). Bearers all worked excellently and Bourlon trench was cleared well & quickly. Evacuation was helped by the Casualties were cleared by wheeled stretcher-carriers possible from the Bearer relay post at (F.19.d.5.2 Sheet 57c) to the A.D.S. LA JUSTICE (L.1.d.9.6) late, to 2/6 S. Staffs, in posted, in Medical officer, in place Capt. MacDonald was evacuated to Hospital Graincourt (W) and evacuation of Capt. Owens who was under shell-fire for some time. The A.D.S. at La Justice was under shell-fire for some time by his Ambulance to the main Dressing Station at Hesquières by Motor Ambulance From there the drivers of ambulances did the evacuation difficult & dangerous but the A.D.s. also carrying inspection was rendered and the personnel of the A.D.S. were in places of constant danger from shell. The result was excellent work in spite of the most satisfactory, amounting to nearly 2000 passing through the clutter & all casualties, were all cleared to the main Dressing Station. Advanced Dressing Station were all cleared to the main Dressing Station before midnight. Capt. Watson was posted to Div. H? fro this morning, in acting D.A.D.M.S. and was a place with A.D.S. by Capt. More. The arrangement of Medicine Field Ambulance Units is shewn in Appendix 1 — Appendix 1 F.N.	Appendix 1 F.N.

Vol. XII Page 2

2/2nd North Midland Field Ambulance

WAR DIARY

INTELLIGENCE SUMMARY

Army Form C. 2118.

Place	Date	Hour	Summary of Events and Information	Remarks and references to Appendices
METZ Q.14.c.8.8 Sheet 57d [Trans approved]	1-12-17		Capt Meenan evacuated to hospital [gassed] (W). Relieved the bearers in the Relay posts & at the Reg. Aid posts tobay. Visited Advanced Dressing Station with A.D.M.S. & also the Bearer posts. Capt Malcolm opened sick collecting station at Harincourt wood (Q.14.c.8.8) Capt Whitehead remained in charge of Sick Collecting near Metz. Capt Whitehead and self there was considerable shelling. The station at TRESCAULT and so there was considerable sick cases also in the villages & roads in this neighbourhood, and numerous local cases dealt with. He converted the post into a Temporary Dressing Station & dealt with them. There was difficulty in evacuating the cases, over 200 having been accumulated during the night 30/11/17 – 1/12/17 and a message having been sent to A.D.M.S. M.A.C. Cars and 8 Ambulance sh[e]ll cars were evacuated. The light railway proved most useful. Night trains could only be started after much trouble; late, & could only be established at Rib[e]court, and one at Trescault owing to hostile shelling, rendering a loading post here to be abandoned but the former had Visited headquarters this afternoon, remaining there for the night. F.N.	
"	2-12-17		Returned to Main Dressing Station Flesquières this morning. Visited Advanced Dressing Station, La Justice & also Bearer posts. Fairly quiet day. Came the Ravine. bearer killed & not very numerous. The Ravine bearer killed & two wounded.	B.P.

Vol XLI Page 3

2/2nd North Midland Field Ambulance

WAR DIARY
Army Form C. 2118.

INTELLIGENCE SUMMARY

Place	Date	Hour	Summary of Events and Information	Remarks and references to Appendices
METZ [Q.14.c.8.8]	3.12.17		A.D.M.S. visited the A.D.S. & Relay Post this morning. The Relay Post was badly shelled & partially destroyed during the morning. The bearers of the 47th Division on the left of our front have become the D.this post, as well as our own bearers to the Confederate movement of this point, & since Tremators no doubt accounts for this. He considers well withdrawn today & a commencement made with a new relay post in the sunken road 3 at F.25.6.6.4, 200 yds further back. Capt. Young returned from temporary duty with 2/8 Sherwood Foresters & was posted to the Advanced Dressing Station today with Capt. Moe. Information received from Div H.Qrs that a withdrawal of the line might take place this evening, so this morning a commencement was made with the removal of stores from the Advanced Dressing Station. Later in the day definite instructions were received from A.D.M.S. that all equipment, stores & personnel were to be withdrawn to Flesquières by midnight. The large Dug-outs & shelters were thoroughly cleaned up and the Dressing Rooms, besides a considerable amount of Medical comforts & medical stores being accumulated & stretchers blankets Kit equipment which had been collected from the Main Dressing Station were all removed & evacuated from the Advanced Dressing Station. All personnel were withdrawn from the A.D.S. by 7 p.m. to the Main Dressing Station except Capt. Young & bearer parties to the tune of 12 men who remained until the troops had all withdrawn from the position except the rear-guard.	
"	4.12.17		The Main Dressing Station was evacuated by the 2/3 N. Mid. F. Ambl. this evening & an Advanced Dressing Station was established in its place. J.W.J.	

Vol XII Page 4

2/2nd North Midland Field Ambulance

WAR DIARY

INTELLIGENCE SUMMARY

(Erase heading not required.)

Place	Date	Hour	Summary of Events and Information	Remarks and references to Appendices
METZ (Q.14.c.8.8)	5-12-17		Proceeded to Ribécourt and established an advanced Dressing Station in the village at L.2.5. central (Sheet 57C). Transferred its personnel & stores here from Flesquières (notes Capt. C.J.D. Bergin & Capt here was hesied here). Capt Young remained with 12 bearers in a Bearer Post at Flesquières. The Bearer post was moved into the cellars today & officials. The casualties were brought in during the preceding 24 hours & Very few casualties were taken place since the withdrawal from the 130 up to Wood position has taken place since no enemy action has taken place near them for All R.A.M.C. personnel attached 8 Battalions remain with them for the present. There was very little cellar accommodation, and the new A.D.S. at Ribécourt sheltly of the flagstones the roof & She was considered safe on the building but no casualties There direct hits were made on the building, & were placed in the cellars, & All patients fit to walk were placed in the dressing-room occurred. the few stretcher cases in the J.W.Y. which is fairly safe.	
"	6-12-17		Very busy day at the A.D.S. Wounded in trains & arrive the whole day, principally from the 36th & 6th Divisions. A small proportion from our own. Winded Capt. Young of the Beaver-Post Flesquières found that the building had been heavily shelling & the building & a good number of wounded was at the time in the dressing-room casualty evacuation. Capt. Young assisted by No. 419378 Pte Kingston C. 2/2 N. Mid. F.A.C. behaved excellent work under heavy shell fire in getting the patients transferred to the cellars. There was a joint German attack during the afternoon in the was forming in front of Flesquières, but it was beaten off about 40 casualties being dealt with after the action. J.W.Y.	

Vol. XII Page 5

Army Form C. 2118.

2/2nd North Midland WAR DIARY Field Ambulance

INTELLIGENCE SUMMARY.

(Erase heading not required.)

Place	Date	Hour	Summary of Events and Information	Remarks and references to Appendices
ETZ (14.C.8.8)	7-12-17		Large number of blankets & stretchers were salved today at the bearer post. Stretchers removed by ambulance to the A.D.S. Ribécourt. Also a good deal of Red Cross medical store, all salvaged were safely removed to Ribécourt. Evacuation of wounded proceeding smoothly — not so many casualties today. F.W.	
"	8.12-17		Visited bearer post at Flesquières this morning. Found the building very much damaged by shell fire. Visited headquarters of the 3 later & also A.D.M.S. at Div. H. Q. Ribécourt. F.W.	
"	9-12-17		Returned to Wounded Descripn Station Ribécourt visiting the Walking Wounded Collecting Post at Trescault on the way. A.D.M.S. called here & gave me instructions to take over this post, & to be responsible for the evacuation back from the Division of all wounded, though to the train. All wounded sick from the Division except those of serious & urgent nature were today sent to 5 M.A.C. Cars were attached as also ambulance from the Trescault. Three divisional cars were also sent today, one by sledge & five by mechanical traction. Just two wounded were got through to the main dressing station to Royal count. F.W.	
"	10-12-17		Took over the charge of the Walking Wounded Collecting Post at Trescault, we being relieved by 36th Div. party today at Trescault. The O.C. of 59th Div. & Maj of 47th Div. visited here. F.W.	
"	11-12-17		47th Div. representatives were relieved by 36th Div. party, & wounded from 59th & 47th Divisions are received here, evacuated by light railway & by motor ambulances to main dressing station Royal count. F.W.	

Vol XVI page 5

Army Form C. 2118.

2/1 West Riding Field Ambulance

WAR DIARY

INTELLIGENCE SUMMARY.

(Erase heading not required.)

Place	Date	Summary of Events and Information	Remarks and references to Appendices
METZ Q.14.c.8.8.	12-12-17	Lt. Kennedy 2/1st W.R. 1st ad. wrote to Advanced Dressing Station Ref. card, in relief of Capt. Hone, 2/2 N.M.F. ad. who returned to his quarters. had 3 Visited A.D.S. Ribecourt, & made a tour of inspection of cellars in the village with a view to discovering one suitable cellar accommodation to the Town hall. Found a good cellar adjacent to ice in a battalion Stretcher-case Station under the Brasserie on the Havincourt Road. Had quarters under the Town hall to have the use of the cellar in case of emergency. Always into Town hall to have the use of some of the support trenches behind Visited bearer post Flesquières & some of the support trenches behind Flesquières. Reported to brigade on the insanitary condition of the latter. Capt. Mitchell returned from temporary duty with 2/1st Leicesters Brasseries (Read?) at Metz. W.I.	
	13-12-17	ADMS 59th Div, ADMS 61st Div. + ADMS 36 Div. all cases of Walking Wounded Collecting Post Trescault this morning. 36 Div. replies none material for construction of some splinter-proof shelters for wounded. Visited headquarters later. Found the camp had been shelled & the Officers' mess & two dugouts destroyed. No casualties. Arranging Removed considerable number of blanket, stretchers etc. to train Dressing Station, Ribecourt, from Ribecourt Trescault. Visited 177th Bde. Head qrs. & explained present arrangements for the support Brigade. W.I.	

Vol. XII Page 87

WAR DIARY
or
INTELLIGENCE SUMMARY

Army Form C. 2118.

Place	Date	Hour	Summary of Events and Information	Remarks and references to Appendices
METZ (214.c.8.8.)	14-12-17	a.m.	Working party of 20 of this unit & 20 of the 36th Div. started work today on excavation for new shelters at Trescault. Trench boards laid down there, & new cook-house commenced. J.W.	
	15-12-17	2 p.m.	One N.C.O. & 8 men of 63rd Div. arrived at Trescault in replacement of 36th Div. Work of excavating shelters continued to-day. J.W. representatives to-day.	
	16-12-17	a.m.	New medical arrangements came into force to-day. All troops in this area are now in 5th Corps, all wounded are evacuated through Havrincourt. 59th Div. was extended to include Havrincourt. 59th Div. has arranged relays of motor ambulances to Main Dressing Station, Ruyaulcourt, & arranged trains on light railway for casualties. 63rd Div. has control of all evacuation over tops & is not carried to-day. Also 1 to 6 P.M. are arranged this evacuation from Trescault. He dug out is not carried out 7 walking wounded from 61st & 63rd Div. as wounded evacuated from 61st & 63rd Div. as walking by 5.9 & 7.17 to Dumains & wounded. A first man the light railway. J.W.	
	17-12-17	p.m.	19th Div. representatives (O.H. & S.O.2) replaced 63rd Div. party at Trescault. Went to the Frères O.C. 20th Corps Light Railway Co. & arranged time table within two trains daily to Trescault & Havrincourt for evacuating back & slightly wounded. Visited the Advanced Dressing Station, Ruyaulcourt, at present being 25 minutes by personnel of 47th Division. s.a. Brig v. Colo visited Trescault. J.W.	

A5834 Wt.W4973/M687 750,000 8/16 D.D. & L. Ltd. Forms/C.2118/13

WAR DIARY

2/1 North Midland Field Ambulance

INTELLIGENCE SUMMARY

(Erase heading not required.)

Army Form C. 2118.

Part XII
Page 75 No. 7/12

Place	Date	Hour	Summary of Events and Information	Remarks and references to Appendices
METZ Q.14.c.8.8)	18-12-17		Capt. Whitehead posted to 2/1 Newcastle in place of Capt. Clark seconded M.C.R. Placed personnel of the Ambulance trains on the D/Railway. Interviewed O.C. 467 R.O.E.S. G.R.E. respecting his advice re the dug-outs at "Trescault". JW.	
	19-12-17		A.D.M.S. 19th Div. called to see the work at Trescault. A.D.M.S. 5th Div. & D.D.M.S. 17th Div. visited all the front area this morning. I accompanied them to Ribécourt, Flesquières & Havrincourt. Several casualties to R.A.M.C. personnel at A.D.S. Ribecourt this evening, 2 Bty (Kelly) F1 severely wounded. JW.	
	20-12-17		Two bearer officers 1/1 N.M. visited our front posts & A.D.S. visited today & made arrangements for taking over from this Field Amb. on the 21st & 22nd inst. JW.	
	21-12-17		Bearer-Sergt & R.A.P. personnel at Flesquières were relieved this morning by 51st Field Amb. party - also the Staff of the advanced Dressing Station at Ribecourt & Staircourt this afternoon. Trescault was closed & the walking wounded (incl. Trescault) handed over to 51st Field Amb. All personnel returned to this unit near Hut 5. See Copy an Ap Ron. Slem noted. JW.	

2/2 North Midland Field Amb.

WAR DIARY Vol XII

Army Form C. 2118.

INTELLIGENCE SUMMARY Page 9.

(Erase heading not required.)

Place	Date	Hour	Summary of Events and Information	Remarks and references to Appendices
Quh C.8.c METZ. (Sheet 57.c)	22/12/17		Happis at Qu.h C.8.c, sheet 57.c, were relieved by 3rd F.Amb. and the Unit proceeded to LE TRANSLOY and took over Det. Amb. site at N.24.d.6.4. (Sheet 57.c) from 3/3rd F.d Amb. Att.746. Lt Col H.W. Johnson proceeded on one month's leave to England, on Au.F. L.1.2322 of 19.12.16 and I Corps L.I.955 of 29/12/17, and handed over temporary command of the Unit and control of the advance account to Capt. H.F. Malister. Att.746.	
	23/12/17		In relief at N.24.d.6.4, sheet 57.C.	
	24/12/17		Transport, lins & Nursing O.S. and 1 Waterfort proceeded under Capt. Welker with 178. Rd. Bde. Transport to ARMET-LES-PETIT. (LSMS.N.V.0000). Journey to MIDWIMEAUX. completed on 25/12/17 under orders of O.C. 576 Coy R.E.C. M.746.	
	25/12/17		Personnel and remainder of Transport moved by train to FREVENT and marched to MONIHEAUX Hqrs were established at H.1.a. & S. sheet 57.c. M.746	
	26/12/17		Opened small Reception Hospital of 10 beds for 178 Inf. Bde. Accommodation at ground MH46. 59th D.R.O. no.154 of 24/12/17 received in this it was announced that 4.4372 Pte Kingston, C. and 4.9382 Pte Carlin Pat J.A. of this Unit have been awarded the Military Medal. 28/746.	
	27/12/17		Permission received from 178 Inf. Bde. to send the Unit from MIDINCHEBAUX to BIVNEVILLE. Since then a letter has been received. 2.D.R.O. 256 of 26/12/17 it was announced that the Military Medal has been awarded 5469.32796. Pampe. Unit moved to BIVNEVILLE (LSMS.N.V.0000) Hqrs established at A.24.a.6.2 (sheet 57.c) and Division Hospital for out patients established. M.746.	
	28/12/17		Nothing of note.	
	29/12/17		Ammunition received in train. Nothing of note M746.	
	30/12/17			
	31/12/17		Leaves complete School 50 men were installed. M.P.M.D Say the men Received Leaflets and little fitted etc. M.746.	

[Signed]

Appendix I

Map references to Sheet 57.C., France 1 in 40,000.

System of Evacuation of wounded from 59th Divisional Front
30th Nov. 1917.

Advanced Dressing Station at La Justice (L.1.d.9.7)
  Personnel 2 M.O.'s & 15 other ranks.

Bearer Relay Post in a dug-out at F.19.b.8.8, near the light railway track. Personnel 1 N.C.O. & 12 bearers.

Regimental Aid Posts:
  Left Subsector – (1) In Chateau, Bourlon Wood (F.13.b.3.8)
  (2) In Quarry, Bourlon Wood (F.18.c.7.5)

  Right Subsector (1) Dug-out in trench at F.20.c.4.4
  (2) Dug-out in trench at F.27.c.3.4

R.A.M.C. personnel at the Regimental Aid Posts consisted of 1 N.C.O. & 20 bearers at the Quarry, Bourlon Wood, 1 N.C.O. & 6 bearers at the dug-out at F.20.c.4.4
1 N.C.O. & 6 bearers at the dug-out at F.27.c.3.4

Evacuation from the Left subsector was by hand-carry to the bearer relay post at F.19.b.8.8, thence by wheel-stretcher carriers to the Advanced Dressing Station.

Casualties from the R.A.P. at F.20.c.4.4 were carried to the bearer relay post & thence by wheel-stretcher carrier to the advanced dressing station.

Those from the R.A.P. at F.27.c.3.4 were carried by R.A.M.C. personnel to the sunken road at L.2.b.5.5 and thence by wheel stretcher carrier to the advanced dressing station.

Sketch plan of Evacuation Route

F.W. Johnston
Lt.Col.

140/2691

2/2nd North Midland F.A.

COMMITTEE FOR THE
MEDICAL HISTORY OF THE WAR

Date -4 MAR. 1918

2/2 11th Mid. F.A. Amb.

Vol. I 1918
Page 1.

Army Form C. 2118.

WAR DIARY
INTELLIGENCE SUMMARY
(Erase heading not required.)

Instructions regarding War Diaries and Intelligence Summaries are contained in F.S. Regs., Part II. and the Staff Manual respectively. Title pages will be prepared in manuscript.

Place	Date	Hour	Summary of Events and Information	Remarks and references to Appendices
BUSNEVILLE A24 d 4.2. (Sheet 57 C France)	1/1/18		Notified that the Division is in G.H.Q. Reserve and is to report at H.Q. Rouen on Jan. 14/18. The supplement to London Gazette issued on 24th & 28th Dec 1917 contained the names of Lieut. Col. F. W. Johnson (Lt. Col. W.W. McCord I) R.A.M.C.(T.F.) and Capt. F.H.G. Waters, R.A.M.C.(T.F.) in his dispatch noted Nov 7, 1917, for distinguished services and devotion to duty. R.2.7.46.	
"	2/1/18		Lieut. Peak has proceeded to N.A.E.R.S. to attend Sanitary Course detailed in 3rd Army A/Q/104/11/18. R.2.7.46.	
"	3/1/18		The following Medical Officers were detailed to attend a series of Lectures arranged by Lt. Entry on 4th, 5th, 7th, 8th, 9th Jan. (Appendix I):- Capt. Davies (2/7 Sherwoods) Capt. Mercer (2/5 Sherwoods) Capt. J.A. Young & Capt. Weldon, 2/1 W.W. R.Amb. R.2.7.46.	Appendix I
"			Summary of R.O. No 878. 7/2/11/18 published the information that Capt. T.A. Young, on officer of this Unit has been awarded the M.C. R.2.7.46.	
"	4/1/18.		Lieut. G.C. Crosier posted for duty to 2/5 Sherwoods in relief of Capt. Watson proceeding on leave to England. R.2.7.46.	
"	5/1/18.		Lieut. Bowden rejoined the Unit. R.2.7.46. Training Programme 31/12/17 - 5/1/18 issued. R.2.7.46.	Appendix II
"	6/1/16.		Nothing of note. R.2.7.46.	
"	7/1/18.		Capt. Welsher posted to 59th D.A.C. in relief of Capt. A. Bergin, on leave. R.2.7.46.	
"	8/1/18.		Nothing unusual, difficulty in collection of rations & water. R.2.7.46.	
"	9/1/18.		Capt. R. Welsh returned from 2/5 Sherwoods, Lieut. of Capt. C. Mercer sent to Hospital R.2.7.46. Capt. J.A. Young proceeded to N.A.E.R.S. for Sanitary Course (3 Army A/Q/10/14/10). R.2.7.46.	
"	10/1/18.		Nothing of note. R.2.7.46.	
"	11/1/18.		"New precautions taken". R.2.7.46. Capt. J.A. Young rejoined the Unit. R.2.7.46.	
"	12/1/18.		During the week a bath consisting of storage was filled up. 2280 men, in addition to certain civilians can be bathed weekly. Weekly Training Programme from 6/1/18. Wt 7/1/18. attached. R.2.7.46.	Appendix III

2/2 h. M. 3rd Amb.

WAR DIARY
or
INTELLIGENCE SUMMARY.

Army Form C. 2118.

Vol I 1916 Page 2.

Place	Date	Hour	Summary of Events and Information	Remarks and references to Appendices
BUMIOVILLE (Sheet 57 C.)	13/1/16		Three men of the Unit, 41586 O.Thompson (4/5 313), 25 C. Kingston (4/4378) and 25 J.Cartwright (4/4432) were presented with the ribbon of the Military Medal by the Divisional Commander. M.M78	
"	14/1/16		Nothing of note. M.778	
"	15/1/16		do. M.778	
"	16/1/16		do. M.778	
"	17/1/16		do. M.778	
"	18/1/16		Capt. L.M. Weedon returned from duty with 59th R.F.C. M.778	
"	19/1/16		Capt. A.L. Bodley Report reported for duty and was taken on the strength, authority naval 57th Div. M.3706 Training programme 13/1/16 to 19/1/16 attached. M.778	Appendix IV
"	20/1/16		Capt. J.A. Young was presented with the ribbon of the Military Cross by the Divisional Commander. M.3726.	
"	21/1/16		Nothing of note.	
"	22/1/16		Lydd y minoc.	
"	23/1/16		Lieut. Col. J.W. Johnson returned from leave and resumed command of the Unit from Lieut. Col. Johnson took over important account withdrawn by A.D.M.S. 6 h.h. 371.90 from Govt. Approaching. M3726. A.D.M.S. visited the Dr. from 2 pm & inspected arrangements in to	
"	24/1/16		Visited the trio de arca & inspected all sanitary arrangements. The four middle officers of the tobies this morning. 30	
"	25/1/16		Training programme proceeded with. Informed management per published was shared today. M.730.	

Vol I 1918
2/2nd North Midland Field Ambulance pg 3

WAR DIARY INTELLIGENCE SUMMARY

Army Form C. 2118.

(Erase heading not required.)

Place	Date	Hour	Summary of Events and Information	Remarks and references to Appendices
BUNEVILLE	26-1-18		Men of the unit bathed this afternoon. Football match.	Appendix V
"	27-1-18		Cards of commendation for Distinguished Conduct for bravery in action issued to the M2/229716 Pte. Field, S.A., M.T., A.S.C. attached to this unit. Church parade (C of E) at 3 p.m. by Lieut. G.C. Crown & Dr. W.H. Rowden. Proceeded to 104 Field Ambulance for 10 days course of instruction. (JW)	
"	28-1-18		Nothing of note. (JW)	
"	29-1-18		Nothing of note. 13 inoculations – winter duty men (PB) C/O promoted to 178th and 132nd. 2nd & 13th men. (JW)	
"	30-1-18		Training programme continued - class for N.C.Os with small practice this morning. Lecture by Capt Young on "Water". (JW)	
"	31-1-18		Attended conference at A.D.M.S. Office this morning. During the month just included a considerable amount of training has been carried out - reinforcements instructed in training to the & equipment rations overhauled & completed to scale. (JW)	

J.W. [signature]
O.C. 2/2 N. Mid 2d Amb.

Appendix I

PROGRAMME OF COURSE OF LECTURES FOR MEDICAL OFFICERS, VITH CORPS.
****

Date.	Place.	Time.	Subject.	Lecturer.
1918.				
Jan. 4th	104th F.Amb. (S.2.b.7.4.)	2.30 p.m.	"Medical Organisation of the Army in the Field."	Col.KATTA, A.D.M.S. 8th Division.
Jan. 4th	104th F.Amb. (S.2.b.7.4.)	3.30 p.m.	"Ordnance Supply in relation to the Medical Services in the Field."	Capt. STRICKLAND, D.A.D.O.S.34th Div.
Jan. 5th.	MOYENNVILLE. (S.28.c.2.4.)	2.30 p.m.	Practical Demonstration in Field Sanitation.	Capt. J.H.STONE, O.C.38th San.Sect.
Jan. 5th.	27 San.Sec.29 (S.28.c.2.4.)	3.30 p.m.	"Sanitation and Water Supplies in the Trenches, Billets and Camps."	Capt. J.H.STONE, O.C.38th San. Sect.
Jan. 7th.	104th F.Amb. (S.2.b.7.4.)	2.30 p.m.	"Treatment of Wounds at the Front."	Capt.K. WALKER, R.A.M.C.
Jan. 7th.	-do-	3.30 p.m.	Demonstration in Splints and other appliances.	-do-
Jan. 8th.	-do-	2.30 p.m.	"Bacteriology as applied to Medical Work in the Field."	O.C.25 Mob. Lab.
Jan. 8th.	-do-	3.30 p.m.	"'A' & 'Q' Work in the Field."	Brig.Gen.J.A.G. TULLOCH.
Jan. 9th.	-do-	2.30 p.m.	"The Organisation and Function of a Field Ambulance."	Lt.Col.ROSS TAYLOR, 3rd Division.
Jan. 9th.	-do-	3.30 p.m.	"'G' Work in the Field."	Major SHERIJKER, G.S.O.2, VIth Corps.

Vol I   Appendix II   War Diary. 1918

PROGRAMME OF TRAINING.
2/2 N. Mid. Fld Amb.   30.12.17. to 5.1.18.

	Sunday 30.12.17.	Monday 31.12.17.	Tuesday 1.1.18.
9 am.	Parade for C.O's Inspection. Fatigues detailed to clear roads. Parade dismissed.	Route March.	Inspection of Anti-gas Respirators.
10 am.	Nil	" "	Anti-gas drill.
11 am.	Nil	" "	Physical drill.
12 noon.	Nil	" "	Squad Drill.
12.30 pm.	Nil	Parade Dismissed.	Parade dismissed.
2 pm.	Nil	Lecture on primary treatment of wounded in the line.	Lecture by Q.M.
3 pm.	Church Parade	Instruction on contents of Medical Surgical, and Hospl Panniers.	Instruction on contents of Medical Surgical, and Hospl Panniers.
4.30 pm.	Nil	Parade dismissed.	Parade dismissed.

	Wed 2.1.18.	Thursday 3.1.18.	Fri. 4.1.18.	Sat. 5.1.18.
9 am	Physical Drill.	Physical Drill	Route March	Internal economy. Parties will be detailed for clean-ing of wagons. Remainder will be employed in clean-ing all billets, store rooms, etc. Issue of Clothing & Equipment by QM
10 am	Stretcher Drill.	Stretcher Drill.	" "	
11 am	Squad Drill	Squad Drill	" "	
12 noon	Company Drill	Company Drill.	" "	
12.30 pm.	Parade Dismd.	Parade Dismd.	Parade dismd	Parade dismissed.
2 pm	Foot Inspection & Chiropody. The M.O. will at same time give short lecture on care of feet. Scabies & Lice Inspection. When inspections are over, men not requiring treatment will be employed on fatigues.	Lecture on Nursing duties at Dressing Stn. Instruction on contents of Medical, Surgical Field & Hospl Panniers.	Lecture on Sanitation.	Parade & Roll Call Necessary fatigues will be detailed & parade dismd.
3 pm			Lecture by Q.M. on Cooking.	
4 pm.				
4.30 pm.	Parade Dismd.	Parade dismd.	Parade dismd.	

Bathing will be arranged for small parties during drill hours.

---O---

OC 2/2 N. M. Fd Amb

War Diary Vol: 1918. Appendix III

PROGRAMME OF TRAINING.
2/2 N.Mid. Fld Amb.   6.1.18 to 12.1.18.

	Sunday 6th	Monday 7th	Tuesday 8th	Wednesday 9th
am	C.O's Parade	Route March.	Inspection of Anti-gas Respirators.	Physical Drill.
10 "		"	Physical Drill.	Stretcher Drill.
11 "	Church Parade at time arranged by Chaplain.	"	Anti-gas Drill.	Squad Drill.
12 Noon		"	Squad Drill.	Company Drill.
12.30 pm.		Parade Dismd	Parade Dismd.	Parade Dismd.
2 pm		Lecture on causes & prevention of Trench feet.	Sections 4-44 of Army Act willbe read on parade also order re reporting at once Venereal Disease	Foot Inspection & Chiropody.
3 pm		15 minutes Squad Drill to promote circulation. Instruction on contents of Medical, Surgical and Hospl Panniers.	15 minutes squad drill. Instruction on contents of Medical, Surgical & Hospl Panrs.	Scabies & Lice Inspection. When inspections are over men not requiring treatment will be employed on fatigues.
4 pm.	Parade Dismd	Parade Dismd.	Parade Dismd.	Parade dismd.

	Thursday 10th	Friday 11th	Saturday 12th.
9 am	Physical Drill	Route March	Internal Economy. Parties will be detailed for cleaning wagons. Billets, storerooms etc. will be cleaned.
10 "	Stretcher Drill	"	
11 "	Squad Drill	"	Kit inspection and issue of clothing & equipment by Q.M.
12 Noon.	Company Drill	"	
12.30pm	Parade Dismd.	Parade Dismd,	Parade Dismd.
2 pm	Lecture on Venereal Disease.	Lecture on Infectious Diseases which are liable to arise amongst troops.	Parade & Roll Call. Necessary Fatigues will be told off & Parade dismissed.
3 pm	15 minutes Squad Drill. Instruction on contents of Medical, Surgical, & Hospl Panniers.	PHYSICAL DRILL	
4 pm	Parade Dismissed.	Parade Dismd.	

Bathing will be arranged for small parties during drill hours.

---o---

F.W. Johnson
Lt. Col.
OC 2/2 N.Mid. F.Amb.

War Diary Vol I. 1918. Appendix IV

PROGRAMME OF TRAINING.
2/2 N. Mid. Fld Amb.   13.1.18 to 19.1.18.

	Sunday 13th.	Monday 14th	Tuesday 15th	Wednesday 16th.
9 am	Parade for Inspection	Route March	Physical Drill.	Bathing. Bath in each case to be followed by one hour's physical drill.
10 am	CHURCH PARADE	do	Inspection of Respirators & anti-gas drill.	
11 am		do	Squad drill.	
12 am		Parade Dismissed	Parade Dismissed.	
2 pm		Lecture on infectious diseases amongst troops.	Stretcher Drill.	Inspection for Lice & Scabies Foot inspection
3 pm		Ten minutes quick marching & doubling.	Company Drill.	Squad Drill.
4 pm.		Parade Dismissed.	Parade Dismissed.	Parade Dismissed.

	Thursday 17th.	Friday 18th.	Saturday 19th.
9 am	Physical Drill.	Route March.	Internal economy. Party will be detailed to clean wagons.
10 am.	Stretcher drill.		All billets, stores, etc., will be cleaned.
11 am.	Saluting Drill.		Kit inspection & issue of clothing etc by Q.M.
12 midday.	Parade dismissed.	Parade dismissed.	Parade dismissed.
2 pm.	Instruction on Panniers.	Field Sanitation.	Parade dismissed.
3. pm.	Company drill.	Ten minutes quick marching and doubling.	
4 pm.	Parade dismissed	Parade dismissed.	

F. Johnson
Lt. Col.
OC. 2/2 N.M. Fd Amb

War Diary 1918 Vol I Appendix V

PROGRAMME OF TRAINING.
2/2 N.Mid. Field Amb.   20.1.18 to 26.1.18.

	Sunday 20th	Monday 21st	Tuesday 22nd	~~Wednesday 23rd~~ THUR. 24
9 am	Parade for inspection.	Route March	Physical Drill	Physical Drill
10am		do	Inspection of Respirators & Anti-gas Drill.	Stretcher Drill
11am		do	Saluting Drill	Squad Drill
12 Midday		Parade dismissed	Parade Dismissed.	Parade dismissed
2 pm		~~Squad Drill~~	LECTURE ~~Stretcher Drill~~ Waggon Orderlies.	Instruction on Wagon loading.
3 pm		Saluting Drill	Company Drill Parade Dismissed.	Company Drill Parade Dismissed.
4 pm		Parade Dismissed.		
6 pm			Pay Parade	

	~~Sunday 24th~~ WED. 23	Friday 25th	Saturday 26th
9 am	Bathing, in each case to be followed by one hours Physical Drill.	Route March	Internal economy. Party will be detailed to clean wagons. All billets, stores etc will be cleaned. Kit inspection and issue of clothing etc.
10am			
11am	do	do	
12Midday		Parade Dismissed.	Parade dismissed.
2 pm	Scabies & Lice Inspection. Foot Inspection.	Lecture on Water.	Roll call.
3 pm	Squad Drill.	Ten minutes Quick marching & Doubling.	
4 pm		Parade dismissed.	

F W Johnson
Lt. Col.
OC 2/2 N.Mid F.Amb

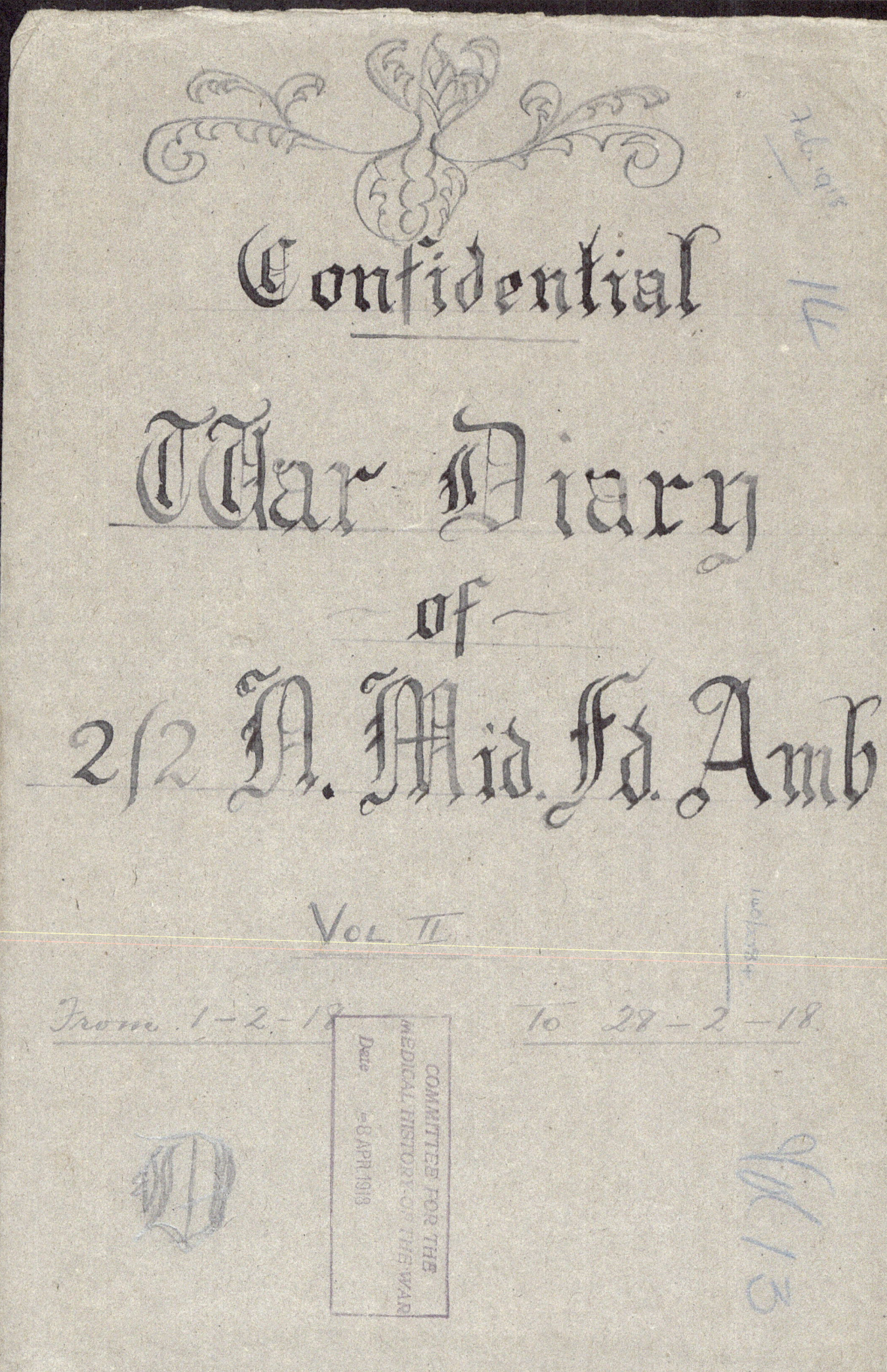

Army Form C. 2118.

2/2d North Midland Field Ambulance Vol. II. Page 1
1918

WAR DIARY

INTELLIGENCE SUMMARY.

(Erase heading not required.)

Instructions regarding War Diaries and Intelligence Summaries are contained in F.S. Regs., Part II. and the Staff Manual respectively. Title pages will be prepared in manuscript.

Place	Date	Summary of Events and Information	Remarks and references to Appendices
BUNÉVILLE Art.d.4.2 Sheet 51C France 1:40,000	1-2-18	Inspected all NCO's & men in full marching order this morn. Training programme continued. Lecture by D.A.D.V.S. on care of horses to pioneer & the Transport section. J.W.	
"	2-2-18	Training programme continued. Afternoon spent in cleaning up equipment & men's kit. J.W.	
"	3-2-18	Church parade at 10 a.m. J.W. 3 officers & men attended meeting of R.A.M.C. officers to inaugurate forming a divisional medical society. J.W.	
"	4-2-18	Inspection of the Unit by A.D.M.S. this afternoon. J.W.	
"	5-2-18	Gave lecture to men on Horsed Ambulances, equipment, uses etc. Orders received from 178 Inf. Bde. to be prepared to move on joining Inf. Bde. J.W.	
"	6-2-18	Packed all equipment on the waggons - J.W.	
"	7-2-18	Orders received to march tomorrow & join with 178th Inf. Bde. Move orders for 7pm till 8am J.W. Capt C.J.D. Bergin posted for temporary duty with 2/1 Sherwood Foresters to follow Ambulance on the march. Visited 178 Bde. Head qrs & arranged for Horsed Ambulance. J.W.	
"	8-2-18	The Field Ambulance marched from BUNÉVILLE at 9.0 a.m. Joining the 178th Inf. Bde. Billeted for the night at BARLY [P.15.d.3.6 Sheet 51.C.] J.W.	
BARLY [P.15.d.3.6 Sheet 51.C.	9-2-18	Capt H. Malcolm proceeded on leave today, but on arrival at BIENVILLERS AU-BOIS instructions from 178 Bde. to march to BIENVILLERS AU-BOIS were obtained. The unit accordingly sent a billetting /pk There were no billets available until tomorrow, he ceased to BERLES-AU-BOIS where billets were obtained. The unit having from today the R.A.M.C. cmce under A.D.M.S. orders the 178 Bde having moved forward in relief of a brigade of the 34 Division. Capt Bergin rejoined for duty from 2/7 Sherwood Foresters. J.W.	
BERLES-AU-BOIS W.15.c.5A Sheet 51.C	"		

A 5834 Wt. W.4973/M687 750,000 8/16 D.D. & L. Ltd. Forms/C.2118/13

Army Form C. 2118.

WAR DIARY — Field Ambulance — INTELLIGENCE SUMMARY

2/2nd North Midland Field Ambulance Vol. II Page 2

1918

Instructions regarding War Diaries and Intelligence Summaries are contained in F.S. Regs, Part II. and the Staff Manual respectively. Title pages will be prepared in manuscript.

(Erase heading not required.)

Place	Date	Summary of Events and Information	Remarks and references to Appendices
BIENVILLERS-AU-BOIS [E.8.a.7.2.] Sheet 57D	10-2-18	Marched from BERLES-AU-BOIS this morning, took over Field Ambulance billets at BIENVILLERS from the 102nd Field Ambulance (34th Div). Capt M. Bowley & Lieut G.C. Corser proceeded to Blaireville to temporary duty with 2/1st N.M. 7 Fd. Amb. (at unit) Ashre a 57 Da.	
"	11-2-18	Bearer subdivision (77 O.R. + rank) marched by road this morning to BEHAGNIES [H.2.a.3.5.sheet57C] for duty with 2/1st N.Mid. Fd Amb., who moved there today. Proceeded with Capt Whitehead as an advance party to ERVILLERS [B.13.d.2.7] Sheet 57C to take over the VI Corps Scabies Station & Div. Rest Station at that place from the 137th Field Amb. (40th Div). left Capt Whitehead, Capt Walker + 10 V.Cos. & men to be attached to 137th Field Ambce until tomorrow, then returned to BIENVILLERS.	
ERVILLERS 12-2-18 [B.13.d.2.7] Sheet 57C	12-2-18	The Field Ambulance marched this morning from BIENVILLERS to ERVILLERS, and took over the VI Corps Scabies Station, Gas Treatment Centre & sick collecting station from 137th Fd Amb. Capt C.J.D. Bergin handed over to 2/3rd N.Mid. Fd. Amb. Treatment centres at MORY (B.21.d.5.5) and ERVILLERS Also took over French-foot treatment centre. 23 Nissen Huts, 2 Adrian huts various small patterns. The hospital site consists of scabies treatment quarters with spray baths, inspection & Adrian hut fitted up as a dining hall. Three Nissen huts are the other is equipped as a hospital ward. The remainder are at present about 120 scabies & 50 other sick in hospital. Officers billets mess are allotted to medical Officers rooms. Here are at present We personnel we accommodated in reception & dressing rooms. on the opposite side of the Corps road. Hospital formed out Divisions of the Corps. 3 Nissen huts on the opposite side of the loading front on the ERVILLERS-BEHAGNIES Road Established as R.A.M.C. loading off loading front. 1 Cpl. 2 men & an operative lieut, then by the 5th Light Decauville Railway carry to 157 Decauville Station & than to ambulance cars 2nd by 60 Light road patient from the Decauville Station & than to ambulance cars	

WAR DIARY 2/2nd North Midland Field Ambulance Vol. II Page 3

Army Form C. 2118.

1918

INTELLIGENCE SUMMARY.

Place	Date	Summary of Events and Information	Remarks and references to Appendices
ERVILLERS [B.13.d.2.7 Sheet 67c.]	13-2-18	Fatigue parties employed in building parapets round the hospital huts & billets as protection from aircraft bombs. A.D.M.S. visited the hospital. F.W.	
"	14-2-18	Capt. Young M.C. detailed as M.O. i/c 1 Scabies treatment. Capt. Whitehead / medical cases. Capt. T. W. Blow however still parade, which is attended by various units in the area. Capt. W. Blow worked in the hospital & also the "entertainment party" known as "The Armadillos". Such canteen started in the hospital during the recent period of rest is now set to give amusement to 16 patients & others in the evening. F.W.	
"	15-2-18	Attended conference at A.D.M.S. Office this morning. Instructions given to convert the Scabies station into a divisional head Dressing station, the Scabies hospital being sent to BLAIREVILLE. Their sanitation system this afternoon. Visited the camp at ERNMYLESR and inspected. 6 huts are now allotted F.W.	
"	16-2-18	Commenced work in enlarging the Gas Treatment Centre. Visited the three reserve battalion camps at Mory this afternoon & inspected sanitary arrangements. 17 members present. D.D.M.S. VI Corps visited the hospital today. F.W.	
"	17-2-18	Meeting of the 59th Division medical Society here this afternoon by Capt. Stanley & Capt. A. Meeres. A.D.M.S. here. A.D.M.S. in the chair - 17 members present today to about 50 to the Corps Rest Station. D.A. Rest Station	
"	18-2-18	Transferred a good many sick to the Corps Rest Station. 2/3 N.M.F.Amb. who will act as D.R. Rest station to-day. In the evening hostile aeroplanes visited A.D.M.S. area & dropped bombs at Behagnies and Ervillers. Six bombs burst near the hospital one falling on Ford Ambulance destroying it completely. Both damaged the car of a second below in the next 4 aircraft huts. T. Ward & stables & left in the hospital area. No casualties occurred to patients & personnel but vast till on the ground. I found the huts proved good protection in the absence of direct hits. F.W.	

WAR DIARY 2/2d North Midland Field Ambulance

Army Form C. 2118.

Vol: 1918 II Paper.

INTELLIGENCE SUMMARY.

(Erase heading not required.)

Place	Date	Summary of Events and Information	Remarks and references to Appendices
ERVILLERS	19-2-18	Visited the 2/3 N.M.F.a.b. at HAMELINCOURT this afternoon and stones a good deal of main dressing station equipment from there - F.W.)	
"	20-2-18	Cleared out all patients except scabies & flu cases today, and equipped four huts as reception rooms, dressing room &c. F.W.	
"	21-2-18	Capt. H.W. Taylor joined for duty. F.W.	
"	22-2-18	A.D.M.S. inspected the hospital &c today. Capt Taylor took charge of the gas wards F.W.	
"	23-2-18	Visited loading-post on the BEHAGNIES - ERVILLERS road - F.W.	
"	24-2-18	Capt. H.P. Malcolm reported for duty from leave to Ireland. F.W.	
"	25-2-18	D.D.M.S. VI Corps visited the hospital & inspected the gas treatment wards and new dressing station arrangement. F.W.	
"	26-2-18	D.M.S. III Army, accompanied by D.D.M.S. VI Corps & D.M.S. 59th Div inspected the field ambulance this morning. F.W.	
"	27-2-18	D.M.S. III Army issued congratulatory order expressing his satisfaction with the field ambulance & the medical arrangements. F.W.	
"	28-2-18	Capt. A. Dewar reported for duty (on transfer fr. 2/1 Highld FA w.3/D.V.) During the past fortnight the two Mobile Baths has been considerably improved. The surroundings of the camp have been cleaned, the unoccupied huts have been dug up & the area of cultivation arranged. A garage is existence F.W. Visited the camps in the right reserve area today & inspects their sanitary condition F.W.	

F.W. Moran Lt.Col. RAMC(T)
O.C. 2/2 N. Midland Field Amb.

140/2900

O/C. 2nd Nth. Mid. Field Amb.

COMMITTEE FOR THE
MEDICAL HISTORY OF THE WAR
Date -6 JUN 1918

5/6/918

WAR DIARY 2/2nd North Midland Field Ambulance

INTELLIGENCE SUMMARY

1918. Vol. III Page 1   Army Form C. 2118.

Vol 14

Place	Date	Hour	Summary of Events and Information	Remarks and references to Appendices
ERVILLERS B.13.d.2.7 Sheet 57C	1-3-18		The bathing apparatus and sulphur cabinets were all removed today to the Field Amb. at BLAIREVILLE which is to be the new Corps Scabies Station. The patients will have to remain here at present + treatment carried out as well as possible without the apparatus. JWL. About 12 patients suffering from shell-gas poisoning were admitted today — from a working party of 1/6/7 Royal Scots Fusiliers (Pioneers) JWL.	
"	2-3-18		Capt. Wasbro posted to Company duty with 2/5 Lincolns in place of Capt Lacey. United A. Divns. at Div. Hd.Qrs. JWL. Evacuated sick.	
"	3-3-18		Meeting 1/59 tt w. Medical Society this afternoon at 2/3 N.M. F. Amb. JWL.	
"	4-3-18		Nothing to note. JWL.	
"	5-3-18		Nothing to note. JWL.	
"	6-3-18		Conference J. Field Ambulance commanders with A.D.M.S. at Div. Hd.Qrs. this morning. Probability of German attack within 24hr front – was communicated to us. Received instructions to make preparations to receive widely wounded in large numbers within the next few days. JWL. Received 10 casualties at this Fd. Ambulance site. Draw up plan this afternoon of the possible improvement of the approaches + managers (in + out) + the moving of the ablution room & incinerator for a new road to be used so as to relieve the heavy traffic on the main road & that the large huts may be approved as hospital today + approved. The huts are visited.	
"	7-3-18		A.D.M.S. + O.C. units visited today + approved the hospital scheme. Working parties / men ft. unit & about 50 light duty patients commenced work on different parts of the new road. Received statistical instructions for medical arrangements in case of active operations. JWL.	

WAR DIARY 2/2 North Midland Field Ambulance
Army Form C. 2118.

Vol. III Page 2

INTELLIGENCE SUMMARY

Place	Date	Summary of Events and Information	Remarks and references to Appendices

ERVILLERS | 8-3-18 | A.D.M.S. (Col. McCabe) visited hospital and the latter expressed his approval of the alterations being made. F.W.J. Visited the camp in the right reserve area this afternoon & inspected sanitation. Considerable progress was made with the new road today. The invite concert party gave a successful entertainment at Bethanies this evening. The buildings have been renamed. |

" | 9-3-18 | The new road is now ready for metalling: the ⅔ Lincolns were working in the way & re-erected shelters. F.W.J. Capt. Walker this evening. Capt. Bailey went up to the ⅔ Lincolns in relief. F.W.J. To relieve officer required to sit on medical board. F.W.J. Made final arrangements for re-billeting. |

" | 10-3-18 | Visited the A.D.M.S. with O.C. 2/1 N.M.S. F.A. & made a final arrangement for the clerical work during active operations. Inspected the hospital & the G.O.C. VI Corps, accompanied by D.D.M.S. expressed himself pleased with the afternoon. He made a brief inspection. The arrangements for duty as M.O. & 5/7 Div. Machine Gun Battalion today when Capt. H.W. Taylor proceeds to (nothing adv. 5 day) [relieve] 3rd Section. |

" | 11-3-18 | Arrangements were made today to transfer 50 of the 150 Scabies patients to the Corps Scabies Station at Blairville together. These were seen this afternoon. The new road is now walkable throughout. About 50 bns. 4 brick with and check has been cut-up to the present. F.W.J. the attack is expected to helpers for casualties early tomorrow, to the dressing room, |

" | 12-3-18 | D.D.M.S. received the day was spent in fitting up the bath-house into a up Jamm. Clears office & evacuation room. At moment I handed the bath-house into large receiving room. All sick except the Scabies patients were evacuated by evening. The Scabies patients we now to rejoin their units in the receipt of orders. F.W.J.

1918 Vol. III Page 3.

2/2nd North Midland Field Ambulance

WAR DIARY

INTELLIGENCE SUMMARY.

Army Form C. 2118.

(Erase heading not required.)

Place	Date	Hour	Summary of Events and Information	Remarks and references to Appendices
ERVILLERS 3.13.d.2.7 Sheet 57C.	13-3-18		Heavy bombardment by our artillery during last night. The expected attack did not take place. 40 more cadres/patients transferred to the rear. Scabies started. Blaineville evacuated. The remaining 58 are fit for light duty & did more work in the new road today. A.D.M.S. VI Corps visited the hospital. (7W.)	
"	14-3-18		A.D.M.S. visited us today & inspected the alterations. (7W.)	
"	15-3-18		All remaining scabies patients transferred to 5 Blaineville (7W.) The conversion of the dining hall into a dressing room was begun. General clear out & disinfection of all wards this afternoon. (7W.)	
"	16-3-18		G.O.C. 59" Div. inspected the Field Ambulance this afternoon. (7W.) Further work done today on the levelling & improvement of the fence & the hospital. 40 men trained, believed not relieved, being in reserve Capt. A. Bostock reported for duty. Visited 4-5 C.C.S. & chat to hand this information to made arrangements for the working of 69 Divisional clerks during active operations (7W.)	
"	17-3-18		Meeting of 59" Div. Medical Society this afternoon at Noailles & Brus. 71 who was present. Capt. & Sermon proceeded on course of instruction to 142 Field Ambulance near BOISLEUX. (7W.)	
"	18-3-18		Nothing to note. The conversion of the hospital into a main hopping station now completed. The bath house has been converted into a large reception room and the dressing-half into a large dressing room. Clerks room & resuscitation room. The casualty centre is fully equipped & separate from the rest of the hospital. A.D.	
"	19-3-18		Nothing further to (7W.)	
"	20-3-18		All men employed on finishing off the digging over of the ground in the front of the hospital. Food program today (?) (?) The Armistice gave a successful performance in the units' Concert party "The Borzois" Behagnies this evening. The Corps Cinema Hall. (7W.)	

WAR DIARY or INTELLIGENCE SUMMARY

Army Form C. 2118.

2/2nd North Midland Field Ambulance

Vol. III Page 4
1918

Place	Date	Hour	Summary of Events and Information	Remarks and references to Appendices
ERVILLERS [B.13.d.2.7. Sheet 57.C.]	21-3-18		Early this morning the long expected German offensive began. A heavy bombardment of the divisional front & the back areas commenced about 5.30 a.m. and this village came in for some attention. One shell wrecked the unit's canteen. Local counter barrage began to arrive about 6.30 and up to 9.30 a.m. we had dealt with about 50. The arrangements already impressed went into force at 9 a.m. i.e. 5 bearers to this unit were sent to 45 C.C.S. ambulance front, 59th F.W. patient unit to the 2/1st N.M. F.A. & 3 C.C.S. bearers to the "7" special dump to their dump, 5 F.W. patients units to O.C. 2nd N.M.F.A. reported there with 2 horsed ambulances proceeded to their hqrs. O.C. 3rd M.A.C. reported at 6 a.m. 34.d.55.) he horsed ambulances were 20 horsed ambulances & all the 57th divisional ambulances, four lorries reported here sent to report to O.C. 2/1 N.M. F.A.L. at Dysart Camp, about to collect. Wounded. Walking wounded began to arrive about 10.0 a.m. from the front line and a continuous stream of casualties were received from the front (when necessary) given anti-tetanic serum, feet, & all clerical particulars taken cleaned between 10 and 2pm. Capts Bostock, Young, Watkins & Elliot worked in relief in the dressing room. Capt. Balcolm had charge of the jarred patients. Evacuation proceeded smoothly and satisfactorily up to 2pm. but apts. that cars were a long time returning as the C.C.S. at Sirames Leferme, Haveleu, & Ledgehill, near Albert had to evacuate back casualties being directed to the enemy had captured the Doullens. Reports came in that the enemy had captured Croisilles, Ecoust - Norevie line and that 10th adv. dressing station had been cut off, these had been forced to withdraw to a replace but those of 1st hore 69 captured. The walking wounded collected post at Mory Albey had been counted an evacuated from Left, the evening reports that Capt. J.a. Young M.C. was posted to 2/5 divisional & was hit Capt. L.M. Webber, was wounded have evacuated to C. S. all cases have been wounded & contd. evacuation to arrive all day some to ambulance, lorry or light railway, cleared to C.C.O. by 10 miles lorry, 18 miles by ambulance & 50 being evacuated. The lating day by the rheum. Over 700 casualties were passed through this unit. H.B. - S. debited the day, beginning 6 S.9. 34" & 40° drowsinss, & Co for Lev 7/0. © Douchy-Ayette this evening. All surplus handful was sent 70.l.

2/2nd North Midland Field Ambulance
Vol. III Page 5
1918

Army Form C. 2118.

WAR DIARY or INTELLIGENCE SUMMARY.

(Erase heading not required.)

Place	Date	Hour	Summary of Events and Information	Remarks and references to Appendices
ERVILLERS 13.10.d.2.7. (sh. 57.c)	22-3-18		Heavy firing continued all night but no further casualties were brought in early this morning. When the firing ceased about 10 a.m. there was a considerable number of wounded cases in ERV. 7.30 a.m. and by 10 a.m. there was a congestion of cases about can in ERV. The Motor Ambulance Service was not sufficient to clear cases to evacuated to C.C.S. He advises the moving forward of MDS. made such long journey. It became necessary to ask permission of 3rd Army. There most of the night & day. About 3 p.m. the enemy was reported advancing to proved very useful. The position of the main Dressing Station was becoming to upon ERV., and were received at it 4pm. Orders were sent back to the subplaces to evacuate the captured. Stretchers, & necessary and staff cases (& cases) reconnoitred all the Trolleys, stores that were left in these were places in H.Q., 7th & 8th Fld. Amb., and hospital store DRT for care to set up to ERV. Approaching to move. The enemy barrage in the meantime was suddenly effectively the main road and it was known DRT was difficult for cars to get up to ERV. at 4p.m. he C.O. was to any point beyond DRT camp. about back to ERVILLERS as soon as I to take the whole unit back to ERVILLERS and I considered this point the reputation to sanguine at 6 p.m. I sent all personnel except a small situation became to sanguine back to AyETTE under charge Capt E. Malcolm. Also had been reached & accordingly AyETTE before leaving to hand over their writing staff back to so were left advised. Stated the heaviest in the there which all the staff were being formed by the 135th Field Ambulance (46th Div.) remained was 3 the rear main heavy Capt. Watson SCRMo) Capt. Elliot, 1 Sergeant & 3 men and attended to the Casualties which were still arriving. About 7.30 sheds began to burst in Ervillers & about 30 a.d.s. as well. and the hospital tents were cover - then several cases - there can but a long way to carry on, and by about 30 a.d.s as well at 8 p.m. it was no longer safe to carry on, and the lightwinty paravant stabling latents were sent off to HAMELINCOURT, which as yet was fairly lightly shelled (report)	

WAR DIARY / INTELLIGENCE SUMMARY

1/2 North Midland Field Ambulance

1918 Vol III Page 6

Army Form C. 2118.

Place	Date	Hour	Summary of Events and Information	Remarks and references to Appendices
ERVILLERS (continued)	22-3-18		At 8 p.m. I evacuated the Main Dressing Station with the remaining personnel and proceeded to Douchy-les-Ayette where we rejoined the rest of the Field Ambulance. An hour previously (7 p.m.) the O.C. 2/1 N.M.F.A. had reported to me at Ervillers that he had evacuated the A.D.S. & the walking wounded collecting post and was withdrawing to Ayette. Shortly after I left, a bearer party of the 46th Division got into communication with Capt. Kelly M.C. & 2/Lt. Vercoe R.A.M.C. who established a bearer post in the village, thus ensuring the continuity of the line of evacuation from the front line to HAMELINCOURT. Capt Young M.C. reported to me at Douchy-les-Ayette about 11 p.m. with a badly sprained ankle. J.W.	
DOUCHY LES-AYETTE F.10.a.8.8. Sheet 57D	23-3-18		Early this morning orders were received for the transport to march to MIRAUMONT & there entrain for BOUZINCOURT. Suitable arrangements for the disposition of the Field Ambulance diminishing the Unit to the 133 Field Amb. on the marches via BUCQUOY. Left DOUCHY-LES-AYETTE at 12 noon, marched to AVELUY near ALBERT. Halted & detrained there at 4 p.m. and proceeded to BOUZINCOURT arriving about 7 p.m. The transport arrived by road about 9 p.m. J.W.	
BOUZINCOURT AVELUY near ALBERT W.15.a Sheet 57D	24-3-18		Morning spent in overhauling equipment & re-packing wagons. Much hostile bombing of ALBERT & surrounding camps railway sidings & the night. J.W.	
"	25-3-18		Left BOUZINCOURT at 4 a.m. during a bombing raid by hostile aircraft. Marched with 29th Div: Train & other units arriving at PONT NOYELLES at 9 a.m. Enemy reported advancing towards ALBERT. Capt. Dewar posted to 176 Brigade Headqrs. Billetted at PONT NOYELLES for the night. J.W.	

1918 Vol. II Page 7

2/2nd North Midland Field Ambulance

Army Form C. 2118.

WAR DIARY or INTELLIGENCE SUMMARY.

(Erase heading not required.)

Place	Date	Hour	Summary of Events and Information	Remarks and references to Appendices
PONT NOYELLES Amiens-Albert road	26-3-18		Marched from PONT NOYELLES under the orders OC 59th Div. Train at 8am and arrived at next destination BONEVILLE near CANDAS about 1pm; and unit is now attached to 178th Brigade group. F.W.	
"	27-3-18		Holiday granted – all ranks rested today. F.W.	
"	28-3-18		Entrained this morning at CANDAS station having previously marched by road under C.R.E. 59th Div., long day in train, finally arriving at Lapugnoy near Bethune. Here the unit detrained. Motor lorries then conveyed us to FREVILLERS, which was reached at 2 a.m. 29th inst. F.W.	
FREVILLERS [T.1.d.5-8 Sheet 36 B.] [1:40,000]	29-3-18		Billetted here for a few hours at FREVILLERS and the marched to BETHENCOURT (U.30.d.) Sheet 30.B.) + C.6.t. (Sheet 51.C.). Here foot billets were obtained and the men were able to have a few hours rest. Transport section arrived during the day. F.W.	
BETHENCOURT C.6.t. Sheet 51.C	30-3-18		Day spent in cleaning up kit, equipment, transport etc. F.W.	
"	31-3-"		Easter Sunday – Church parade at N.3. Bn hr. F.W. During the recent operations this unit supplied all its bearers to the field ambulance in charge of the Advanced Dressing Station of there, most were relieved to 8 Bearers in reserve on the night of the 20th inst, so that the majority were able to get away safely, only 6 + 10 being unaccounted for. There are either killed + wounded. Much good work was done by the rest of the N.C.Os + men at Fresvillers, including the smartening of the new road + conversion of an irregular collection of huts into a good 8 main clearing station	

T.W. Johnson
Lieut. C.R.
O.C. 2/2 North Midland F.A.

CONFIDENTIAL

WAR DIARY

of

2/2ND NTH. MID.

FIELD AMB.

for the month of

APRIL, 1918.

VOL. - 4

Vol. IV Page. 1
1918

Army Form C. 2118.

2/2nd NORTH MIDLAND WAR DIARY FIELD AMBULANCE
INTELLIGENCE SUMMARY.
(Erase heading not required.)

Instructions regarding War Diaries and Intelligence Summaries are contained in F.S. Regs., Part II. and the Staff Manual respectively. Title pages will be prepared in manuscript.

Place	Date	Hour	Summary of Events and Information	Remarks and references to Appendices
BETHENCOURT c.b.t. Sheet 51c	1.4.18		The Division received orders to return this morning to HOUDAIN. The north marched to HOUDAIN and entrained at 1 p.m. for a destination in the north. After a long & tedious journey the unit detrained at PROVEN [F.7.central Sheet 27, Belgium] and marched with the 177. Inf. Bde. to SCHOOLS CAMP, near POPERINGHE [L.3.c.6.2, Sheet 27]. The unit was accommodated in huts, in a very dirty & incomplete camp.	
SCHOOLS CAMP, POPERINGHE L.3.c.6.2 Sheet 27, Belg: 7 trap 1:40,000	2.4.18		Established a small detention hospital in camp for the brigade. The transport section, which had marched by road from BETTENCOURT arrives this afternoon. A.D.M.S. visited the ambulance today. JW.	
"	3.4.18		G.O.C. 2nd Army inspected the Brigade (infantry) today. Received orders from A.D.M.S. to take over the divisional rest station at BRANDHOEK tomorrow from the 101st & 102nd ambulances (33rd Div). 3 horses to Brandhoek this afternoon with the Q.M. and arranged details of the 101" & 102"d relief with O.C. 107" FA. Sent clerks on this event to take over the returns remaining. JW. Capt. G.S. Henning Reunie. (T.C.) reported for duty today & was taken on strength the following promotions were notified today in 59th Div. Routine Orders:- Captains H.P. Malcolm and F.H.C. Watson to be acting-majors, and to command Sections 1 & 2/2nd North Midland Field Ambulances dated Jan. 4. 1918. JW.	Authy ADMS 594. Authority
BRANDHOEK G.12.f.6.8. Sheet 28 I/1 Belg: Pr 40000	4.4.18		Advance party under Capt. J.A. Young [I.C. marched at 1 a.m. to BRANDHOEK and took over the divisional Rest Station from the 101st Field Ambulance. The remainder of the unit followed at 1 p.m., relief being completed by 3 p.m. O/C. H.P. Malcolm having received an appointment as No. 8 Stationary Hospital / proceeds to BOULOGNE for duty. From which date the activity Major, never to his permanent rank. Major H.P. Malcolm relinquishes the acting rank of Major, reverts to his permanent rank of Captain from this date on ceases to command 1 Section. 1 Div: H.Qs. this afternoon. Capt. A. Bevan returned from temporary duty with 176. Inf. Bde. (author's a Dws 578w.) Belgium interpreter M. de Jonghe attached to the unit today. JW.	

Vol. IV Page 2

Army Form C. 2118.

2/2nd NORTH MIDLAND FIELD AMBULANCE

WAR DIARY
INTELLIGENCE SUMMARY.
(Erase heading not required.)

Place	Date	Summary of Events and Information	Remarks and references to Appendices
BRAND HOEK G.12.d.6.8 (sheet 28)	5.4.18	Capt. McMinn (2/3ºN.M.F.Amb.) and Lieut. F. Wreh (2/1ºN.M.Fld) were attached to this unit today for temporary duty. The Div. Rest Station is a camp consisting of 5 large hospital Marquee "huts" and a number of Marquees. Medical, slight surgical & scabies cases are admitted. Accommodation 300. At present there are 250 cases in hospital, mainly 33rd Division. J.W.	
"	6.4.18	Major F.H.C. Watson rejoined the unit today as 2nd in command, having relinquished his appointment of D.A.D.M.S. 59th Division. Capt. B. Whitehead proceeded to 59 Div. as acting D.A.D.M.S. Went G.C. Cowan rejoined from temporary duty with 60º H.A. Brigade. Capt. McMinn has returned to this unit 2/1 ºN.M.F. (coll) today. J.W.	
"	7.4.18	A.D.M.S. visited the D.R.S. today. Capt. Dewar proceeded for a course of instruction at the VIII Corps Gas School STEENVOORDE today. Church parade in the recreation room this afternoon. J.W.	
"	8.4.18	Commenced the reorganization & rearrangement of the hospital wards today. They were too scattered & mixed up. Capt. Fleming proceeded to 4th Lincoln Regt. for temporary duty, in relief of Capt. Dudolf (authg. 2/2 N.a.S.9.Dw.) JW. Lt. G.C. Cowan proceeded this morning.	
"	9.4.18	Capt. Ludolf reported for duty this morning in place of Capt. Mackenzie, M.C., I.M.S, who to 2/5th Sherwood Foresters for duty to the 1st Division. JW. A.D.M.S. VIII Corps visited the hospital & made various suggestions for improvements. JW.	

2/2nd North Midland Field Ambulance   Vol. IV p. 3

Army Form C. 2118.

WAR DIARY
INTELLIGENCE SUMMARY.
(Erase heading not required.)

Place	Date	Hour	Summary of Events and Information	Remarks and references to Appendices
BRANDHOEK G.12.b.6.2 (sheet 28)	10-4-18		The work of improving the hospital was continued today. There was considerable shelling of Ypres, Vlamertinghe and Poperinghe today; in conjunction with a great enemy attack near Armentières and against the Messines Ridge. 7W?	
"	11-4-18		The rear orderly room was partially built today. The Brigade at WATOU was moved up to BRANDHOEK today; the Brigade Rest Station at WATOU was closed. The 36 patients being transported to us, about 10 then sick to-night were admitted from the forward area. There are now nearly 300 sick & slightly wounded in this Rest Station, chiefly belonging to the 33rd Division. 30 were evacuated today to C.C.S. 7W?	
"	12-4-18		At 11 a.m. called today & gave warning order for the move of the ambulance tomorrow. Packed up all equipment not in use, except parcels of medical & surgical equipment for the Main Dressing Station, YPRES. received late today; as the M.D.S. is to be transferred from the Prison (Ypres). 7W?	
"	13-4-18		Orders received for Division to move by rail-road to Corps area today. The transport left at 3.30 p.m., the three Field Ambulances marching in succession under the Council Ipt. Gen School. The 140 Field Ambulance (141st Div.) arrived and took over the Rest Station & the hospital remaining. The personnel entrance of BRANDHOEK R.B.P. and details of 2/2 NORTH MIDLAND (Q.18.m sheet 27) and were accommodated for the night in huts tents & vacated by No.11 C.C.S., Transport proceeded to the neighbourhood of K.24.c.5.5. north of 140 tomorrow code. (sheet 27).	
ODEWAERSVELDE R.7.C.2.5 (sheet 27)	14-4-18		Remained in camp till 5 p.m. then marched with transport to KOKEREELE farm near WESTOUTRE (R.17.b.6.3 sheet 27). Here a walking wounded collecting post was established, with provision for accommodating about 30 sick. The Division is now astride the line between BAILLEUL & NEUVEÉGLISE. 7W?	

Vol IV Page 4

2/2nd North Midland Field Ambulance

WAR DIARY
INTELLIGENCE SUMMARY

Army Form C. 2118.

Place	Date	Summary of Events and Information	Remarks and references to Appendices
KOKEREEL FARM, near WESTOUTRE [R.17.b.5.3 Sheet 27]	15.4.18	The morning was spent in converting a large dining-hut into a waiting room for walking wounded, with provision for cloak and for feeding the patients. One hut was equipped as a dressing-room and six Nissen huts were cleared to receive Stretcher cases - sick grounded. About 2 p.m. wounded began to arrive and continued in a steady stream all the rest of the day and through the night. A second dressing room was fitted up as numbers increased by evacuation was carried out by M.A.C. Cars which had 67 stretcher-cases between them - Towards evening about 200 sitting cases also accumulated owing to the fact that ambulance and motor lorries for trans to Trains and message for Ambulance was made to the M.A.C. cars, clearing all small numbers. Ultimately were sent. These of the M.A.C. cars clearing all 6 buses eventually were sent. These of the 2/1st N.M.F.A. having been wounded by 7 am on the 16th. About 4 p.m. Field Ambulance notes no. 10 remained here shelled out their main dressing station at LOCRE reached to this place, and have been moved to this Field Ambulance. Every case wer Main Dressing Station. During the 12 hours ending 6 a.m. 17/4/18, 47 Stretcher cases and 320 sitting were passed through the dressing station - Every case was given Anti-tetanic serum & fed, and particulars of every case were entered up by the Clerks. Rather more than half the latter were from the 59th Division, together with French troops and several German prisoners. Capt. W.F. Cornwall was posted to this unit for duty to-day. 60 easy cases from 10 am - during the day. Evacuation carried out by troops M.A.C. cars.	
"	16-4-18		

M.

Vol. IV Page 5.

Army Form C. 2118.

2/2nd North Midland Field Ambulance

WAR DIARY
INTELLIGENCE SUMMARY.

(Erase heading not required.)

Instructions regarding War Diaries and Intelligence Summaries are contained in F. S. Regs, Part II. and the Staff Manual respectively. Title pages will be prepared in manuscript.

Place	Date	Hour	Summary of Events and Information	Remarks and references to Appendices
KOKEREEL FARM near WESTOUTRE [R.17.b.5.3. Sheet 27.]	17.4.18		About 9.30 a.m. a heavy bombardment of the whole area commenced, extending from the front line, over the range of hills she [we] overlooking it and back to the road & villages in rear. The barrage gradually reached the Main Dressing Station and for two hours it was under heavy shell fire. There were only 15 patients remaining at the A.D.S. and these went at once away by ambulance. The kit + transport, which was stationed here, inclusive of all the three field ambulances, was at once sent back to GODEWAERSVELDE, and was her[e] led at a farm north of that village. Many she [we] were billetted in the Dressing-station premises several direct hits being made on the farm buildings. Accordingly at the end of 2 hours I reported the situation to the A.D.M.S., sent all personnel not required for duty, under Capt. Young to entrain to a sheltered position half a mile short of the road. Major Watson + Capt. Ludolf with a strong Tent Subdivision and 60 reserve bearers were detailed to remain + carry on the work of the Dressing Station. This they did during the whole morning with great gallantry, devoted to duty. There was no protection from shell fire and many explosions in close proximity during the morning and I were cruising the whole time, and every case was properly dressed + safely evacuated. Exceptionally good work was done by Major J.H.G. Watson, Captain H.G. Ludolf, 20.419 [Pte. J. Waterfield], 20 [illegible] Pte. M.E. Wolfe and 20 [illegible] Pte. H. Peters.
After mid-day the bombardment ceased) instructions were received from the A.D.M.S. to carry the foot as an advanced Dressing station at A BEELE by the 2/1st N.M. 3rd N. M. D S. having been established the Main Dressing Station has not until handed to the staff details. (Cowusby) the remainder of the personnel not needed to form the harr. subsection were writhdrawn to B.D.Rs. and marched to join us [illegible] at the farm north of Godewaersvelde. (L.35.d.9.1. Sheet 27.)	

A5834 Wt.W4973/M687 750,000 8/16 D.D. & L. Ltd. Forms/C.2113/13.

Vol. IV Page 6

2/2nd North Midland Field Ambulance

WAR DIARY or INTELLIGENCE SUMMARY
Army Form C. 2118.

Place	Date	Hour	Summary of Events and Information	Remarks and references to Appendices
KOKEREEL FARM near WESTOUTRE (R.17.b.2.5 Sheet 27)	18-4-18		In trenches at KOKEREEL Farm this morning and found the night had been quiet & uneventful. No wounded had been admitted since 7pm last night. The stores acquired from the original advanced Dressing Station & Main Dressing Station at LOCRE were brought here this morning to be held over the A.D.M.S. & O.C. During the afternoon orders were received to hand over the 176 Brigade 2/3 N.M. F.Amb., and a march was to be handed over to O.C. 2/3 N Mid F.Amb. at 5 pm. All store & equipment were taken over to BOESCHEPE & ABEELE picking up the hand-cart and remainder of the personnel at the cross-roads between ABEELE and STEENVOORDE. Billets were allotted to us at TERDEGHEM (P.10.a.7.3 Sheet 27) J.W.	
TERDEGHEM [P.10.a.7.3 Sheet 27]	19.4.18		Orders received during the night for a further move this morning. Marched with the 176 Inf. Bde. via Steenwoorde & Watou to the St Sixte area east of PROVEN, a 17 mile march, which the men accomplished very creditably. Occupied huts at DOZINGHEM lately vacated by No. 47 C.C.S. A bombing raid by hostile aeroplanes was carried out near Hospital during the night. No bombs actually fell in the camp. J.W.	
DOZINGHEM [F.II.d.9.5 Sheet 27]	20-4-18		A quiet day was spent in camp. All ranks were able to have a hot bath. J.W.	
"	21-4-18		Marched at noon with 177 Inf. Bde. Group, via PROVEN to the HOUTKERKE area, near Camp, near HERZEELE (D.11.c.2.5. Sheet 27), the personnel the unit occupied 'Road Camp', a short distance away. A small Inpat. hospital was being billetted in two farms & est. established at Road Camp, with accommodation for 30 sick. J.W.	

Vol: IV Page 7

2/2nd North Midland Field Ambulance

WAR DIARY
INTELLIGENCE SUMMARY

Army Form C. 2118.

Place	Date	Hour	Summary of Events and Information	Remarks and references to Appendices
HERZEELE (Road Camp) D.11.c.2.5 Sheet 27	22-4-18		Equipment and Stores were overhauled today, deficiencies indented for, and waggons cleaned. A.D.M.S. visited the camp.	JW.
"	23-4-18		Major Walton visited M.O.s 2/5 Lincolns & 2/4 Leicesters — made arrangements for collecting sick of the Brigade each morning, by Motor Ambulance.	JW.
"	24-4-18		Capt. Dewar posted to 59th Div. Artillery for duty today (authority A.D.M.S 59' Div.) Visited Quarters of 4th Lincolns & M.O. Pte B Dakin of this Unit notified to rejoin the field to No. 419 Advanced Military today Divisional Routine Orders. Authority A.D.M.S 59' Div.	JW.
"	25-4-18		Capt. H. G. Ludolf rejoined to 6 & 4th Lincolns (under authority A.D.M.S 59' Div.) Box respirators of unit inspected today. Gas drill carried out.	JW.
"	26-4-18		The Unit moved up today, with the 177th M.F. Bde. to Schools Camp, St Jan ter Biezen. JW. (L.3.b Central Sheet 27) JW. (L.3.b Central Sheet 27) 177th Bde. moved by ?	
SCHOOLS CAMP, ST JAN TER BIEZEN L.3.b central Sheet 27	27-4-18		Rested in camp today. In the evening the infantry of the 177th Bde. took & the to reserve line near Reninghelst, leaving this Field Amb. & the Brigade transport here. M. Captain W.F. Cornwall — notified by 1st Division Military Cross awarded to Captain W.F. Cornwall.	JW.
"	28-4-18		Messages received from 177th Bde. H.Qrs asking for a Car-body post & motor Ambulance, so it took up a party of about 7 Officers & motor ambulance at L.24.c.3.8 (Sheet 28) with instructions to clear Infantry casualties to the Corps main Dressing Station at Reninghelst (C.22.d). Notified A.D.M.S. & 177 Bde. of this arrangement.	JW.

2/2nd North Midland War Diary Field Ambulance
Vol. IV Page 8

Army Form C. 2118.

INTELLIGENCE SUMMARY.

Place	Date	Hour	Summary of Events and Information	Remarks and references to Appendices

SCHOOLS CAMP ST JAN TER BIEZEN
[L.3.b.central sheet 27]

29-4-18 — Received orders from 177 Bde to send handcart & details back to the Houtkerke area at 7.30 am. Accordingly all except reserve bearers and headquarters were sent back to Farm 4, E.8.c.2.8 (sheet 27), north west of Houtkerke. I then visited the A.D.M.S. to make my head quarters at Remy Siding with the section 2/1st N.M. F.Amb. who have today taken over the Divisy Station for the S.African Field Amb. at L.22.d.9.3 (sheet 27). Accompanied the A.D.M.S. on tour of inspection of the car loading posts. Cpl. B/g A. Young M.E. was placed in charge of Car post at 177 Bde. Hdqrs at L.29.d.0.9 (sheet 27). A Cpl & 4 men at L.24.c.2.9 (sheet 27) for clearing the 177th Brigade Casualties. One car at each post. Loading front was the establishment at G.21.c.9.5 (Sheet 28) a third car, loading in charge and two cars, for clearing the Casualties with Capt. Cornwall in charge of Outposts & Trenches for Ousedom to the 176- R.l.Bde. who are keeping reserve bearers by the Remy belt. Capt Cornwall now relieves this evening by Capt Pritchard 2/3rd N.M. F.Amb. Command of his Brigade.

The regimental aid posts of the two brigades are as follows, in farmhouses or cottages in all cases:–

4th Lincolns	G.26.c.3.2 (sheet 27)	2/6 N. Staffords	G.22.d.1.1 (sheet 28)
2/4 Leicesters	G.26.a.2.9 "	2/6 S. Staffords	G.28.b.4.3 "
2/5 Lincolns	G.32.a.3.7 "	5th N. Staffords	G.29.b.7.3 "
177 Bde.		176 Bde.	to each of these R.A.P.s

Sight R.A.M.C. Bearers were posted to each of these R.A.P.s.

REMY SIDING (L.22.d.9.3 sheet 27)

30-4-18 — Head quarters were now established at REMY SIDING (L.22.d.9.3 sheet 27) with the Left Sect of No 2. Canadian C.C.S. 30 reserve bearers have been left at Farm 4 Clearcoat with Capt Watson Lawson Road quarters of the 177th Bde. Visited with Capt. Young this morning & got into touch with the R.M.O.'s of the 177 Bde. A.M.O.'s. JW.

Vol. IV Page 9

Army Form C. 2118.

1/2nd North Midland Field Ambulance

WAR DIARY

INTELLIGENCE SUMMARY

(Erase heading not required.)

Place	Date	Hour	Summary of Events and Information	Remarks and references to Appendices
REMY SIDING L22.d.9.3 sheet 27	30.4.18 (continued)		Fitter up & staffed & F- receiving tents & dressing rooms &c. Capt Bonner was sent back til the transport lines to A.D.M.S. Major Medical Change the sick here. Military head awarded to No. 419342 Pte. Waterfield J. this unit by N. Corps Commander - was published in today's Div. Routine orders. This Field Ambulance is now responsible for collecting sick & wounded Divisional dressing station, all casualties of the two brigades which are at present occupying reserve lines. Arrangements are now complete, and are sufficient for present conditions. Should the situation change so that these lines become forward trenches, further posts would have to be established. JNO.	

J.W. Osborne
Lt Col. R.A.M.C.
O.C. 2/2 N. Midland Field Amb.

Confidential

War Diary
~ of ~
2/2 N. Mid. F̄d Amb

From 1-5-18.   To 31-5-18.

Volume V

Army Form C. 2118.

WAR DIARY
2/2nd North Midland Field Ambulance
INTELLIGENCE SUMMARY.
(Erase heading not required.)

Vol V. Page 1.

Place	Date	Summary of Events and Information	Remarks and references to Appendices
REMY SIDING L.22.d.9.3 sheet 27	1-5-18	Visited the 176th Bde. hartqrs. Car loading-post and all the Regimental aid posts of the Brigade. 1st & 7th S. North Staff. was found to be a very long carry from R.A.P. to the Car loading Posts. A Car loading post of the 19th Div. 600 yds from the R.A.P. is therefore being made use of. Not many casualties to clear during the last 24 hours - about 15 ill & several sick. JW).	
"	2-5-18	Nothing of note. JW).	
"	3-5-18	Visited 177th Bde. Headquarters and all three R.A.P.'s of the Brigade, also own two Car loading posts in this Brigade area. The dispositions of medical personnel are as shown in following illustration by the sketch below of attached -	Oppendix 1.
		Main Dressing Station at REMY SIDING (L.22.d.9.3, sheet 27) & also head quarters of this Field Ambulance.	
		Car loading post No.1. { 1 Capt & 3 Men } (L.29.b.0.9 (Sheet 27))	
		Car loading post No.2. { (Capt Young M.C. & 4 men) } at L.24.C.2.9 (sheet 27) { serving 177th Inf. Bde.	
		Car loading post No.3. { (Capt Pitteroff (Sgt. & 4 men) } at G.21.C.9.5 (sheet 28) " 176 Inf. Bde. { 2 ambulance cars.	
		The R.A.P.s are as follows:- 4th Leicesters at L.29.b.0.9 (Sheet 27)	2/6 N. Stafford G.22.a.1.1 (Sheet 28)
		2/4 Leicesters at 2b.a.2.7 sheet 27	2/6 S. Stafford G.28.d.4.3 " "
		2/5 Lincolns at L.32.a.3.7 " "	5.N. Stafford G.29.b.7.3 (" ")
		Arrangements are working satisfactorily. JW).	
"	4-5-18	Major Watson visited the 176th Bde. & 2w 3. Car loading post to JW).	
"	5-5-18	Both Brigades were withdrawn today & marched to the HOUTKERQUE area, and all attached bearers and Car loading posts were returned to head quarters of REMY SIDING this evening. HOUTKERQUE and all the unit was concentrated at the Transport Lines, at Farm No.41, E.8.c.2.8 (Sheet 27). JW)	

Army Form C. 2118.

Vol. V Page 2

2/2nd North Midland Field Ambulance

WAR DIARY
INTELLIGENCE SUMMARY.
(Erase heading not required.)

Place	Date	Summary of Events and Information	Remarks and references to Appendices
HOUTKERQUE area E.8.c.2.8 [Sheet 27] 1/40,000	6-5-18	Marched this morning by road via HERZEELE, WORMHOUDT to ROUBROUCK. The remainder of the Brigade being carried on busses & lorries to ST. MOMELIN (near ST. OMER). Billet & stables in farms at HOGENHIL (H.12.b.3.6. sheet 27) 7.W.	
ROUBROUCK (Hogenhil) (H.12.b.3.6) [Sheet 27] 1/40,000	7-5-18	Left billets this morning and marched to NIEURLET, 6 kilos from ST. OMER, where tents were obtained and a camp pitched, near the 177th Brigade Head Quarters. 7.W. Visited A.D.M.S. at ST. OMER this afternoon and made arrangement for collecting sick from 177th Brigade. Commander/Asked for Divisional Commander Sen. for Cards for No. 419342 Pte. J. Waterhead, No. 447336 M.E. Wolfe & No. 419241 Pte. Peters - now in action receiving treatment for influenza. Names & Regt. numbers of four others today No. 419342 Pte J Waterhead to Staff Peach Battn. 7.W.	
NIEURLET M.8.b.2.2 Sheet 27	8-5-18	All the infantry of the 177th Brigade except a small has gone to Staff Peach Battn. Company very far too sick and were sent to the Base Reinforcement depot today. 7.W. now requiring treatment. 7.W.	
"	9-5-18	Marched this morning with the Brigade details remaining to ECQUES (4.D.30.10. Hazebrouck 5A) and billeted there for the night. Lt. 7.W.	
ECQUES 4.D.30.10. Hazebrouck 5A 1/100,000	10-5-18	Marched again today to SAINS-LES-PERNES (H.13.a.3.5 sheet 36B) a distance of 20 miles. Busses were obtained for 2/3 7th men the remainder doing half the distance. Capt. H. W. Taylor rejoined for duty from the 59th Machine Gun Battn., on the disbandment of that unit. 7.W.	
SAINS-LES-PERNES H.13.a.3.5 sheet 36B	11-5-18	Visited 177th Bde. H. Qrs & there R.M.O's who are all billeted at PRESSY-LES-PERNES 2½ kilos from here & arranged for collection & next daily. 7.W.	
"	12-6-18	For farriers from battalions attached to the 177th Bde. H. Qrs today. 7.W. Bde H. Qro moved to ESTRÉES-CAUCHIE. Visited Bde H. Qro this morning & learned.	
"	13-5-18	For a Field Ambulance site in the neighbourhood. Nothing could be arranged. However today and a temporary arrangement for collection of sick by motor ambulance from SAINS-LES-PERNES was the best that could be done. 7.W.	

Army Form C. 2118.

Vol. V Page 3

WAR DIARY

2/2nd North Midland Field Ambulance

INTELLIGENCE SUMMARY

(Erase heading not required.)

Instructions regarding War Diaries and Intelligence Summaries are contained in F.S. Regs., Part II. and the Staff Manual respectively. Title pages will be prepared in manuscript.

Place	Date	Summary of Events and Information	Remarks and references to Appendices
SAINS-LES-PERNES H.13.a.3.5 Sheet 36.B	14-5-18	Sent motor ambulance 18 miles to Estrée Cauchie & Divion to collect sick from the Brigade. As unit figures no hospital accommodation they had to all tent at the C.C.S. near PERNES. Capt. F.A. YOUNG M.C. promoted to acting Major, whilst commanding ambulance. — F.W. Warrant order received from A.D.M.S. to be ready to move. F.W.	authority G.H. & a list
"	15-5-18	Unit moves this morning to LES-QUATRE-VENTS, 3 mile south of ESTRÉE CAUCHIE.	
"	16-5-18	The dismounted portion will convey in lorries. The camp on an old field ambulance site, hurriedly being occupied by a Canadian Dental Section. The huts are in a very dilapidated condition & there is much work to be done to make the place habitable. F.W.	
LES 4 VENTS W.9.c.9.9 Sheet 36 B.	17-5-18	Visited 177th Bde. H'qrs and the northern portion of the Brigade this morning, including the camps of 2/6 Warwicks 2/3 Durham L.I. & 11th Hants Somerset L.I. at J. Trick are in neighbourhood 7 to VIELFURT J.2.6. t. sheet 36B] north & HOUDAIN. A.D.M.S. indicates all sanitary arrangements in the afternoon visited the battalions in the southern portion of the area viz 2/5 and 2/8 Kings Liverpool Regt at W.C.3.5.2. & 15" K.G. Batt. Essex Regt at Q.27.b.6.3 (Sheet 36B)	
"	18-5-18	A.D.M.S. 59" Div. visited Field Amb. H'qrs and accompanied him in a tour of the camps in the Brigade area. F.W. D.A.D.M.S. 10" Corps visited H'qrs today. Capt. H.W. Taylor & Capt. W.J. Carmichael M.C. ambulants A.D.s (57 & 59 Div) & A.D.M.S. (authority A.D.M.S 59 Div) joined for duty from 2/1st N. Mid. Fd. Amb. Lieut F.E. Webb. F.W.	
"	19-5-18	Sent three lines ambulances & two motor ambulances to convey men unable to march & follow bus bad china (i.e. (I.G.E.) B) of the 176 Brigade from MAGNICOURT en COMTÉ early this morning, authority A.D.M.S. 59 Div). This afternoon visited the HOUDAIN area where B.M. 25-5 9 B. Divisional Rest at their Camps. Church parade (C.of E.) at 11.15 am at 176 Bde. 4 m.c. was with Major Young M.C. must endeavour to find accommodation for a section of the Field ambulance to provide a small hospital for the 177 Bde. troops in this area. After much difficulty a site was found at BARAFFE [P.17.A.5-3 sheet 36 B] for a small Canvas Camp & billets for personnel. Capt. H.G. Luhoff M.C. reported for duty from & therefore (authority A.D.M.S 57" Div.) F.W.	

WAR DIARY

2/2nd North Midland Field Ambulance

INTELLIGENCE SUMMARY

Vol. V Page 4 Army Form C. 2118.

Place	Date	Hour	Summary of Events and Information	Remarks and references to Appendices
LES 4 VENTS [W.9.c.9.9. sheet 36.B]	20-5-18		All three horsed ambulances & 2 motor ambs. again helped to bring two G.S. Waggons from HABARCQ to MT NICOURT COM. CEM. this morning, returning to 176th Fd Bde. Major Young, I/MC & Capt. Duddy MC. went 25 the road & proceeded to BARAFFLE (P.17 d.6.3. sheet 36.3) and opened a small hospital (canvas) with accommodation for 20 patients. Ful.	
"	21-5-18		The field sub. Kenyon is now much improved. The huts have been repaired, the proper cleaned, drainage & latrine arrangements put in satisfactory condition. The large hut accomodates about 50 patients & admitted scabies hospital (cases) with bathing accommodation. Men in isolation several days. Horse transport was sent up from three horse transport to the 9 N.C.O.R.T. The nursing & move the hind 2 battalions of 176th Bde to a reserve line of trenches, standing to. The 177th Brigade are engaged in trench instruction [J.20.6. sheet 36.B] in the north to CAPELLE FERMONT [E.3.d. sheet 57c] from the BRUAY-ST POL Road. This is the southern portion of the "BB" line of defence in the south. This is the "B.B." line of defence we devise upon this road. The medical arrangements for all troops engaged in this line are done by a motor ambulance as regards collection. Sick & wounded, and also from BARAFFLE for the troops in the VIELFORT Camps each morning, and also for two units in the OLHAIN Wood [Q.13.a. & 14.C sheet 36B] viz 2/North San. S.Bn. and 71st Chinese Labour Group. These units in the ESTREE-CAUCHIE are served by horse ambulances which collect each morning. Visited "C" Section Camp at BARAFFLE this morning, and reconnoitred the ground in front of behind OLHAIN wood with Major Young, with a view to evacuation in the event of from this enemy of the "BB" line if required. Thence on to Tch "BB" line in front of CAMBLAIN L'ABBÉ. I traversed the Southern section of the "BB" line in this sector and reconnoitred the roads & ground generally. During the night about 1 Gen. Hosts, aeroplanes visited this neighbourhood dropping bombs to right about & again south to falling within half a mile of the Fd. Amb. Head quarters. Ful.	

Vol. V Page 5

2/2 North Midland WAR DIARY
Field Ambulance
INTELLIGENCE SUMMARY.
(Erase heading not required.)

Army Form C. 2118.

Place	Date	Hour	Summary of Events and Information	Remarks and references to Appendices
LES 4 VENTS [W.9.C.9.9] [Sheet 36.B.]	22-5-18		This morning I reconnoitred the "BB line" and ground behind it in the sector from the ST.POL-BRUAY road & N.E. of HOUDAIN. Suitable sites for R.A.P.'s & Car-loading posts were noted. Also noted M.O.s of 11th Sevens L.I. & 3rd Nov. 9.9 Batt., the latter having just arrived near LE VIEL FORT. The work of rapid anti-aircraft protection round the huts at "les 4 Vents" was commenced. Today further sites identified for. JW.	
"	23-5-18		Visited camp of 118th Chinese Labour Coy. at CAPELLES FERMONT (E.3.C.2.2 Sh. 151c) and arranged for a Medical Officer to visit its camp daily. Also see sick cases daily & rule (authority A5thG 579 JW) between this & inspected bath d'Institution at "53 line" (between Houdain & CAMBLAIN L'ABBÉ, mostly evacuation routes for wounded JW).	
"	24-5-18		Nothing of note. JW.	
"	25-5-18		A.D.M.S. visited the hospitals & inspected all arrangements at headquarters at Barcaffle. JW.	
"	26-5-18		Reconnoitred the rail roads & country behind the "BB" line in the AUBIGNY neighbourhood & reconnoitred the evacuation routes for wounded.	
"	27-5-18		Visited section at Barcaffle in front of Mag village. JW	
"	28-5-18		Reconnoitred The evacuation routes for wounded between Houdain & neighbourhood & also between Houdain & Main Dressing Station. JW	
"	29-5-18			
"	30-5-18		Nothing of note JW. D.D.M.S. X Corps inspected the hospitals this morning JW.	
"	31-5-18		Completed scheme of medical arrangements for this Brigade area, in connection with the defence scheme for the "B13 line". ------- Appendix ii JW.	

J.S. Johnson
Lt. Col. R.A.M.C.
O.C. 2/2 N. Midland J. Amb.

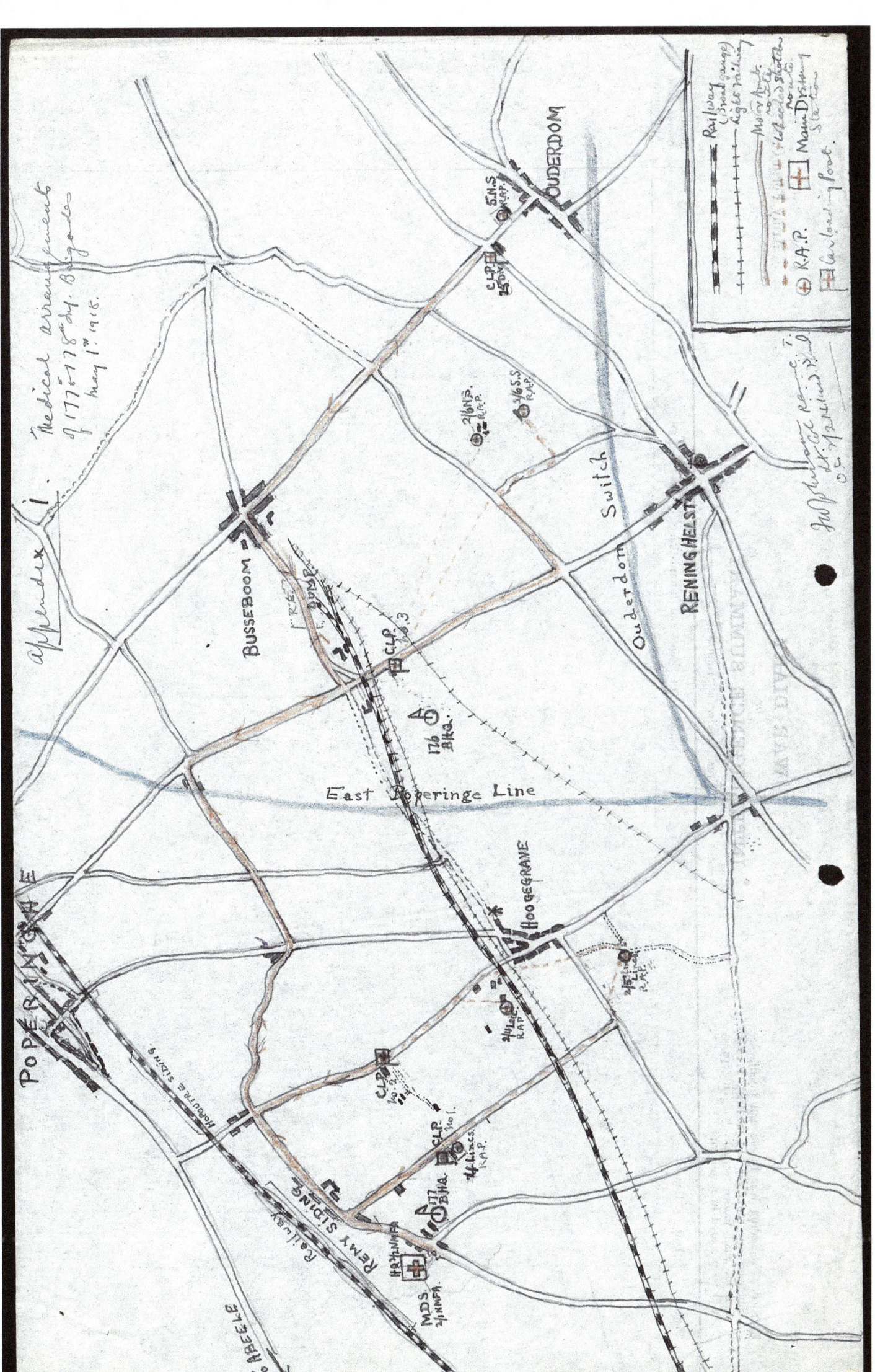

Army Form C. 2118.

WAR DIARY
or
INTELLIGENCE SUMMARY.

(Erase heading not required.)

Instructions regarding War Diaries and Intelligence Summaries are contained in F. S. Regs., Part II. and the Staff Manual respectively. Title pages will be prepared in manuscript.

Place	Date	Hour	Summary of Events and Information	Remarks and references to Appendices

Appendix II

△ Car loading Posts.
⊕ Advanced Dressing Sta.
⊞✠ Main Dressing Sta.
⊞✠✠ Cas. Clearing Sta.
⌇⌇⌇ Motor Ambulance route
⎯⎯⎯ Railway

Plan of Medical Arrangements for Defence of the BB line, Southern Section.

Confidential.

War Diary.

2/2nd NTH. MID. FLD. AMB.

Vol. VI

1-6-18 to 30-6-18

"A" Form. Appendix 2. Army Form C.2?

MESSAGES AND SIGNALS.

TO	2/2nd	WM	Fd. Ambce.

Sender's Number	Day of Month	In Reply to Number	AAA
G4	26/2		

You will march tomorrow 27th inst to billet at BAYONVILLERS AAA Report on arrival to Town Major who will allot billets

From 59th Div
Time 11.15 am

Vol VI Paper

2/2nd North Midland Field Ambulance

Army Form C. 2118.

WAR DIARY or INTELLIGENCE SUMMARY.

(Erase heading not required.)

Place	Date	Hour	Summary of Events and Information	Remarks and references to Appendices
LES 4 VENTS [W.9 central] [Sheet 44b]	1-6-18		The Division is still engaged on the construction of reserve lines of defence. The Garrison found battalions are now becoming before accustomed to the fatigue & work they are engaged on, and the number of men admitted to hospital this average p keeps down to about 50 sick. 2/1th Brigade & hospital & this average keeps about the same. C.F. was attached to the unit today. The Rev. A.G.Kemp. C.F. J.W.J.	
"	2-6-18		Church parade in camp this morning. Visited the camp of the 25.y. Bn. K.R.R. in OLHAIN WOOD reconnoitred the camp & No.13 B "" in front of the wood. The line was received today which necessitates an alteration in the medical arrangements for the Brigade. Recces in connection with the Defence Scheme. J.W.J.	
"	3-6-18		A.D.M.S. called this morning. Spent the whole day reconnoitring the roads & villages in rear & the sector of the Bde line allotted to us for medical organisation. A.& Q.M. Sitwell indicated in camp on temporary duty is acting D.A.D.M.S.3rd Dn. leave to England. Capt. H. G. Dudley M.C. proceeded on temporary duty is acting D.A.D.M.S.3rd Dn. J.W.J.	
"	4-6-18		This morning an outbreak of ptomaine poisoning occurred in A company of the 25.y. Bn. 1.K.R.R. while it work. The result of defection of beef 35 of which had been made into rissoles. 42 men were affected # they were sent to hospital, hurdle enquiries into the occurrence was instituted the 9.M. 7/the Batt. an epidemic of mild suffering 2nd cases having occurred the 2/6 Durham L.I. have to-day your visited the Batt. & advised the M.O. re isolation ets etc. J.W.J.	

2/2nd North Midland Field Ambulance War Diary Vol VI Page 2

INTELLIGENCE SUMMARY

Place	Date	Summary of Events and Information	Remarks and references to Appendices
LES 4 VENTS [W.9 contd] sheet ref 6]	5-6-18	Visited the 25th K.R.R. today & obtained further details of the influenza (?) prevalent pattern yesterday. A further 16 cases occurred this morning, several being held again. Supplies is amongst the company & have all found that the M.O. has already visited the camp & given all necessary instructions. I therefore completed my report & obtained a sample of the food, which was sent to the mobile laboratory for analysis. Military Cross awarded to Capt. Henry Price MALCOLM, (late) this Field Ambulance, now at No. 6 Stationary Hospital — included in King's Birthday Honours list 3rd June 4/18.	
"	6-6-18	Visited Brigade H.Qrs today and endeavoured to obtain the use of the divisional Threshing disinfector for the use of 7th Brigade. Staff-Capt. promised to apply for an allotment & pass to the Brigade. F.J.	
"	7-6-18	Visited C Section Camp Today.	
"	8-6-18	Progress made today with the public ye acting anti-aircraft revetments. normal. Capt. F.C. Smith M.O. R.C. U.S.A. (2/1 7 N.M. F. Amb.) attaches for temporary duty.	
"	9-6-18	Church Parade at 10.0 a.m. Major J.A. Young M.C. proceeded on leave to England. Lt. West posted to C Section at BARAFFLE. F.J.	
"	10-6-18	Visited Camp of 13th S.G.B. West Riding Regt. in Bois de Bozois, near DIVION. Inspected Sanitary arrangements. F.J. H43015,	
"	11-6-18	D.D.M.S. 18th Corps called this morning to see that accommodation was there is here the 2/6 Durham L.I. moved from LEWELFORT to CAMBLIGNEUL today. Sent hired motor to move the men & baths to march. F.J.	
"	12-6-18	Capt. Forsyth C.A.M.C. w.o./c. 13th Northumberland evacuated to hospital today. Army for Lt. Welfed to see their sick every morning. Capt. Smith posted for temporary duty with 11th Somerset L.I. Vice Capt. Fowler (No.0/C) sick in hospital. F.J.	

Vol.VI Page 3

2/2nd North Midland Field Ambulance

Army Form C. 2118.

WAR DIARY
INTELLIGENCE SUMMARY

(Erase heading not required.)

Place	Date	Hour	Summary of Events and Information	Remarks and references to Appendices
LES 4 VENTS W.9.c.4.7. (Sheet 44b.)	13-6-18		Nothing of note (W.D. J.W.)	
"	14-6-18		The disinfection had changed for the 7th Brigade in a dry heat disinfector of the 74th Field Amb. at Estrée Cauchie (XVIII Corps Show Centre) J.W. All blankets of this unit & two battalions were disinfected this morning. Received orders from A.D.M.S. to leave two Camp Equipment 7ts. ready for a suitable station in the neighbourhood for the field ambulance. Secured field in Estrée Cauchie, but no hospital accommodation could be obtained. I.A.D.M.S. 62 Div. & O.C. 2nd North Mid. F.Amb. called to day with orders to ship our LES 4 VENTS tomorrow. J.W.	
"	15-6-18		Sick patent seen all stopped this morning either	to C section hospital or heaven't loaded mess to 2nd North Mid. F.A. of BARAFFLE or to C.C.S. & Stretcher ambulance moves to ESTREE CAUCHIE Stores packed up this morning and the ambulance moves to BARAFFLE at 2pm. billeting there for the night. J.W.
ESTREE CAUCHIE W.2.6.2.9. [Sheet 44b.]	16.6.18		Orders received from 177th M. Bde. to move to further move tomorrow. Marched this afternoon, arriving in billets at DIVION. Closes the section hospital at BARAFFLE about 5pm. Sending all patients either to C.C.S. or to duty, handed over BARAFFLE 30 patients to 2nd North Mid. F.A. and at Les 4 Vents C section rejoined the unit from BARAFFLE this evening. Hostile air raid in the district several casualties in one 7th battalion near DIVION. J.W.	
DIVION I.24.d.10.9 [Sheet 44b.]	17.6.18		The whole of the 177th M. Bde. moved this morning to the HESTRUS area. We marched at 8 a.m. and arrived in billeting area of HERBEVAL about 2pm. Sent ambulance up to pick up the sick en route fall out on the march. They were walking all day & carried before so too 30.0 Billets are our personnel in barns. No hospital so cooks tents of 200 & 30.0 Tents to vaccinated and a satisfactory small hospital established in field. J.W.	
HERBEVAL I.2.c.7.2 G.33.a.7.2 [Sheet 44 & 44b]	18-6-18		Capt. F.C. Smith (M.O.R.C. U.S.A.) returned today from temporary duty with the 11th F.D. Somerset L.I. Crippled hospital inoculations except a cook-house + conducted latrines with the places. Capt H.J. Lindsay has been ordered on leave to England. J.W.	

WAR DIARY / INTELLIGENCE SUMMARY

Army Form C. 2118.

2/2nd North Midland III Field Ambulance

Vol. VI Page 4

Place	Date	Hour	Summary of Events and Information	Remarks and references to Appendices
HERBEVAL G.33.a.7.2 [Sheet 44b]	19-6-18		Visited M.O. 1 2/6 Durham L. Inf. also Brigade H.Qrs. Not many sick coming to hospital at present. J.W.	
"	20-6-18		Carried on the work of erecting the necessary latrines, ablution benches etc. There is no sanitary arrangements in the village. Sent 6 skilled men to work at the 2/2nd Sanitary Section, PERNES, to expedite the matter. Sufficient influenza at the 4.Q.M. Addllaer reported on duty, returning from leave in England. J.W.	
"	21-6-18		Two tent-subdivisions complete. (One Officers) with the necessary equipment & one tent sub-division nos ceases to (CAMBLAIN L'ABBÉ) to reopen & support one H.W.B. Qrs. XVIII Corps - authority A.D. no 59-"I.D. This is for the purpose of assisting in the treatment of large numbers of cases of "influenza" which is now epidemic in that locale. Attended a lecture at the 15th Army School as No. 1 C.C.S. Ten nursing Sisters 2/11 N.M. F.A and 6 being on complete of temporary duty with this unit. (acting A.D. no 57 Div.) I went over with Lt J. Doyle Capt. F.C. Smith (M.O.R.C. U.S.A.) returned to this unit. J.W.	
"	22-6-18		The 177 hy. Bde moving by N. to the CYECQUES area. — midwife arrangements for billets and inspected the village billets to this unit — midwife arrangements for billets and not available. Also Sisters permission to use the Field Ambt. arrive tomorrow about Nantes lid J. for Savoure, also when we admitted the Dumfries etc ~~J.~~ ~~10 hospital for Inf~~ Quartermain ~~The 4th Davy.~~ have 40 to 50 cases Influenza (E ~?), all from number 1 packing up to 860.	
NOUVEAUVILLE Q.22.a.9.1 Sheet 30D	23-6-18		Handed at 9am to NOUVEAUVILLE with all transport (and) Vance party. proceeded early and the hospital 60 to 70 patients to the new area. Arrived at NOUVEAUVILLE at 3.30 p.m. was ready to receive them by midday. Sisters & the rear party were now by km 2/6 Durham L.I. All kinds to transfer sick. Sirs & the rear party. Leaving from the 2/6 Durham L.J. to take 80 cases influenza were collected this evening from the Opened a trench hospital into a barn at CAPELLE, ¼ mile distant. J.W.	

2/2 nd North Midland Field Ambulance Vol. VI Page 4

Army Form C. 2118.

WAR DIARY or Field Ambulance
INTELLIGENCE SUMMARY.
(Erase heading not required.)

Place	Date	Summary of Events and Information	Remarks and references to Appendices
NOUVEAUVILLE [Q.22.a.9.1 Sheet 36.D]	24-6-18	The epidemic of influenza (or 3 day fever) is increasing in the 2/6 Durham L.I. and all the staff were down this morning. I accordingly sent Lt. WEBB to take the sick parade and attached an orderly to the battalion. (temporarily). In A.D.M.S. office reported progress. 54 cases admitted to hospital to-day. Visited the A.D.M.S. office to obtain some extra canvas. But this appears difficult to obtain. jw).	
"	25-6-18	40 fresh cases admitted today. Several the earlier patients are now returning to duty. The average time in hospital being about 4 days. Handed in hospital staff and have built hutted cookhouses latrines etc. Have now taken charge. 2/6 Durham L.I. sick parade twice daily. Lt. WEBB there at Nouveauville the latter also taking the 2/6 Durham L.I. sick parade twice said. The hospital staff are now getting the epidemic in spite of prophylactic gargling etc. and it is becoming difficult to find sufficient men for necessary fatigues. A.D.M.S. visited. This field ambulance is expected all arranged for stay. jw).	
"	26-6-18	Major J.A. Young we returned from leave today & took over the hospital at Nouveauville. Lieut. Watts proceeding to the 2/6 Durham L.I. for temporary duty. Capt. BOYLE (No. 7C) we have now evacuated sick. We have now 230 cases in hospital. jw).	
"	27-6-18	The Durham L.I. epidemic is now almost over only a few fresh cases having occurred. jw).	
"	28-6-18	Major Watson attended a conference at A.D.M.S. Office, I myself being unable to attend though rather ... jw).	
"	29-6-18	Myself + 16 O.R. have influenza - very few fresh cases now. Hutt next the brigade having huts have which it is hoped to carry out this week being headed by sending the Quebec hutments, on account of the hole units & ... being in hopes to be able to commence some training in the course of another week. jw).	
"	30-6-18		

W. Johnson Lt. Col.
O.C. 2/2 N. Midland F.A. Amb.

ORIGINAL.

Confidential
War Diary
of
2/2 A. Mid. Fd. Amb.

FROM 1-7-1918.   To 31-7-1918.

VOLUME VII

Army Form C. 2118.

WAR DIARY of 2/2nd North Midland Field Ambulance
INTELLIGENCE SUMMARY.

Vol: VII Page 1.

(Erase heading not required.)

Place	Date	Hour	Summary of Events and Information	Remarks and references to Appendices
NOUVEAUVILLE (Q.22.a.9.1) [Sheet 26D]	1-7-18		The epidemic of influenza has now subsided in the 2/6 Durham L.I. but today the 15th B. Batt. Essex Regt. commenced to send in a good number of cases. There are 150 cases still in hospital. 7W.	
"	2-7-18		Nothing of note. 7W.	
"	3-7-18		45 cases of influenza admitted today from the 15th Essex. The two tent subdivisions lent to the 18th Corps were returned here today. There are about 20-30 cases a day of influenza arriving. 7W.	
"	4-7-18		Nothing of note. 15th Essex Regt. 7W. chiefly from the	
"	5-7-18		Practice levering up + hooking in ready to move. Carried out today by the Transport section. 7W.	
"	6-7-18		Lt. Col. J. W. Johnson proceeded on 14 days leave to England. Major + H.C. Wolford took over command of the unit during his absence. 7W.C.W.	
"	7-7-18		Capt. H.J. Endolf R.A.M.C. returned from leave. Capt. E.J.P. Notley of R.S.C. 7W.C.W.	
"	8-7-18		Capt. C.T. Falmouth M.C. was posted to H.Q.W. Mid. Fld. Amb. + reported for duty. 7W.C.W.	
"			Troops returned from 2/6 Bn. D.L.I. 7W.C.W.	
"	9-7-18		Received warning orders from 177 Bde. to be ready to move to HABRICOURT area. Lt. H.C. Little, M.O.R.C. U.S.A. appointed for duty. 7W.C.W.	
MAISNIL-LES-TENEUR 32.A [Sh.44C]	10-7-18		Moved to MAISNIL-LES-TENEUR. Established Brigade Reserve Hospital. Over half under canvas and half in huts at TENEUR. Commenced influenza cases received. 7W.C.W.	
"	11-7-18		Nothing of note. Capt. J.W. Anderson M.C. reported for duty.	

WAR DIARY

Army Form C. 2118.

2/North Midland of Field Ambulance. VOL VII PAGE II

INTELLIGENCE SUMMARY.

(Erase heading not required.)

Place	Date	Hour	Summary of Events and Information	Remarks and references to Appendices
MAISNIL-LES-RUITZ L.32.A Sheet 44C	12.7.18		Proceeded with constructional work in villages & camps. sanitary.	
"	13.7.18		Capt. J.W. ARCHIBALD M.C. proceeded for duty with 2/5.13 LRFA, vice Capt. A.W. Bodley R.A.M.C. on leave. 7MGW.	
"	14.7.18		Nothing to note.	
"	15.7.18		The number of sick in hospital having decreased by 50% and influenza epidemic now practically over, hour hospital was consequently since all patients recovered to camp. D.A.D.M.S. visited hospital 7MGW	
"	16.7.18		A.D.M.S. visited hospital in afternoon. 7MGW.	
"	17.7.18		Nothing to note. 7MGW.	
"	18.7.18 19.7.18		Nothing to note. 7MGW.	
"	20.7.18		D.M.S. 1st army visited hospital with A.D.M.S. & D.D.M.S. 1st under red temporary duty with 1st army Artillery about 11am	
"	21.7.18		D.D.M.S. 17th Corps visited hospital with A.D.M.S. 5th D.J. and inspected all arrangements Capt. Aylward M.C. posted to 1/1 Bn. Somerset L.J. and relieved of the clerical guard. 7MGW.	
"	22.7.18		Lt. Col. F.W. Johnson returned from leave and resumed command of the unit. 7MGW.	
"	23.7.18		Nothing of note. 7MGW. Warning now received to be prepared to move tomorrow. 7MGW.	
"	24.7.18		Packed up all stores, equipment and disposed of all patients remaining either to C.C.S. or to duty. Visited VI Corps Rest Station 90B4 m. ARTOIS, which is the takeover by this unit tomorrow. 7MGW.	

A 5834 Wt. W4973/M637 750,000 8/16 D. D. & L. Ltd. Forms/C.2118/13.

Vol VII Page 3

2/2nd North Midland Field Ambulance

WAR DIARY
INTELLIGENCE SUMMARY
(Erase heading not required.)

Army Form C. 2118.

Place	Date	Hour	Summary of Events and Information	Remarks and references to Appendices
GOUY-EN-ARTOIS Q.19.a.7.7 Sheet 51C	25-7-18		Advance party proceeded at 7.0 a.m. to GOUY-EN-ARTOIS and took over the VI Corps Rest Station, with 230 patients, from the 10th Canadian Field Ambulance. The Remainder of the Personnel proceeded by buses, leaving at 2 p.m.; the transport travelling in Brigade transport column, marched at 8.30 a.m. The whole arriving at GOUY by 7 p.m. Lieut. F.E. WEBB reported for temporary duty at 1st Army H.A. School.	
"	26-7-18		Went round the Corps Rest Station & noted the various improvements required. All the huts require recreating a general Cross is needed and various improvements in connection with the kitchens, sanitation and the Officers' Quarters. VI. also paid a brief visit to the hospital, also ADMS 59 Div. Borms VI also paid a temporary duty with 17th Bath. Royal Sussex Regt. — instead of ADMS 59 Div. Lieut F.E. WEBB located sick transmit the 178 Bde who were in reserve in BARLY & GOUY. Arranges for Collection of the first line between MERCATEL & NEUVILLE-VITASSE to-day, the Division took over the line, 177 Bde. in support at BEILACOURT 113° RETENCOURT, 176 Bde being in the line, & 177 Bde also reverting to Bde.	authority ADMS 59 Div
"	27-7-18		Commenced work on construction of Ground Cross and also reverting Regt. huts to Lt. F.E. WEBB (noted [?]) duty as M.O.i/c 17th Br Royal Sussex Regt. FW).	
"	28-7-18		ADMS 59 D.S. visited the hospital FW.	
"	29-7-18		Working parties continued the recreating & ground cross construction. D.D.M.S. VI Corps visited the hospital. 2nd Lt. 59 Div. concert Party ("The Crumps")	
"	30-7-18		Work continued. In the evening the tents & personnel gave an entertainment to the patients & personnel. 2nd Lt. R.F.A. reported for duty from 295 Bde. 2nd Lt. R.F.A. reported for duty from 295 Bde.	
"	31-7-18		Nothing of note. Enemy aircraft bombed the neighbourhood Astruo Capt. A.L. Bodley M.C. reported for duty from 295 Bde. 2nd Lt. R.F.A.	authority Astruo 59 Div
			Nothing of note. Enemy aircraft bombed the neighbourhood during the night. No bombs to fall in this hospital precincts.	

H.B. Musgrave Lt Col
O.C. 2/2 N. Midland F. Amb.

Confidential

War Diary
~ of ~
2/2 A. Mid. Fd. Amb

FROM 1-8-1918.   To 31-8-1918.

VOLUME VIII

Army Form C. 2118.

Vol. VIII Page 1.

2/2nd North Midland WAR DIARY Field Ambulance
of
INTELLIGENCE SUMMARY.
(Erase heading not required.)

Place	Date	Summary of Events and Information	Remarks and references to Appendices
GOUY-EN- ARTOIS Q.19.a.7.7. (sheet 51c) FRANCE 40,000	1-8-18	Inspection this morning of the VI Corps Rear Station by Maj-Gen. Darwin, D.M.S. 3rd Army, who was accompanied by D.D.M.S. VI Corps & A.D.M.S. 59th Div. The work of protecting the huts against aircraft bombs is being proceeded with daily.	F.W.?
"	2-8-18	Attended Conference of F. Amb. Commanders at A.D.M.S' Office this morning.	F.W.?
"	3-8-18	Nothing of note.	F.W.?
"	4-8-18	Special Service in commemoration of anniversary of commencement of the War was held today.	F.W.?
"	5-8-18	Visited the billets of 17th R. Sussex Regt. with M. O/c, arrangements.	F.W.?
"	6-8-18	D.D.M.S. visited the Rear Station today. Work proceeding as usual.	F.W.?
"	7-8-18	Clinical meeting at 19 C.C.S. FREVENT this afternoon - 3 or 4 M.O's form here attended. Re-organised the accommodation for the men suffering from scabies - erected a marquee as 2 mess & equipped the existing ward Hut B.R. C.S. stores.	F.W.?
"	8-8-18	Visited billets of the two battalions at BARLY and inspected sanitary arrangement. Condition and much work remains to be done. The sanitary section is providing urinals, new latrine seats and grease traps, also water pits for ablution, filtration pits for ablution water is proceeding and the work of making proper filtration pit for ablution water is proceeding.	F.W.?
"	9-8-18	Attended Conference of F. Amb. Commanders at A.D.M.S' Office this morning. Commenced work of the construction of a new cookhouse, the old one being dilapidated & insanitary. Also pulled down the old cook house in order to use as much of the material as possible in constructing the new one.	F.W.?
"	10-8-18	Continued the work necessity huts.	F.W.?

Vol. VIII Page 2

2/2nd North Midland Field Ambulance

Army Form C. 2118.

WAR DIARY

INTELLIGENCE SUMMARY

(Erase heading not required.)

Place	Date	Summary of Events and Information	Remarks and references to Appendices
GOUY EN-ARTOIS	11-8-18	Church Parade Service for Patients (CVE) in Cinema Hall today. JW.	
"	12-8-18	Capt. A.L. Bodley M.C. posted to 295 Bde. R.F.A (59 Div. Arty) today for temporary duty. [Q.19.a.77.] Capt. H.G. Ludolf M.C. posted to 10/11 Royal Scots today for temporary duty. Sheet 51c No 5 There are at present about 400 sick in the rest station, 90 being on light duty, in and about the camp. Discharged about 60 today to duty. JW.	patients authority ADMS 59 Div. patients arrived 59 Div
"	13-8-18	1st Lieut W.N. Sweet, M.O.R.C., U.S.A. posted to this unit for duty today.	
"	14-8-18	The new DDMS VI Corps visited the Rest Station today and inspected all arrangements.	
"	15-8-18	The new cook-house is now half-finished but the work is being delayed for want of sufficient materials, our indent having been cut down. Visited the Battalions at BARLY & inspected their sanitation & billets. Found the crickwalk [?] much improvement since last week. JW	
"	16-8-18	Attended Conference of DMS/Ps [?] & Commanders at DMS office this morning. Visited B.R.C.S. Stores at Henu, & obtained some necessary equipment for the Officers' Ward & Mess.	
"	17-8-18	ADMO visited the hospital today. Erected the portable dry-heat disinfector which has been brought here from the last billetting area. Also removed a small hospital Leastocks [?] from BARLY needed it here.	
"	18-8-18	Nothing of note.	
"	19-8-18	Another Convoy [5th] has arrived in the Coffro, and sent in a great number today. Another division has arrived & its men being sent to 19 inform the total admissions today reaching 160. In order to infix [?] those the Cinema Hall had to be converted into a ward. Capt. Ludolf M.C. returned from temporary duty with 11 R. Scots Fros. JW	

Army Form C. 2118.

2/2 n North Midland Field Ambulance Vol VIII Page 3.

WAR DIARY
INTELLIGENCE SUMMARY.
(Erase heading not required.)

Place	Date	Summary of Events and Information	Remarks and references to Appendices
GOUY -en- ARTOIS	20-8-18	Many sick admitted today, from 62nd Div. which two first arrived in the Corp, also from three other divisional Rest Stations. Total number in hospital by 8pm was 704. Cleared the Cinema hall & Recreation Room & converted them into wards, also evacuated the two remaining marquees & filled them with sick. Rumours of an impending attack by this Corps reached us this evening, but no definite information. F.W.	
"	21-8-18	Early this morning the VI Corps attacked on a wide front carrying all their objectives. As actual operations now appeared to have commenced and the medical arrangements during such operations include the provision of walking wounded collecting posts. The arrangements for Lorries to AVESNES-LE-COMTE to evacuate from there the banked wounded I emptied the Advn Hut occupied by R.A.M.C. by train to CCS at Frevent. I emptied the Advn Hut occupied by R.A.M.C. personnel & accommodated the wounded in bell tents. He Advn Hut was made ready to receive walking wounded from the main Dressing Station. About 7am the first batch arrived, and they continued at intervals all day. Sent Major Watson & a merc'y to AVESNES-le-COMTE to make arrangements for a service of trains for the accommodation of walking wounded while waiting for the train. I regarded service as arranged and the Church Army Hut by the station was utilised as shelter & much day used. Cpl. Weddy rationed them on arrival in the day. About 340 walking wounded was fed at the Rest Station. Through by train to CCS Frevent. This number included 26 wounded German prisoners. A.Q. Those at the C. Main Dressing Station for the purpose two lorries were obtained from GOUY to AVESNES, & there with the help of our Convoy, of the motor ambulance, successfully cleared all casualties by 8pm from the cases from GOUY to AVESNES. F.W.	

Vol VIII Page 4

2/2nd North Midland Field Ambulance

INTELLIGENCE SUMMARY.

Place	Date	Hour	Summary of Events and Information	Remarks and references to Appendices
GOUY en-ARTOIS	22-8-18		More walking wounded continued to arrive during the night and by 7 am. Coy 702 had been sent through the B.pa Rest Station & fed, and all had been sent by train to C.Cos. There was no further attack today, the gains of yesterday were being consolidated. Several German counter attacks were repulsed, and more walking wounded arriving today, some evacuated in the same way. D.D.M.S. called this morning expressed satisfaction with the arrangements here. Two more divisions joined the Corps today and sent in over 200 sick during the day - In order to accommodate them I had to utilize the Officers Ward & heavy tent, and afterwards on a Field Ambulance site at WARLUZEL (not in use at present) on my way from the Corps Horse Show found near COUTURELLE and there obtained D.Div's authority to take over and there others from the Corps Horse Show, and all patient under cover - Total numbers evacuated by evening (and walking wounded sick in hospital is now 850, exclusive of walking wounded.	
"	23-8-18		The attack was renewed early this morning, with great success - The 52 Div. passes though our own division's lines to attack. Walking wounded again began to come in about 7 am. Up to this hour 1108 walking wounded has been passed through since the commencement of the attack. Large numbers came in during the morning, and the two lorries (proved insufficient to keep pace with the cases arriving. Supplies for extra lorries that could only be obtained after much delay. Received orders to hand over the Rest Station to 1/3 Northants F. and 52 Div. by 6 pm. so all equipment was packed this afternoon and the unit mached out by 8 pm. bivouacked for the night at SAULTY. left behind to clear up a rear party to complete the loading over - There were 100 sick in hospital by 10 pm & these were were accumulating. F.N.?	

A 5834 Wt.W4973/M687 750,000 8/16 D.D. & L. Ltd. Forms/C.2118/13.

Vol VIII Page 5

2/2nd North Midland Field Ambulance

WAR DIARY
INTELLIGENCE SUMMARY

Army Form C. 2118.

Place	Date	Hour	Summary of Events and Information	Remarks and references to Appendices
SAULTY V.2.C. [Sheet 51C]	24-8-18		The 59th Division, which concentrated at SAULTY last night, entrained today. This unit entrained at SAULTY at 4pm and travelled to AIRE, where it detrained and marched to TILLES at WITTERNESSE (Q.13.b.8.8, Sheet 36A). The transport marched by road and had just arrived by the time the unit was in billets. The officers & rear party returned in time to join the train. J.W.	
WITTERNESSE Q.13.b.8.8 Sheet 36 A.	25-8-18		Reported at ADMS Office this morning, now situated at NORRENT-FONTES, & received information that the Division takes over the Robecq Sector from the 74th Division tomorrow. Accompanied DADMS 59 Div. to the ADMS 74 Div. who gave us all details of the medical arrangements of the sector. This unit is to take over the Main Dressing Station at BERGUETTE and the Advanced Dressing Stations at St Venant and ROBECQ, & be responsible for clearing casualties from the line. J.W. took over the	
"	26-8-18		Went up with an advance party to BERGUETTE and M.D.S. from the 230 Field Ambulance. He O.C. 230 F.A. then took me round the A.D.S. at ROBECQ and the battalion R.A.P.s & Beau(..)arts. Arranged to release all those forward posts tomorrow morning. Posted Major Young up to the A.D.S. at ROBECQ; Capt Linds(..) of the A.D.S., St Venant, and a skel(..)on party at each Regl Aid post (Beau(..)art Capt 17(..)). Quarter master Lieut A. Sidwell promoted to be Hon. Capt. 175(..). J.W.	Gazette Aug. 24/18
"	27-8-18		The Unit moves today by march route to BERGUETTE and took over the Main Dressing Station at Q.16.C.7.0 from the 230 F. Amb.(74 Div.) An advanced party proceeds earlier & relieves all personnel of the 74 Div. at Advanced Dressing Stations at ROBECQ (P.24.b.5.3) and St VENANT (P.5.a.2.1). The Advance Dressing Station at Calonne Q.4.c.3.4 + Q.3.C.8.8) & Q.21.a.5.0 and the Regl Aid post at Calonne (Q.3.d.7.2) & Car loading post was also relieved at Calonne. J.W.	

A 5834 Wt. W4973/M687 750,000 8/16 D. D. & L. Ltd. Forms/C.2118/13

Army Form C. 2118.

Vol VIII Page 6

2/2nd North Midland Field Ambulance

WAR DIARY
INTELLIGENCE SUMMARY.
(Erase heading not required.)

Place	Date	Hour	Summary of Events and Information	Remarks and references to Appendices
BERGUETTE O.16.c.7.6 (Sheet 36A)	27-8-18		(Contd.) A tent subdivision of the 2/3rd N. Mid. Field Amb. was attached for duty today. JW.	
"	28-8-18		This morning the Main Dressing Station at BERGUETTE was cleared up, and various improvements made. More personnel were sent up to both Advanced Dressing stations. The system of evacuation from the front line are now as described in appendix I. Evacuation for sitting cases to cat. & car is only retained for being ready (relay), to Bequatt. The A.D.S. out of Quant is only nine from Mu Adeurentin Cassities.	appendix I.
"	29-8-18		This morning the Main Dressing Station this morning. The D.M.S. XI Corps visited the A.D.S. at Robecq and also called at 177th Brigade. In the afternoon I visited the A.D.S. The line was moving forward. Headqrs in Robecq. Here information was obtained that the Regimental Aid Posts the enemy having retired. Accordingly went up to the places of the vacated & made arrangements for new sites. Relay posts to be the car loading posts at R.A.P. to maintain the line forward. The line moved forward about 3000 yards. Calonne and before night a car loading post was established at Q.5.a.3.0. Today and before night had been posts at Quentin (Q.22.b.3.3) had not the bridge at Q.14.b.6.3 been down for reconstruction. A reasonably good let the Clerin bridge at Q.14.b.6.3 been down for reconstruction. A rendezvous post at and another (Q.21.a.3.0) was therefore established to complete the chain the late right R.A.P. (Q.21.a.3.0) was therefore established to complete the chain and cat established in the late R.A.P.	
"	30-8-18		Moved up the Advanced Dressing Station to Calonne, and occupies the mined house at Q.9.b.7.7. Brigade H.Q. having occupied a mined house in repair station in the village. The Staff of the A.D.S. did much valuable work in repair of the house & buildings in short time. Visited St. Venant & inspected the Asylum remains & ruins which is selected for the main aid station. Arrangements for a leaf I one of the there tonight. The building chosen is very little damaged building. The M.D.S. there tonight. The bridges have crossed the troops in excellent spirits though LESTREM & the troops have crossed the large distance line now. Russian Canal.	JW.

Vol VIII Page 7
2/2 A North Midland Field Ambulance

WAR DIARY
INTELLIGENCE SUMMARY

Army Form C. 2118.

Place	Date	Hour	Summary of Events and Information	Remarks and references to Appendices
ST. VENANT ASYLUM [P.9.d.1.8. Sheet 36A.]	31-8-18		Moved the Main Dressing Station up from BERGUETTE to ST. VENANT ASYLUM and occupied the building already chosen. It is well suited to the purpose, there being rooms with a good floor & two on the first floor, in good condition. Captain Dudley this personnel from the A. D. S. at the eastern end & looks that post being no longer required. S. VENANT that post being no longer required. Visited the A.D.S. at Calonne and also what moved the supplied battalion in Paradis & the Regimental aid posts in Eastern — Placed a bearer relay post in L'Epinette in rear of the Western entrance to Eastern and a bath [?] post at Q.11.D.8.5. this being the nearest point a Car can be taken at present, on account of the cross-roads having been blown up. 177 Bde H.Q.s are now in Eastern and the line is still advancing. Selected a site for the Advanced Dressing Station in LESTREM as it will be necessary to move it up to this point so soon as the road is passable. 130th Reg. aid posts are moving forwards from LESTREM tonight. The horizon [?] however posts and the evacuation routes are shown in Appendix 2. Up to the present the casualties of the division have been very light — on average about ten a day — but quite to S Venant have been several rounds either of chest abdomen or head.	Appendix 2.

J.W. Johnson
Lieut. Col. R.A.M.C. (T.)
O.C. 2/2 N. Midland Field Amb.

War Diary – 2/2 North Midland F.d. Amb.   Vol. VIII.
Appendix I.

Positions of Main Dressing Station,
Advanced Dressing Stations and
Regt. Aid Posts on 28th Aug. 1918.
Casualties were cleared from the Main Dressing Station
by M.A.C. cars to AIRE (39 Sta. Hosp. & 54 C.C.S.)

J W Johnson Lt.Col.
O.C. 2/2 N. Midd. F. Amb.

War Diary – 2/2nd N. Midland Field Amb. Vol. VIII
Appendix 2.

Position of Main Dressing Station, Advanced Dressing Station and R.A.P.'s on Aug. 31st 1918.
Evacuation of casualties by wheeled stretcher to Car post north of PARADIS, thence to A.D.S. by car.
Cases cleared from M.D.S. by M.A.C. cars to AIRE.

F W Johnson Lt Col.
O.C. 2/2 N. Mid. Fd Amb.

Vol 20
14/3257

Confidential
War Diary
of
2/2 A. Mid. Fd. Amb

From 1-9-1917   To 30-9-1917

Volume VI

Ref 9-1917
17B

Army Form C. 2118.

Vol IX Page 1.

2/2 North Midland Field Ambulance

WAR DIARY INTELLIGENCE SUMMARY.

(Erase heading not required.)

Place	Date	Summary of Events and Information	Remarks and references to Appendices
ST. VENANT ASYLUM [P.g.d.1.8 P.Sheet 36A]	1-9-18	Visited the A.D.S. at Calonne and the Regtl Aid Posts at Lestrem - also Brigade H.Qrs. The Bearer relay posts at L'Epinette and Lestrem. The road is both repaired & craters are now traversable by cars. He went on to the Colonne through Merville to Lestrem. Began Young reconnoitred the road from Colonne through Merville to Lestrem & found it possible to get a car up that way as far as Lestrem. Posted an ambulance at the Support R.A.P. The Brigade is again advancing, but has been held up village in both places. Lestrem is still being shelled at intervals. If theirs do not get beyond a move up the R.A.P's from the village. (Position) medical posts shown in Appendix 1. Forward area in Lestrem moved up the	Appendix 1
"	2-9-18	Again visited the R.A.Ps. Forward area in Lestrem both Cairo there. Bearers stationed from Calonne as a supplementary bearer station brought as the kept at the A.D.S. at Calonne & one of rams was two been today, and placed new A.D.S. is not quite finished & the whole place cleaned. Ambulance tins repaired. Colonne today & looked over the A.D.S. A two V.C.ps visited. The Period's route being Evacuation is now west by Beaupre Merville, the Period's route being seen very rough. J.W.J.	
"	3-9-18	Several severe casualties last night. Ballaterio advanced little distance last night to both R.A.Ps have gone forward. The left to PONT RIQUEUR (R.10.c.3) position as shown in appendix 2 the right to Bout Deville (R.21.c.a.3.3) Positions are shown in touch with the A.D.S. J.W. Post I Bearer always at their late sites, to keep. Went to LESTREM this afternoon	Appendix 2
"	4-9-15	Further advanced by the battalions of 2000 & 3000 yards to saw the Brig. & 176 Bn. at H.Q. He had made the hardest position with R.A.Ps that are Major Young reconnoitred the roads & got into touch until Bn. He posted further bearer relays a car loading point in front of Lestrem just west of BOUT DEVILLE (R.17.d.7.7.) LESTREM was shelled during the night - several shells falling very near the A.D.S. J.W. (Position) medical posts as shown in appendix 3	Appendix 3

2/2nd North Midland War Diary Field Ambulance Vol. IX   Page 2

Army Form C. 2118.

INTELLIGENCE SUMMARY.
(Erase heading not required.)

Place	Date	Hour	Summary of Events and Information	Remarks and references to Appendices
ST VENANT ASYLUM (P.9.d.1.8) (Sheet 36A)	5-9-18		Commenced work today on clearing debris & rubbish from a house in LESTREM with a view to moving up the Main Dressing Station as soon as possible. Visited the right Bearer relay post & Car loading post at M.19.d.7.9 and R.17.d.7.7 (Neufacture), & reconnoitred the roads in front of the (sheet 36 SW) (Sheet 36 A.S.E.) Major Young visited the L/S Car transport at R.5.d.6.5 (Sheet 36A) (Pont-Rocham) and the L/B Bearer relay post at M.7.6.1.2 Sheet 36 SW (Riez Bailleul). There are several large craters in the roads which need filling before Cars can be brought forward & the present site of Car-posts. Sent in request for R.E. labour to do this. Work at the Main Dressing Station is proceeding smoothly. J.W.J.	
"	6-9-18		Visited Lestrem again this morning. The neighbourhood of the A.D.S. was shelled again last night & one horse wounded. Not the A.D.S. but into the house in the right of R.9.d.1.7 (Sheet 36A), and made a fairly good Dressing room in the front part of the building. The remainder of the house forward proved quite unsuitable as the roof was badly damaged & heavy rain that night came through and penetrated the rooms. Hauled the Left sector Bearer posts at M.7.6.1.2 and M.2.C.8.8 (Sheet 36) and moved up two Car-loads (not been filled in, see appendix X 3) at M.19.d.7.9 (Sheet 36) and between these points along the former beaten part the right R.A.P. having moved forward. Moves the right Car post forward to M.15.C.7.7 the right R.A.P. having moved forward. Established a new Head post at M.15.C.7.7. Visited the right Advanced Dressing Station at Riez Bailleul & M.2.3.a.2.2. arranged to move the A.D.S. there tomorrow to be prepared from the right sector to the high forward the Chateau Stables as soon as the road found all satisfactory, so arranged for the Chateau Stables & work was begun on that today. Meanwhile learning was Started and work was begun on that today. For the next 3 wks Main Dressing Station. Visited Lestrem J.W.J. J.A.P.M.O. (Wilkes) returned from leave.	
"	7-9-18		Capt. A.L. Bodley M.C. returned for duty from the 295th Bde. R.F.A. Visited the new A.D.S. at RIEZ BAILLEUL (M.7.6.1.2) having moved up there this morning. Or party continued to work Chateau Stables and cleared out several rooms & prepared the M.D.S. in a joy on time. J.W.J.	

Vol. IX Page 3

2/2nd North Midland Field Ambulance

WAR DIARY

INTELLIGENCE SUMMARY.

(Erase heading not required.)

Army Form C. 2118.

Place	Date	Hour	Summary of Events and Information	Remarks and references to Appendices
ST VENANT ASYLUM (Pg.d.1.8 sheet 36A.)	8-9-18		Col. Franken Cavalry Surgeon 5th Army visited the Main Dressing Stn, and inspected the building with view to picking up advanced Dressing Stns there shortly. I went with the A.D.M.S. to Lestrem and inspected the progress made with the work at the chateau stables. Visited the A.D.S. at Riez Bailleul, and the right subsector car loading post, right battalion R.A.P. and subsector R.A.P. Tested it subsector car loading post. Much shelling of the right battalion H.Q. pink road. Brigade Headquarters forward to M.15.c.7.7 with our troops further forward to the moves the right car post forward to leave the chateau stable & been there and we left.	
"	9-9-18		Div. Headqrs received all personnel. Work on ascending of Stables there – Building is suspected of being mined – 5 Nissen huts vacated by Div. Head Qrs at night. The A.D.M.S. has asked to secure the village having been shelled again last night. The south end of LESTREM, the village from young women the left sub sector. To-day I visited the A.D.S. & will begin young women nominal. (M.9.a.8.8), the left R.A.P. at M.12.a.central Calling at the bearer post in M.10.c.3.2. LAVENTIE is the beaver post & in approx. six moved the left car road up foot up & loading posts have been approx. in approx. to jug. at M.2.T.c.6.8.	appendix 4
"	10-9-18		D.M.S. 5th Army visited D.H.Q. & agmo 5th Div. at Les Lreux Inry, Station Wagon with D.D.M.S. XI Corps & adno 59th Div. D.S. Station. Today we started on the new site for the Honorary Cook house & Dressing Hut have the ground of huts – built a catering hut on our right. Capt. Bodley took charge of the work. Fair giving the rid is now Catania. His evening the village under shells dain wings totally now Station horse 54 C.C.S. arrives at if Venant with a voice Sports from 54 C.C.S. Lieut Little M.O.R.C. USA forward this way to it's site & the new at M.D.S. (by authority A.D.M.S. 59 x Div) with the V/II E Somerset Light Infantry

J.W. | |

2/2nd North Midland Field Ambulance

Vol. IX Page 4

Army Form C. 2118.

WAR DIARY
INTELLIGENCE SUMMARY.
(Erase heading not required.)

Place	Date	Hour	Summary of Events and Information	Remarks and references to Appendices
ST VENANT ASYLUM (P.9.d.1.8 sheet 36A)	11-9-18		Orders received to move the headqrs of the unit to destination tomorrow. Visited the new site today with the Q.M. and inspected the arrangements. Arranged billets accommodation for the personnel in dug out barracks and for the Q.M. Stores in a building close through to LESTREM and clean for M.A.C. Cars not run through to LESTREM and clean camouflage from stable today as the main Dressing Station functioned at the new site from position, since evacuation shown in appendix to the party for 54 C.C.s, and now. No portion, since evacuation shown in appendix to the party for 54 C.C.s, and now.	
LESTREM R.9.C.3.b (sheet 30A)	12-9-18		Handed over the building at St Venant Asylum commenced work on the ground, clearing the unit by hand moved to LESTREM making a good job. away debris and arranged a plan for the neighbourhood of posts with Major Young Visited the A.D.S. and the left subsector of the M.D.S. during the night let 9/7th A few shells fell in the neighbourhood built road leading into the Trj.	
"	13-9-18		Commenced work on the construction. But on the new site M.D.S. Re-erected one Nissen Hut. The casualties commenced for the Division front were not numerous, but they are being more severely wounded each night - they are being evacuated as quickly as possible we feared. We are using hand wheeled stretchers more severely wounded by wheeled stretchers, but 1500 yards from entity. The road is very heavy. Car loads are going & evacuation from R.A.P. to the 1 N.A.D.S. via PONT REQUEUR. the centre leaving the A.D.S. is now direct to the heavy Car loads to the 1 N.A.D.S. via PONT REQUEUR. all been filled in. J.W.	
"	14-9-18		A.D.M.S. visited the M.D.S. Good progress made with the new road, and the repair of the F.M. Stores, hot & small hut was so insanitary, and water laid on for baths. The latter was equipped with a stove & a buffer for hot drinks etc. In the afternoon a larger house near the original cottage Visited the A.D.S. in safe by the R.E.s & we move to the A.D.S. here today & has not been passed as safe by the R.E. There is now room of the hutments made a much better dressing Station retained as an Base centre. cleared the old site used now by the R.A.P.s a/b Rank if required. Arranged for a car to collect from any 9th R.A.P. if required. J.W.	

Vol. IX Page 5

2/2nd North Midland Field Ambulance

Army Form C. 2118.

WAR DIARY
INTELLIGENCE SUMMARY.
(Erase heading not required.)

Place	Date	Hour	Summary of Events and Information	Remarks and references to Appendices
LESTREM [R.9.c.3.6] [Sheet 36A]	15-9-18		Moved another Nissen Hut to its new position today. Completed the enlargement of the Cook-house to their work about the camp. Several bad casualties admitted during the day - one or two as the result of shelters being blown up by delay-action fuses.	
"	16-9-18		The weather has now improved and good progress is being made with the work of the M.D.S. Major Watson proceeded on leave to England. Capt. Grant & 36 I.R. were attached from the 2/3 N. Mid F.A. and were attached here for duty. As the majority being detailed is working parties to construct the 2/1 N. Mid 3 A. M. to contract a new Divisional Rest Station half a mile south of Lestrem the huts is now almost complete. A.D.M.S. visited the M.D.S. today.	F.W.
"	17-9-18		Visited 177th Bde H.Q. and they a.D.p. this morning Captain[?] visited the M.D.S. today. R.A.p's found post & inspected the work. F.W.	
"	18-9-18		T.S.M.S. called at the M.D.S. Commenced the construction of Capt. Botley visited the M.D.S. site more shelters for personnel. Repaired formed cross on the M.D.S. is now under canvas. Some shelters are still under canvas.	F.W.
"	19-9-18		Major Grey inspected the tomes post (R.a.p.) to-day. M.D.S. is reported the 177th Brigade tents (in poor condition) as the events of might. A good deal shelling of Lestrem during the evening & night.	F.W.
"	20-9-18		Much work done on the M.D.S. today. The M.D.S. is now well equipped & clean. Visited the A.D.S. which is now well equipped and also Those shelling of the village during the night.	F.W.

WAR DIARY / INTELLIGENCE SUMMARY

Army Form C. 2118.

2/2 North Midland — Field Ambulance

Vol. IX Page 6

Place	Date	Summary of Events and Information	Remarks and references to Appendices
LESTREM (R.9.c.3.6) sheet 36A	21-9-18	Consulting Surgeon 5th Army (Col Handley) and Consulting Physician (Lt Colley) visited the M.D.S. today — also A.D.M.S. today. B/G. rear found in another Marrec that was moved.	J.W.
"	22-9-18	Capt A.L. Botley M.C. proceeded on a course at XI Corps Gas School. L/Cpl. 59 Barrow inspected the horse Dressing Station today. Shaped hunt near the M.D.S. Six a/eight times this afternoon — Visited the A.D.J. + left car-loading front in Laventie, with wiring.	J.W.
"	23-9-18	Prospected a new road between RIEZ BAILLEUL and the A.D.S. main ESTAIRES - LA PASSEE road which will shorten the journey to the A.D.S. from the car-loading point. It is already passable, but not good; all the N roads are at the M.D.S. is now functioning, and their personnel the found-arms at present in possession are otherwise moved to stand sanitary appliances which are at the houses near the A.D.S. today to stand sanitary appliances visited 76 Sanitary Section of A1RE today to return uplifted section of the M.D.S.	
"	24-9-18	Capt Ludolf M.C. took charge at the A.D.S. today, St Sweet M.R.C. U.S.A. was sent to join him there from the Heads pa at the M.D.S. have shaped our this camp today — no casualties	
"	25-9-18	Capt dicksby visited forward posts today. 11 casualties admitted this evening from 2/6 Durham L.J. Muses in reserve — all shrapnel wounds. Lt Neff M.R.C. (USA) Lt Sweet posted for temporary duty with 295 Bde. R.F.A. 6 the A.D.S.	
"	26-9-18	3/1 N.W. 70 Amb. reported for duty. conveyances such att this unit was posted. two men from R.E. dump today — J.W. two men Pioneers these were drawn for R.E. dump today — J.W. Capt Grant, 2/3 N.W. F Amb., rejoined his unit on arrival of Division S.T. Div.	J.W.

WAR DIARY
2/2nd North Midland Field Ambulance
INTELLIGENCE SUMMARY

Vol. IX Page 7
Army Form C. 2118.

Place	Date	Summary of Events and Information	Remarks and references to Appendices
LESTREM (R.9.c.3.b) Sheet 36A	27-9-18	A.D.M.S. paid a visit to the Main Dressing Station today. I visited the Advanced Dressing Station. The Reg. Adjutant of the Support battalion and the right battalion in line; also the right Car loading post. The Right R.A.P. is now moved to "Road Bend Post" at M.17.d.10.b (Sheet 36) and the R.A.P. of the Support batt. is now on the La-Basseé-Estaires road, at M.14.d.9.9. RAP Lt. Wall visited the left car-loading post at Laventie and the Left battalion R.A.P.	
"	28-9-18	Heavy rain this morning made the ground very bad, & evacuation heavy. Received warning that operations would commence in a day or two, I accordingly made preparations for obtaining an increased stock of dressings, tablets, another supply of anesthetics, etc. The A.D.S. was pushed on with all speed. Received & put up of [?] blankets from the Corps Reserve, bringing our stock up to about 600. Capt. A.L. Bodley M.C. returned from the San School course today. The neighbourhood of the Main Dressing Station was shelled by a long range gun this evening, several hits being made in the Artillery transport lines close to the hospital entrance. No casualties.	
"	29-9-18	The attack by the 11th R. Scots Fus. is to take place early tomorrow. I sent up supplies of morning splints to Stations, blankets & medical comforts today, to the A.D.S. Visited the A.D.S. this afternoon. Hospital 30 extra to the M.O. i/c 11th R.S.F. at the Right R.A.P., four extra stretcher bearers to the 11th R.S.F. and two extra motor ambulance cars reported for duty from the 2/3 N.M.F. and Capt. Bodley proceeded to the A.D.S. for duty, relieving Sgt Webb, MRC. U.S.A. who returned to the 2/1st W. 3rd N.M. Fd. Amb. ten other wounds. The Main Dr. Station was again shelled. This evening one H.E. exploding over the Camp-probably intended for the artillery lines. No casualties.	

J.N.

Vol IX Page 8

Army Form C. 2118.

2/2nd North Midland Field Ambulance

WAR DIARY

INTELLIGENCE SUMMARY.

(Erase heading not required.)

Place	Date	Hour	Summary of Events and Information	Remarks and references to Appendices
LESTREM (R.9.c.3.6) Sheet 36A	30-9-18		At 7.30 a.m. the N.M.R. took Pra. Winners their first about 1000 yards, taking all their objectives in rough stormy weather. Casualties amounted to about 50, and evacuation was carried out satisfactorily especially considering the A.D.S. at 5 p.m. and arranged with Capt. Hardy to visit the A.D.S. at 5 p.m. and arranged with Capt. Hardy to hand bearers to the extra R.A.P.'s in front of Laventie, the 178th Brig. not having come into line on the left with two battalions in line and two bns. come into the line on the right with two battalions viewing. The 177th Bde. came into Battalion position. Four R.A.P.'s were ascertained, and bearers with blankets stretchers, wheeled carriages, located track. The Right Car-load host at M.15.c.7.7 (Sheet 36) was retained but a forward Car loading host for Jours Camp was established at M.22.a.1.1. The final position of all medical posts is shown in Appendix 4. Evacuation routes (including the new one between La Bassée & La Becque Rd.) & Rue Biszet) as in use at the end of the month.	

W.H.Johnston Lt. Col. R.A.M.C.(T.)

O.C. 2/2 N. Midland Field Amb.

Appendix 1.

Position of M.D.S., A.D.S., Car loading post and bearer posts, & the R.A.P.'s on the 1st Sept. 1918. The road from Lestrem to Merville is still bad, and Evacuation is carried out via L'Épinette & Paradis.

.... Wheeled stretcher routes
———— Motor amb. routes.

1.9.18

F.W. Johnson Lt Col
OC 2/2/4 M.F. Field [Amb]

Appendix 2.

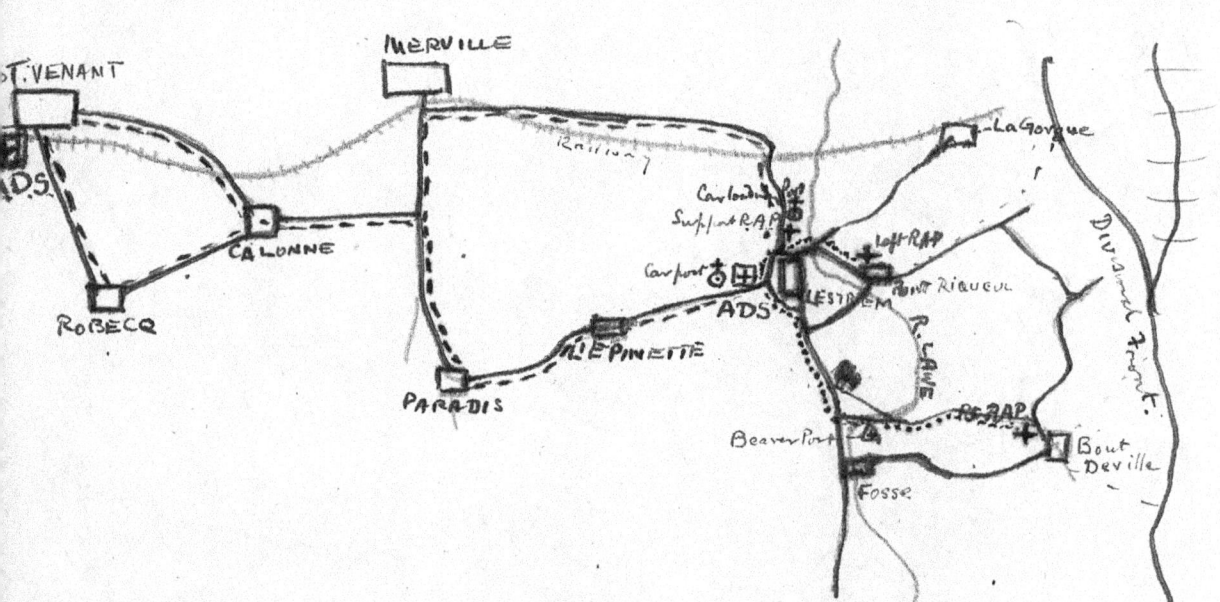

Position of M.D.S, A.D.S, Car-loading posts, bearer-relay posts & R.A.P's on Sept. 3rd 1918.

············· wheeled stretcher routes
— — — — motor amb. routes.

3–9–18

F.W. Johnston Lt Col.
OC. 2/2 N. m. F. amb

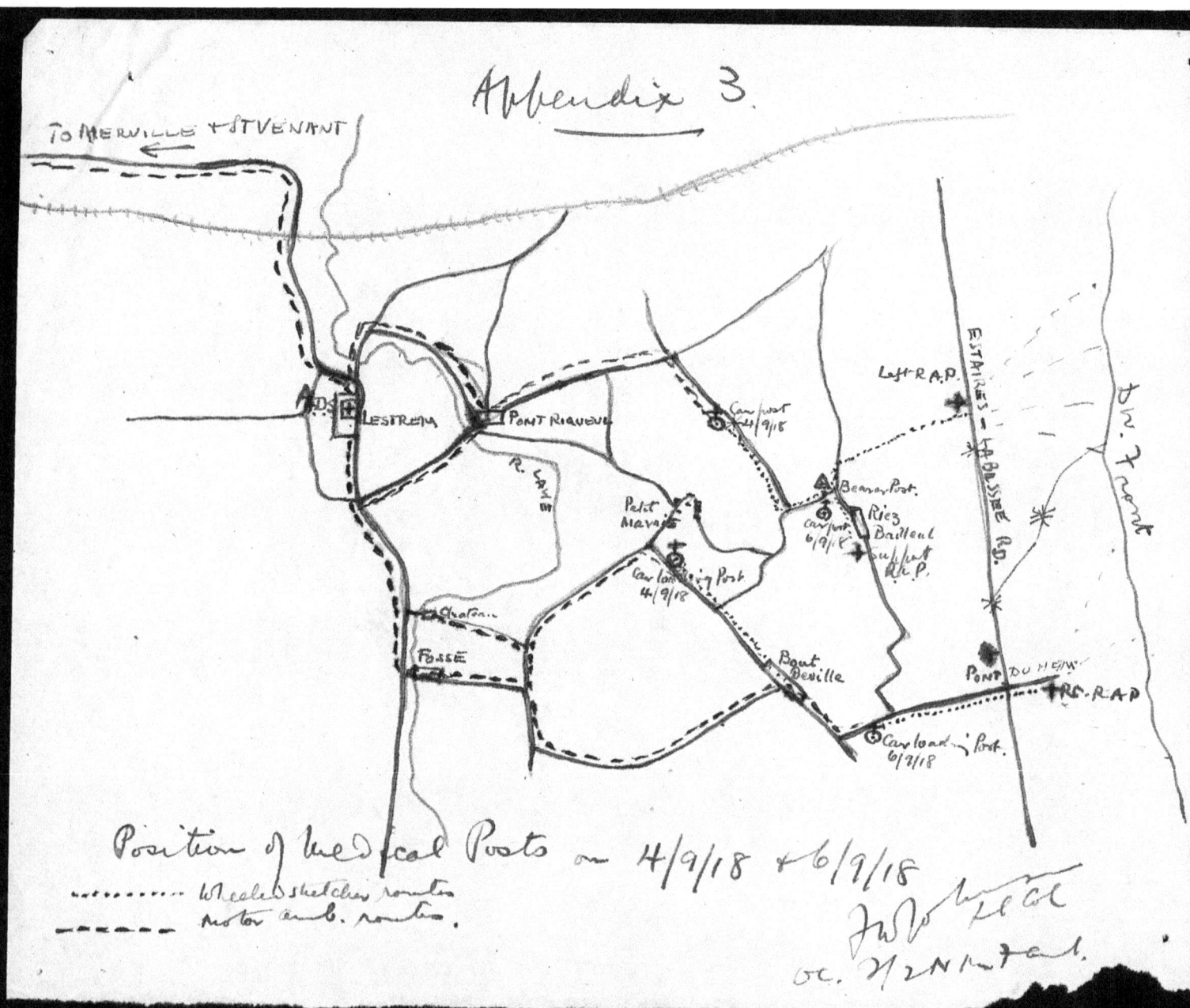

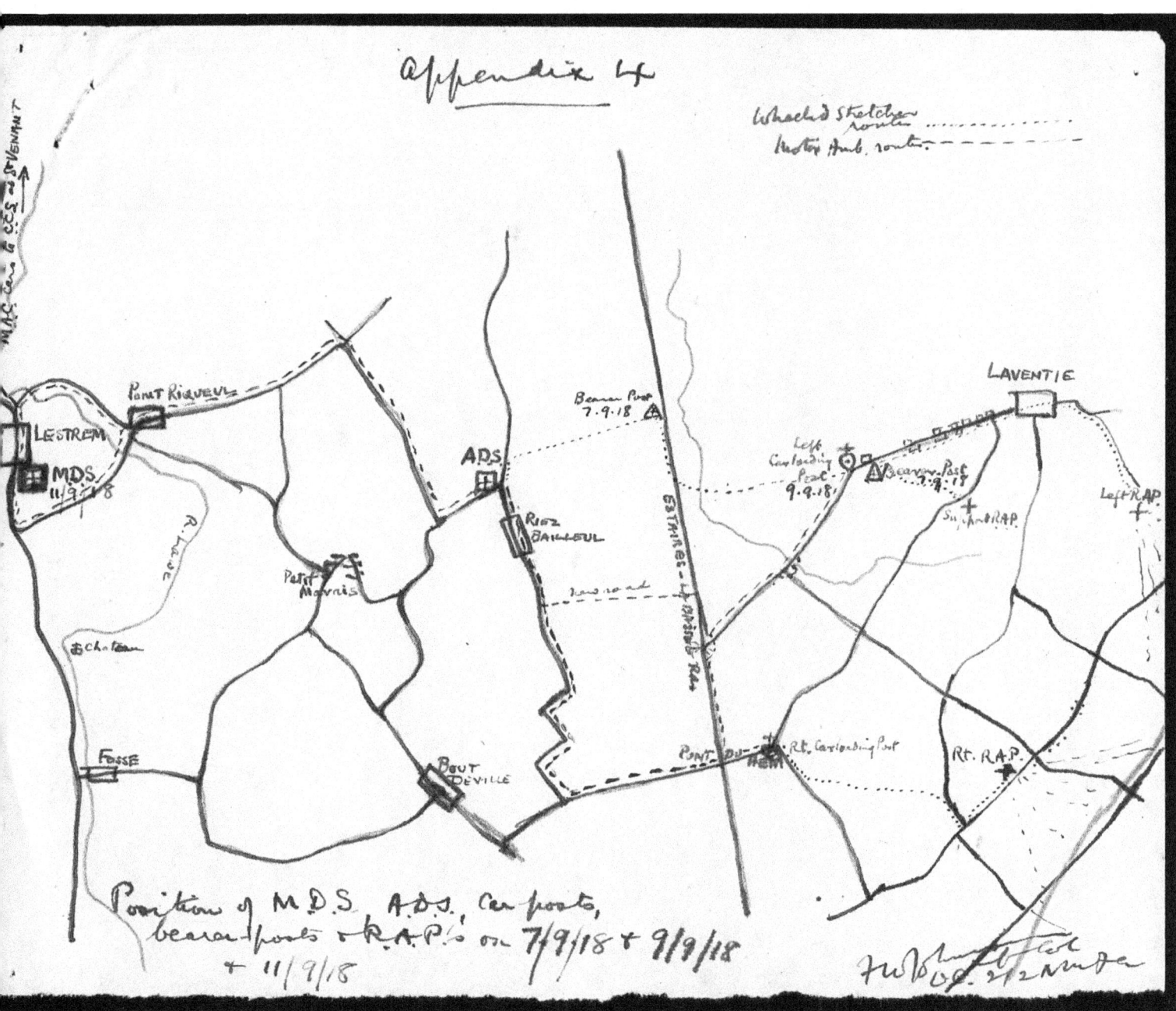

Confidential

War Diary

~ of ~

2/2 N. Mid. Fd. Amb

From 1-10-1918. To 31-10-1918.

Volume X

Vol X. Page 1

2/2nd North Midland Field Ambulance

Army Form C. 2118.

WAR DIARY
INTELLIGENCE SUMMARY.
(Erase heading not required.)

Place	Date	Hour	Summary of Events and Information	Remarks and references to Appendices
LESTREM [R.9.c.3.6] (Sheet 36A)	1-10-18		The ADMS visited the Main Dressing Station. I visited the Advanced Dressing Station at RIEZ BAILLEUL & with Capt. Bodley visited the right car loading post r/the R.A.P.'s on the right sector. Established an advanced car loading post at M.22.a.1.1 (Sheet 36). J.W.	
"	2-10-18		This morning the 46th R. Welsh Div. attacked and captured a Strong point known in Two Basefarm on the left 1/th division front. About 40 casualties reached were all evacuated from the M.D.S. by 11 a.m. I inspected all our arrangements this morning. D.M.S. 5th Army visited the M.D.S. & Shared over to the 47th Div. tomorrow. Orders received & the patients to be moved this evening & camped alongside the M.D.S. The 1/5 London F.Amb. arrived this evening. The unit is taking over the A.D.S. & formed also the 1/4 London F.Amb. The former unit to be instructions for this new bivoucac. The 1/4 London F.Amb. The latter the M.D.S. A.D'S. carrier advanced forward posts to take over the present 61st Div. Rest Station at Haverskerque tomorrow. This afternoon I visited HAVERSKERQUE and arranged details of relief with C. 2/2 South Midland F.Amb. J.W.	
"	3-10-18		This morning I took the O.C. 1/5 London F.Amb. round & shewed him this R.A.M.C. post & carloading posts & all bearer posts. The final programme of relief in Appendix 1. The unit is shown in touch with O.C. 1/5 London F.A. & assisted on relief of this unit. Reconnoitres the ground in front & Carboy's post at Two-tree farm and Road- Bend post near H.D.S. & Carboys-post at Two-tree farm. Hauled over the Main Dressing Station Withdrew all my personnel on relief at 2a.k.m. by O.C. 1/4 London F.Amb. hauled out bearers at 4pm and arrived at HAVERSKERQUE about 7am advanced party having already proceeded Car Master in rear H.D. Rest Sta. Wt 100 stations. J.W.	see Appendix 1.

Vol X. Page 2

2/2nd North Midland Mobile Ambulance

WAR DIARY

INTELLIGENCE SUMMARY.

(Erase heading not required.)

Army Form C. 2118.

Place	Date	Summary of Events and Information	Remarks and references to Appendices
HAVERSKERQUE [J.27.d.cent.] sheet 36A.	4-10-18	Major Watson reported for duty on return from leave to England. The day was spent in arranging details of administration including stores etc. Late in the day Orders instructions were received to send advance party to recce on the site of the present Main Dressing Station of the Division, which is being evacuated this morning, & convert it into 2 Div. Rest Station. Lt. Major Watson & Capt. Archer toured this duty today. I visited the place, which is situated at Chapelle Duvelle (L.26.c.6.8. Sheet 36A.) "Trade avenue" & "Sir Conway" Stores there tomorrow. The Division has ordered the Front line from J. to 61°8in, & the line is now east of the advance, so that the present D.R.S. at ARMENTIERES - BOIS-GRENIER Road will be too far back.	
"	5-10-18	There are about 150 patients in hospital today. Sent is many informed back to duty. Packed up as much of the equipment as possible & sent forward with all blankets & stretchers to begin Watson. The Div. line having advanced further, Chapelle Duvelle was evacuated to day & Major Watson to this section moved into a new site at Fort Rompu, east of Bac St Maur (H.7.d.7.3. Sheet 36) who set up an extra ambulance party & 20 men to assist in preparing a Div. Rest. Station there.	
"	6-10-18	Visited the new site for the D.R.S. & noted Capt. Butler to meet Major Watson. Much work was done there today in cleaning the Brewery buildings for hospital and erecting marquees & repairing & resetting a large tent for a person's billet. Sick were admitted at Fort Rompu today, but being in hospital there this evening. About 140 remain at Haverskerque and there are being evacuated by about 30 or 40 daily to duty or CCS. Waggons are being sent up daily with stores from Haverskerque. J.W.	

Vol X Page 3

Army Form C. 2118.

2/2nd North Midland Field Ambulance

WAR DIARY
INTELLIGENCE SUMMARY.
(Erase heading not required.)

Place	Date	Hour	Summary of Events and Information	Remarks and references to Appendices
HAVERSKERQUE J.27.d.central (Sheet 36A)	7-10-18		Patients at Hospital were reduced to 85 this morning. Visited Fort Rompu this afternoon & inspected the progress made there. 1/20 latrines were erected. Floor and trench in room for another 50 or 60. Sent up more tents & floor boards & erected a Nissen Hut there for scabies cases. J.W.J.	
"	8-10-18		Sent up another load of stores to Fort Rompu J.W.J. by 6 G.S. wagons. R.M. Store + hospital clerks were transferred there J.W.J.	
FORT ROMPU 9-10-18 H.7.d.7.3 Sheet 36N			Transferred head quarters and the rest of the unit to Fort Rompu this morning, leaving a rear party in charge of Major Young at Haverskerque, to look after the 60 patients still remaining there until they are disposed of. There is now a good billet for personnel with 110 bunks, Q.M. stores, equipment store, cookhouse, orderly room & offices, dispensary, officers quarters, and hospital accommodation for 150 patients. J.W.J.	
"	10-10-18		Commenced work in erection of pack store, reception room, clerks office & a spray bath etc. 160 patients in hospital here, about 30 remaining at Haverskerque. J.W.J.	
"	11-10-18		A.D.M.S visited the D.D.S. Day inspected the work done. Capt Luddy M.C. proceeded on leave to Paris. Visited the Divisional Baths. Nick and Camp erected at Bac St Maur. J.W.J.	
"	12-10-18		The rear party at Haverskerque rejoined today bringing with them the few patients remaining there. Much work for them to-day. Spray bath completed & working. Pack store nearly finished, clerks office complete, Marquees erected where commenced. About 180 patients in hospital. J.W.J.	

Army Form C. 2118.

Vol X Page 4

2/2nd North Midland Field Ambulance

WAR DIARY
of
INTELLIGENCE SUMMARY.
(Erase heading not required.)

Instructions regarding War Diaries and Intelligence Summaries are contained in F. S. Regs., Part II. and the Staff Manual respectively. Title pages will be prepared in manuscript.

Place	Date	Hour	Summary of Events and Information	Remarks and references to Appendices
FORT ROMPU (H 7.d. 7.3) (Sheet 36)	13-10-18		Continued work of the D.R.S. All stores & near-parts have not been transferred to hospital. 210 patients in hospital today. Received warning orders to prepare to move at short notice, as an infantry retirement of the Enemy, on a large scale, is expected. Attended Conference of F. Ald. Commanders at A.D.M.S. Office, Fleurbaix. J.R.	
"	14-10-18		Attended Conference of F. Ald. Commanders at A.D.M.S. Office, Fleurbaix. J.R.	
"	15-10-18		Nothing of note. J.R.	
"	16-10-18		The Divisional front has been advanced about 2000 yards. Lt Sweet, M.R.C., U.S.A. returned from duty on temporary duty with 2/6 Bde R.F.A. 6/6 Brigade – behind hills. The troops are not well kept.	
"	17-10-18		Further retirement of the Enemy. Received orders to move up tomorrow. The town. Received 6/6 Brigade in the S.B.O. to 51. C.C.S. today. There are still 200 patients in Hospital [succeeded] Major Young + 2 Nursing Orderlies (attached A.D.M.S. 59th Div.) J.R.	
"	18-10-18		Sent forward Section under Major Watson & Capt. Bodley to take over a site at St André, a northern suburb of Lille, however the 2/3 N Md F. Amb. whose R. D. F. S. has now moved forward, I found 3 R.S. was established there, in the Hospice with room for 1000 & more patients. 7 civilians who accused the troops the town of Lille & its suburbs with a most wonderful welcome. After 4 years of German rule they rendered every possible assistance in the way I billet & accommodation. From the remains at Fort Rompu were reduced 6125 by this evening. The patients remaining today asthma 6 possible ones, + more tomorrow. All stores were packed today after an possible road. J.R.	

Vol X Page 5

2/2 North Midland Field Ambulance

WAR DIARY

INTELLIGENCE SUMMARY.

Army Form C. 2118.

Place	Date	Summary of Events and Information	Remarks and references to Appendices
ST. ANDRE HOSPICE K.19.c.a.b (sheet 36)	19-10-18	Moved headquarters & the rest of the unit up to ST ANDRE Hospice today, leaving a rear party in charge of Lt Sweet to remain at Fort Rompu until the 125 patients there are disposed of. All the surplus stores & in charge of Lt ... (Lt Sweet). Our unit were deposited at the R.A.M.C. dump which has been formed at Fleurbaix, and two men left in charge. There are 58 patients already at the Hospice St André, & plenty of plants for more. Received news from advance to move the 9 D.R. up to Flers, east of Lille tomorrow, occupying the site of the M.D.S. there on its removal to HEM, 3 miles further east. The 94	
FLERS L.32.C.8.3 (sheet 36)	20-10-18	Marched from ST. ANDRE at 8 a.m. & transferred the whole unit & its stores in a to the school house at FLERS (L.32 c.8.3 sheet 36) patients who remained in hospital. There are half the building, the other half being in the vicinity of established the Div. Rest Station ... line of the R. Schelot being The Division has advanced up to the banks having	
"	21-10-18	Lt Sweet & the rear party rejoined from Fort Rompu this evening, having marched the whole distance of 30 kilos, though Lille.	
"	21-10-	Took over the whole school at Flers today, forming no accommodation for 120 patients. Capt Lindsay returned from leave to Paris, reported for duty. J.W.	
"	22-10-18	There are 110 patients in hospital today. Received instructions to move up to HEM tomorrow; accordingly visited HEM today & arranged to take over the site vacated by the Main Dressing Station, who have gone forward to TEMPLEUVE. Capt Lindsay proceeds to Boulogne duty with 11th Br R.Sat No. ... any Lindsay 67 9w)	
HEM L.24.C.9.1 (sheet 36)	23-10-18	Moved the Divisional Rest Station, all personnel, & the 95 patients remaining to HEM this morning, occupying an aeroplane hanger & a factory as hospital. The afternoon was spent in fitting up the necessary latrines, cookhouses, & emptying the wards, for patients. J.W.	

Vol X page 6

Army Form C. 2118.

2/2nd North Midland Field Ambulance

WAR DIARY
INTELLIGENCE SUMMARY.
(Erase heading not required.)

Place	Date	Hour	Summary of Events and Information	Remarks and references to Appendices
HEM L24.c.9.1 Sheet 36	24-10-18		A fresh number of admissions today – including about 20 cases of influenza, four cases being of the severe epidemic type with pneumonia complications. Arrangements for isolation wards for influenza cases had been made at Collection & the back of the billets 176 & 178 & in bigger huts and tents in reserve in the Touffleurs & Chaos districts, which are not very extensive at present; the empty Thomas hall. The hospital accommodation is occupied by Field Ambulance personnel; shelters of both floors by the upper floor is occupied by Field Ambulance personnel; shelters of both floors by personnel of Divisional HQrs and Divisional Artillery. JW	
"	25-10-18		About 70 admissions to hospital today – more than half being influenza. Total number in hospital is now 135. In view of more influenza cases being likely to occur, further accommodation will be necessary to evacuate 6 cases to 34 Cas. to C.C.C.Sty. Major F. Long R.C. returned to duty from 51 C.C.S. where he has been on a course yesterday. JW	
"	26-10-18		Admitted about 65 patients today. Evacuated 40 JW	
"	27-10-18		The daily rate of admissions remains about 60 and is likely to accrue. Many a portable latents have been placed as there often are formerly. Sick is not very satisfactory; difficult to obtain either billets to Rainc personnel in order to leave the upper floor for patients. JW	
"	28-10-18		A.D.M.S. 5th Div. inspected the hospital and suggested the whole factory block be handed over to the Field Ambulance. JW	
"	29-10-18		D.D.M.S. XI Corps visited the hospital. To know the whole block for hospital purposes today. Also established a separate ward, with both room & dressing room for scabies patients in another part of the factory. JW	

Vol X Page 7

2/2nd North Midland Field Ambulance

WAR DIARY
INTELLIGENCE SUMMARY.

Army Form C. 2118.

Place	Date	Hour	Summary of Events and Information	Remarks and references to Appendices
HEM L.24.C.9.1 Sheet 36	30-10-18		Moved all influenza cases to the large upper floor of the factory, other medical cases being accommodated on the lower floor. Transferred surgical cases to the supply house. Completed the scabies treatment section with a Norwegian dry bath. We have now about 200 patients in hospital – 130 being influenza cases. The 39th Stationary Hospital has not opened in Lille so that cases for evacuation have not far to travel to the C.C.S. Lt. W. Sweat, M.R.C. U.S.A. proceeded to 13th Bn W Riley Regt. Military Gunnery duty, vice Capt. H.K. Merritt A.C. who reports to this unit for light duty. JW.	
"	31-10-18		A.D.M.S. called at the hospital to inspect the new arrangements. The large wards are rather difficult to keep warm – have Canadian stoves were applied for today. The minute to course of sickness apparent the influenza outbreak is at the present, being mainly a mild type. The cases admitted have up to the present, been cleaning up in 4 or 5 days. We have had about 6 or 8 severe cases with pneumonia.	

J. W. Thompson
Lieut-Col. Round 17
O.C. 2/2 N. Midland Field Amb.

Army Form C. 2118.

WAR DIARY
or
INTELLIGENCE SUMMARY.
(Erase heading not required.)

Position of M.D.S., A.D.S., Car-loading posts
stretcher-posts on handing over
647ᵗʰ Division - 3-10-18.

Evacuation routes in red.

Vol 22
465/564/1

Confidential
War Diary
of
2/2 A. Mid. Fd. Amb

From 1-11-18   To 30-11-18

VOLUME XI

Nov 1918

WAR DIARY

2/2nd North Midland Field Ambulance

INTELLIGENCE SUMMARY

Army Form C. 2118.

Vol. XI. Page 1.

Place	Date	Hour	Summary of Events and Information	Remarks and references to Appendices
HEM [L24.c.9.] Sheet 36	1-11-18		The influenza epidemic is increasing slightly. We have more than 230 patients in hospital. Official news received today of the conclusion of an armistice with Austria-Hungary and Turkey. JWL	
"	2-11-18		Patients increased to 300 today — we are beginning to need more accommodation. Obtained more stoves and also stationed for the wounds.	
"	3-11-18		Arranged to take over another portion of the factory as a convalescent ward. JWL.	
"	4-11-18		A.D.M.S. visited the Rest Station. Huts arranged to fit up the other portion of the factory as a large convalescent ward — cleaning out the floors &c today & repairs. By this evening 400 cases in the leaky roof. JWL	
"	5-11-18		Quiet day — started the new convalescent ward; having stoves & mattresses & straw we were able to put in 70 patients this evening. From the more serious wards above. The roof still needs further repairs & stoves for warming the room have now been started. The upper ward of the factory now holds all acute cases, the lower ward the remaining medical cases are necessarily once filled the former ward. At present, but a search is being made for other accommodation in the latter was (?) present for accommodation for them. JWL	
"	6-11-18		D.M.S. V Army visited the Rest Station, made a minute examination of all our arrangements, especially the influenza wards. Something was made in (?) the fitting & repairing of the convalescent ward. The roof is now watertight. An instructor in physical training was attached to the unit today from 178th Bde H.Q. for Capt Burnett gave him a detailed scheme of procedure & exercises &c. for convalescents. JWL	

Vol XI Page 2

Army Form C. 2118.

2/2nd North Midland Field Ambulance

WAR DIARY
INTELLIGENCE SUMMARY
(Erase heading not required.)

Place	Date	Summary of Events and Information	Remarks and references to Appendices
HEM [L24.c.9.1] sheet 36	7-11-18	D.D.M.S XI Corps & A.D.M.S. 51st Div. visited the hospital today. We now have 490 cases in hospital (including 350 influenza). The convalescent ward is now in full working order, the patients being divided into three classes, according to their degree of convalescence. Various exercises, games, boxing, route marches are part of the programme, in addition to light fatigues about the hospital. Saw that Germany has asked for an Armistice. The news was received very calmly - but that is the Western Front. Been referred to the Military Commander in chief. 7W2	
"	8-11-18	The remaining stores of the R.A.M.C. dump at Fleurbaix were cleared today by lorry & the personnel brought away. The influenza outbreak has apparently hit its peak today (an Eng) reached its height. 7W2	
"	9-11-18	A.D.M.S. visited the hospital. Visited the Red Cross depôt at Hammes-Artois, and obtained a number of stores required necessary for the use of latest Official news received that German plenipotentiaries have received the terms of Armistice by Marshal Foch, with Allies representatives present. 7W2	
"	10-11-18	The Division has advanced across the Schelot river. On instructions of D. Div I sent Major Walton forward with an advance subdivision transport to follow the rear Brigade & establish a hospice for sick, in each with the Brigade. He established a post at a house near ESQUELMES (I 13 d, sheet 37). 7W2	

Vol XI Page 3

2/2 North Midland Field Ambulance

WAR DIARY / INTELLIGENCE SUMMARY

Army Form C. 2118.

Place	Date	Hour	Summary of Events and Information	Remarks and references to Appendices
HEM [24.c.9.1 Sheet 36]	11-11-18		Official intimation received that an Armistice has been signed by Germany and hostilities cease from 11 am today. The troops are standing fast in their present position until further orders, but Major Watson reported back here today, under instructions 7 A.D.M.S. J.W.	
"	12-11-18		The influenza epidemic is abating. There are now only 350 patients in hospital. J.W.	
"	13-11-18		A.D.M.S. visited the hospital. Instructions received hereon to evacuate. It came not likely that we shall be held in this area at the rate of 60 to 80 daily. J.W.	
"	14-11-18		Evacuated 70 patients to CCS today. News published today of the abdication & flight into Holland of the German Emperor. J.W.	
"	15-11-18		80 patients evacuated to a few number remaining 200 still in hospital. J.W.	
"	16-11-18		Another 86 patients evacuated today & about 70 returned to duty, leaving only 50 remaining. Received instructions to send an advance party today to visit a Reception camp for Repatriated Prisoners of War at St Andre. Major Watson, Capt Bradley proceeded on this duty, with the personnel of B section (but subsequently returned) P.O.W.	
"	17-11-18		Handed over the patients remaining (48) & the 2/1 N. Mid. 2 F.A. & moved to take over nearest Facilities & all equipment to the tent subdivision marched to St ANDRÉ & took over the Returned P.O.W. rest of the hut arrived (K.14.a.2.9 Sheet 36). This is a large Hock Yards Camp at the Asylum accommodation for about 500 in beds & another 1000 in tents beds. The heating arrangement is only 1 Riper & there is no water supply or lighting. R.E. representative coming tomorrow to take in hand the provision of these necessities	

Vol XI Page 7

2/2nd North Midland Field Ambulance

Army Form C. 2118.

WAR DIARY
INTELLIGENCE SUMMARY
(Erase heading not required.)

Place	Date	Hour	Summary of Events and Information	Remarks and references to Appendices
ST. ANDRÉ (LILLE) K.14.a.2.9 (Sheet 36)	18-11-18		The whole unit was employed today in cleaning out the many wards & moving of the asylum, fitting up beds & fireplaces, equipping a large dining hall, a recreation room, clothing & food stores, baths etc & constructing latrines. 40 Italian repatriated prisoners arrived this evening. J.W.	
"	19-11-18		Heating apparatus is now working. Latter & stores are fitted in wards. Sent the Chaplain to the British Red Cross Depot to obtain a supply of magazines, games etc, which he did, also a Gramophone so that we now have all necessary equipment. About 200 more Italians were received this afternoon, and another 170 at 10 p.m. All these were accommodated with beds & blankets, & all who required it had a bath & clean change. J.W.	
"	20-11-18		A few more British & Italian repatriated prisoners came in this morning. S. Divn. XI Corps visited the Camp. J.W.	
"	21-11-18		200 British P.O.W. arrived this morning having been transferred from TOURNAI reception Camp. Admin 67 Divn visited the Camp today & St Andre Station, where a 67 Divn D.I.R. is. J.W.	
"	22-11-18		Orders received to send all British returned prisoners to a P. and. This division to concentrate at 8 a.m., 240 in number. They were entrained at St Andre Station. A few Russians arrived today managed from more Italians etc. 3rd Corps called today arranging to work according to instructions recd from T. Army. ADMS 80 Div; 3rd Corps to take over this Camp on the 24th. J.W.	

2/2nd North Midland Field Ambulance Vol XI Page 5

WAR DIARY
INTELLIGENCE SUMMARY
(Erase heading not required.)

Army Form C. 2118.

Place	Date	Hour	Summary of Events and Information	Remarks and references to Appendices
ST. ANDRÉ (LILLE) K.14.a.2.9 (sheet 36)	23-11-18		Small advanced party of the 26th Field Amb. (8th Div.) arrived today to arrange the taking over of this Reception Camp tomorrow. Later in the day orders were received from XI Corps cancelling the arrangements. This camp is to be closed tomorrow after entraining all the Italian & Russian repatriated prisoners. All stores, surplus to unit equipment & any other not unlikely remaining, are to be handed over to the Returned P.O.W. Reception Camp at LA MADELEINE.	
"	24-11-18	4.30	Italians & 5 Russians were marched to St Andre station entrained at 12 noon today. The remainder of the repatriated prisoners consisting of 5 British were transferred to La Madeleine Reception Camp, together with all Corps stores (blankets, clothing, rations, medical comforts, Red Cross stores etc.). The Camp was then closed, all Field Ambulance equipment packed, and the Unit marched at 2 p.m. to EMMERIN south of LILLE (P.34.a.9.5) & went into billets. J.W. sheet 36	
EMMERIN P.34.a.9.5 sheet 36	25-11-18		The men are to have several days rest & recreation while in this place. There is no hospital work to be done, and steps were taken to try to fit up a recreation room, a football ground, and a dining room. The men are all in good billets. J.W.	

Army Form C. 2118.

Vol XI Page 6

2/2nd North Midland Field Ambulance

WAR DIARY or INTELLIGENCE SUMMARY.

(Erase heading not required.)

Place	Date	Hour	Summary of Events and Information	Remarks and references to Appendices
EMMERIN [P.1tt.a.65] Sheet 3b.	26-XI-18		Coal miners are being asked for, & will shortly be demobilized for work in the mines at home. Particulars of 10 N.C.O.'s & men of this unit who are qualified for this work were sent in today. The question of manager educational classes in various subjects with a view to refitting men for their civil occupations on demobilization is being considered. Major Young has been appointed Educational Officer for this unit & he has spent much time in obtaining particulars of the nature of instruction required by N.C.O.s & men of the unit. Classes are to be arranged shortly & the Divisional Education Officer will be asked to will be asked to arrange in charge or may be purchases.	Fwd.
"	27-XI-18		Football games were played today. Nothing else to note.	Fwd.
"	28-XI-18		Orders received to send an advance party, with M.T. 1 of Bde., 6th BRUAY area, the Division having received orders to proceed to the 8 lands. Capt. Rudolf Hoscheid with sub of 2 O.R., rolled up serves at RUITZ (K.19.c. Sheet 44b)	Fwd.
"	29-XI-18		Nothing of note.	Fwd.
"	30-XI-18		Nothing of note.	Fwd.

J.W. Johnson
Lt-Col. R.A.M.C. (T)
O.C. 2/2 N. Midland F. Amb.

Original Copy.

Confidential
War Diary
~ of ~
2/2 N. Mid. Fd. Amb

From 1-12-18   To 31-12-18

Volume XII

Vol XIV Page 1

2/2nd North Midland Field Ambulance

Army Form C. 2118.

WAR DIARY

INTELLIGENCE SUMMARY.

(Erase heading not required.)

Place	Date	Summary of Events and Information	Remarks and references to Appendices
EMMERIN (P.24.a.9.5) (sheet 36)	1-12-18	The unit is still resting at EMMERIN; the time is being occupied by the making of arrangements for Educational classes, & the preparation of documents relating to the men's civil occupation, with a view to preparing for demobilization. J.W.	
"	2-12-18	A.D.M.S. called. Warning order received to prepare to move with the 178th Inf. Bde. Army early date. J.W.	
"	3-12-18	Unit transferred to the administration of 178th Inf. Bde. # go today. Orders received this morning for transport detail of 178th to proceed this afternoon or there join the rest of its 178 Inf. Bde. transport. Capt. Lindsey proceeded in charge of the transport at 2 pm & Lieut. in FOSKETT & Lt. ? Orders received in the rear by the rest to proceed by 'Bus tomorrow to the Noeux-les-Mines area. The afternoon was spent in packing all stores etc. [U.I.a sheet 36] Cap. F.A.L. Bodley M.C. proceeded to Pets as M.O. % 36th North'd Fus. Fusiliers ¬ authority A.D.M.S. 97th J.W.	
"	4-12-18	The Unit marched at 8.0 am to Petit Ronchin & entrained there at 9.0 a.m. arriving in the Noeux-les-Mines area at One p.m. Billets were found for the Ambulance at RUITZ (K.19.c. sheet 44 b.) Iwb. hos. 6/2 taken for the Div. Brigade HQ visited all sick of 4/ 10th Div. J.W.	
RUITZ (K.19. C.3.7) Sheet A.44.	5-12-18	There is no hospital accom. to take 100 sick at RUITZ all sick of 6th Div. Battalions or Noeux-les-Mines (Y.3.N.and.) H.H. visited all 10th Div. gp (119.9.) hopes. The morning & evening for sick & execta which J.W.	

Vol XII Page 2

2/2nd North Midland Field Ambulance

Army Form C. 2118.

WAR DIARY
INTELLIGENCE SUMMARY.
(Erase heading not required.)

Place	Date	Hour	Summary of Events and Information	Remarks and references to Appendices
RUITZ [K.19.c.3.3 sheet 44L]	6-12-18		Nothing to note. J.H.J	
"	7-12-18		Warning order received to prepare to move with 178th M/Bde. to DUNKERQUE on the 16th inst. J.H.J	
"	8-12-18		Church parade at 10.00 a.m. J.H.J	
"	9-12-18		Parade for inspection. The unit by A.D.M.S. who also presented the ribbons of the Military Medal to the following N.C.O's & men who had been decorated during the last few months:- No.395038 Sergt. HAILEY, M, No.M/31319 A/sgt COOPER, J, M.F.H.C. attached, No.419342 Pte Waterfield, J, No.44918 Pte Dakin. B. J.H.J	
"	10-12-18		The unit entrained at CALONNE-RICOUART station today, the transport proceeding on the first two trains, and the personnel on the third. Last. J.H.J	
"	11-12-18		The Unit arrived at DUNKERQUE & went into camp at ST POL-SUR-MER. LT.COL. F.W. JOHNSON proceeded on 14 days special leave of England. MAJOR F.H.C. WATSON assumed command of the unit. J.H.J. until 178 Inf. Bde Reinforces from 59 Division. D.L.G.C.	
DUNKERQUE (ST POL-S-MER)	12-12-18		Took over control of medical & sanitary work of Demobilization Camp. Pte A Sidwell returned from leave. J.H.J.	
"	13- "	-12-18.	} Nothing to note. J.H.J.	
"	14- "			
"	15- "			
"	16			
"	17-12-18		Major Young, M.C. proceeded to England on 14 days leave. J.H.J	
"	18 19 20 21 22	F.S.G.	} Nothing to note. J.H.J	
"	23rd-12-18		Capt HE Ludo M.S. proceeded on leave for 14 days to England. J.H.J	
"	23 - 24 - 25 /12/18		Nothing to note J.H.J	
"	27/12/18		Major F.W. Johnson returned from leave & took over the command from Major J H J	

Vol. XII. Page 3
Army Form C. 2118.

2/2nd North Midland

WAR DIARY
or
Field Ambulance
INTELLIGENCE SUMMARY.

(Erase heading not required.)

Instructions regarding War Diaries and Intelligence Summaries are contained in F. S. Regs., Part II. and the Staff Manual respectively. Title pages will be prepared in manuscript.

Place	Date	Hour	Summary of Events and Information	Remarks and references to Appendices
DUNKERQUE (ST POLS-MER)	28-12-18		Visited the Camps of the 36" Northumb. Fusiliers 73" W. Riding at Mardyck, also the bathing & delousing centre near the "Hospice" camp. The men of this unit are employed in working the bathing arrangements & delousing plant for all men passing though the demobilisation centre. Noted that the delousing chambers are not acting well. Tp.?	
"	29-12-18		Visited the delousing plant again & reported to Brig. H. Gr. with the unsatisfactory condition of the delousing chambers, pointing out the defects that require remedying. Major Wilkins also is in charge of sanitary Capt. inefficiency No. "11" R. Scots Fusiliers in the Brigade area, accompanied me & assisted in arrangements for withdrawing me & stores of the camps this afternoon, fill.	
"	30-12-18		Nothing further to fill.	
"	31-12-18		Capt. A. L. Bradley M.C. provides on leave to England. In medical Officers Lieut. Sweet M.R.C. V.S. as N.O. Mardyke camps (36"N. Fus. & 13"W. Riding) the M.O. (Capt. Harfleur?) as M.J.O. Hospice Camps (11"R.S. Fus) and the M.O. (Capt. Harfleur?) as M.J.O. Hospice Camps for the sup of area. Three M.O's (Major Watson and other M.O.t. Sweet) on relief, on the usual inspection duties at the demobilisation centre.	

W. Munson
Lt. Col. R.A.M.C. (T)
O.C. 2/2 North Midland Fd. Amb.

59 DN
Box 2888

Head with and. A.A.

COMMITTEE FOR THE
MEDICAL HISTORY OF THE WAR
Date

1919. Vol IX Page 1 Army Form C. 2118.

2/2nd NORTH MIDLAND FIELD AMBULANCE

WAR DIARY
INTELLIGENCE SUMMARY

JANUARY.

App 24

Place	Date	Hour	Summary of Events and Information	Remarks and references to Appendices
DUNKERQUE (ST. POL-SUR-MER)	1-1-19		Nothing of note — Unit still employed on medical, bathing & disinfecting duties at the demobilization camp. 7x9.	
"	2-1-19. to 31-1-19		Nothing of note. Employment as before. 7x9.w.	
"				

H Howarton
Major

2/2nd North Mid. F.A.

Feb. 1919.

31

2/1st West Midland Fd. Amb. FEBRUARY 1919. Army Form C. 2118.

WAR DIARY
or
INTELLIGENCE SUMMARY.
(Erase heading not required.)

Place	Date	Hour	Summary of Events and Information	Remarks and references to Appendices
DUNKERQUE	1-2-19 to 8-2-19		nothing of nTa. FHcw.	
ST PAL-SUR-MER	9-2-19 to 9-2-19			
	10-2-19		Capt H.G. Ludolf M.B. proceeded to England for demobilization War Office letter - 112/Pers/2/572 AMD1 - 24.1.1919. — FHcw.	
	11-2-19 to 28-2-19		nothing to nTa. FHcw.	

J.H.Wharton
Major.

140/3551

17 JUL 1945

WAR DIARY
2/2 NTH MIDLAND FIELD AMBULANCE
INTELLIGENCE SUMMARY

Army Form C. 2118.

MARCH - 1919.

Place	Date	Hour	Summary of Events and Information	Remarks and references to Appendices
DUNKERQUE	1-3-19		Nothing to note. 7them.	
H/Q-2nd Sn MFA	2-3-19		A/Lt. Col. F.W. Johnson proceeded to England for demobilization & handing over. 6.3.19	Authority - debited notice no DM 32089 (AM)
	3-3-19 to		Own command by Major F.H.C. Watson. Reorganisation of Amb. on two section basis completed. 7them	
	7-3-19		Nothing to note. 7them	
	8-3-19		c/Major F.A. Elliot M.C. reported for duty	
	9-3-19		Assumed Command of this Ambulance on this date. 7them.	STRENGTH
			Capt. A/major F.H.C. Watson proceeded to England for demobilization 10/3/19	
			Authority - Des. etc. issue - no DM. 32411 (AMD) - 13.2.19. Jno. J. Elliot Major	COMMAND
	11.3.19.		Unit (O.R.) engaged as pres. with at Delousing Sta. & Camp Sanitation, M.C.	NORMAL
	12.3.19.		Testing & M.C.	
	13.3.19.		History of Ambulance supplied G/O.	
	14.3.19.		"	
	15.3.19.		"	M/C
	16.3.19.		"	N/W ever or otherwise M/C
	17.3.19.		"	M/C
	18.3.19.		"	M/C
	19.3.19.		"	M/C
	20.3.19.		"	Snowshower M/C

WAR DIARY or INTELLIGENCE SUMMARY

MARCH – 1919.

Army Form C. 2118.

Place	Date	Hour	Summary of Events and Information	Remarks and references to Appendices
DUNKERQUE- ETEL SUR MER.	21.3.19.		Orders received for unit to be reduced to CADRE - M.L.	REDUCTION to CADRE.
	22.3.19.		Acting Report - Some power at night M.L.	
	23.3.19.		Brigade inspection of horses by O.C. 59 Divisional Train (Lt. Col. T. HAZLERIGG DSO) M.L.	
	24.3.19.		Acting Report M.L.	
	25.3.19.		Acting Report M.L.	
	26.3.19.		Acting Report M.L.	
	27.3.19.		Acting Report M.L.	
	28.3.19.		34 horses entrained & despatched Hd.qrs. of Cadre ordered to be stationed at the Camp. M.L.	
	29.3.19.		a/Q.M.Sgt. to the Crew established. — Sgt. Ptn. Pte. St. Sgt. ... 11.3.19. Pte. Butler the left of 1.3.19 Cpl. Smart, the Sgt. ... 11.3.19 ..... 1.3.19 L/Cpl. Thomson the Cpl. 20.3.19 ..... 1.3.19 M.L. Pte. Soden the Cpl. 11.3.19 Others.	PROMOTIONS TO CONFIRM CADRE.
	30.3.19.		Nothing of importance happened. About 4 no. Ord. Est. + instruments ammuny M.L.	
	31.3.19.		" " " " " " " — Snow showers throughout.	

J.T. Short Capt. Dwn Qmt.
for W. ... Major SL ..... Qmt.
O.C. 2/2 york-midland Div Train

140/3050.

17 JUL 1919

WAR DIARY
or
INTELLIGENCE SUMMARY.
(Erase heading not required.)

Army Form C. 2118.

APRIL 1919.

2/2 Mt MIDLAND F.AMB.

Place	Date	Hour	Summary of Events and Information	Remarks and references to Appendices
DUNKERQUE- ST POL-SUR-MER-	April 1.		Nothing to Report	M.
	2.		" "	M.
	3.		Aerator toy gun -	M.
	4.		18 Horses rent to remount dept & veterinary Hospital Calais.	M.
	5.		Nothing to Report	M.
	6.		" "	M.
	7.		" "	M.
	8.		" "	M. Top incident 1 P.O.W. Dunkerque during transport to bo M.
	9.		Capt A.C. Bodley returned from 8 Canadian hosp. Dontry received.	M.
	10.		Bk T.A. Young returning from leave.	M.
	11.		Leave opened.	M.
	12.		Hurricane during night.	M.
	13.		Nothing to Report	M.
	14.		" "	
	15.		Major L.M. SMYTH RC, CB, CD & O.C. & Dr + & STANSFELD G.O. 17th D.L. Arib milic	
	16.		Inspect Stores & Hospital-lorry. Major fm THOMSON. Dunkerque inspects Weights & Quantity stations afternoon	
			ADMS Dunkerque intro to Lt Col. McDonnell O.C. 10 & General	
			Hospital. via letter of ADMS Dunkerque. A. SIDWELL to U.K. on leave Hospital	
			Capt & QM. A. SIDWELL to U.K. on leave Hospital	M.

WAR DIARY
INTELLIGENCE SUMMARY.
(Erase heading not required.)

APRIL 1919

Army Form C. 2118.

Place	Date	Hour	Summary of Events and Information	Remarks and references to Appendices
DUNKERQUE	April 17.		Wea fine dull & cld. M.	
	18.		" warmer " M.	
	19.		fine & bright - warm - Good Friday - Games & bathing. M.	
	20.		Cpl + dull - Easter Sunday - M.	
	21.		Dull & cld " Monday - General Holiday. M.	
	22.		fine & bright 1.30 M. kept. M.	
	23.		dull & cld. M.	
	24.		Dull - cld - showers. Afternoon M. kept. M.	
	25.		fine & bright - warm. " " M.	
	26.		dt. Rain M. Capt. W.H. SWEET left for France. W.	
			BABTIE V.C. noted Disinfectr Stations M.	
	27.		T. Cld. Heavy storm of snow, sleet rain in afternoon & evening M. Lt.Col.Y. O.K.	
	28.		T.Cld. Rain & sleet at intervals. Capt. Boxley returned from leave to H.Q. M.	
	29.		T.Cld - hailstorm - gale - Capt. Stewart been retailed to H.Q. & any 3.15. P.M.	
	30.		Rain & wk. M.	
			Fisted adv - troops	
			1915 on temporary Command of 2nd T.Q. =	
			Major J.B. Chances C.M., M., J.B.M.C. Mior Comdt	
			Ambulance from Major J.B. Chances C.M., Mt. Inches	
			O.C. 2/3 North Midland	
			Field Amb.	

May. 1917

140/3560

2/2nd North Mid. F.A.

2/2 N M 2nd Aust
MAY 1919.
I 28

Army Form C. 21

WAR DIARY
or
INTELLIGENCE SUMMARY.
(Erase heading not required.)

Instructions regarding War Diaries and Intelligence Summaries are contained in F. S. Regs., Part II. and the Staff Manual respectively. Title pages will be prepared in manuscript.

Place	Date	Hour	Summary of Events and Information	Remarks and references to Appendices
DUNKERQUE	MAY 1.		Work continues as before. Porters working.	
	2.		Maj. Gen. N.M. SMYTH V.C. O.C 2nd Divn. visited Camp 9/5	
	3.		" " " " " " 9/5	
	4.		" " " "	
	5.		" "	
	6.		Inspection of Camp & equipment by Col. BIDDIS.	
			Dam open 9/5	
	7.		Men on fatigue Freight + H.P Dock Dunkerque	
			Other " " " St Pol & 166 are bit. 9/5	
			L.C. No 4 General Hospital	
	8.		Maj. Gen. N.M. SMYTH V.C. G.O.C 2nd Divn. + Capt Dyer arrived on the	
			inspection by me of the reserve stores G.J.C.	
			Camp cleared up + inspected - ant to Camp 9/5	
	9.		Details reported to me at H.Q. reserve lines + Cut to Camp & fitted. 9/5	
			(1) O.C. 2/2 Aust. M.D. with dust.	D. Tm
			(2) O.C. 9/2 Aust. Quartermaster	6/5
			(3) O.Rank. Details Camp Hospt. for 1/2 Divn.	
			Officers attached in detail to D.C.I. Ex-2616.	
			Issue store withdraw + reported on detail 45 heater kitchen + loss	HMN
			General Details Cant. Shew sent + report 15 hats. 9/5	
			3 blanket	

D. D. & L., London, E.C.
(50510) Wt W5300/P713 250,000 3/18 E 2688 Forms/C2118/16.

WAR DIARY
or
INTELLIGENCE SUMMARY.
(Erase heading not required.)

Army Form C. 2118

MAY - 1919.

II.

Place	Date	Hour	Summary of Events and Information	Remarks and references to Appendices
DUNKERQUE SPPé-sur-MER	May 9.		Reports K.A.D.M.S. Dunkirk & Major HEPBURN - O.C. No. 004 General took for parade No. 9 par from K.O. ref par. 1+2 letter for host no. 360 Above re charge duty of orderlies - to intimate personnel.	Report.
	10.		Officer now to cont. do. G/c. Capt. Inns Court visits & Col. on no 97 Lieut. Gen. M.	Order to
	11.		Orders received from A.D.M.S. DUNKIRK to hold own crowd to the ambulance & report to O.C. Northern Hospital per lorries. Outlines to the Quartermaster Staff. Orders to A.D.M.S. Lake O.C. No 2 M.O. M.T.T.R. R.C. & Capt. Pat. Bodey R.C. Stone & Matron of the cent. Capt. J.A. Young & Sgt. & report to O.C. 14 G.H. for duty office.	Reduction.
	12.		To 10.5.19. Capt. Young & report to 36. Nothing came Moves to M.H.(Captain) for tel. 10/7 mg. trans. No. 04/1360/19 duted 10/7mg. at 11pm our Tony Cooks	
	13.		Commencement of field amb. to extent & 44 O.R. M.R. holding report. Guesta Australia W/c.	

Army Form C. 2118

WAR DIARY
or
INTELLIGENCE SUMMARY.
(Erase heading not required.)

MAY – 1919.
III

Instructions regarding War Diaries and Intelligence Summaries are contained in F.S. Regs., Part II. and the Staff Manual respectively. Title pages will be prepared in manuscript.

Place	Date	Hour	Summary of Events and Information	Remarks and references to Appendices
DUNKERQUE ST-POL- SUR- MER.	May	14.	Instr. (12) O.R. sent for disposal to try M.C.	
		15.	10 O.R's importance refused to try M.C.	
		16.	Surplus A.S.C. men returned to units. Off.	
		17.	Nil to report – M.C.	
		18.	" " " M.C.	
		19.	" " " M.C.	
		20.	A.&Sgt. & 7 men (cooks) for disposal – list &c. established & approved MC	
		21.	Nil to report. MC	
		22.	" " " MC	
		23.	Closing of "Commands" to be effected by C.O. & 9/4 & SIDWELL for 2nd in Command	
			Also arrangement made with Codn. reg 1050 Aus. & Byrne by Lieut.	
			Sharpe February 13/9 for A. Burton. Maj. + 71 Lieut. (Cont)	
			Capt. Anderson to ?	
			Reports as to outfits were to be proceeded with as he ?	

Army Form C. 2118

WAR DIARY
or
INTELLIGENCE SUMMARY
(Erase heading not required.)

MAY 1919

Instructions regarding War Diaries and Intelligence Summaries are contained in F.S. Regs., Part II. and the Staff Manual respectively. Title pages will be prepared in manuscript.

Place	Date	Hour	Summary of Events and Information	Remarks and references to Appendices
DUNKIRK.	24 May		Took over command of troops also Depot & Regimental Staff	
	25 "		Nothing worthy of note	
	26 "		Transferred Guards room etc to RTO in camp recently vacated by R.F.C. M.T. [?]	
	27 "		Nothing worthy of note	
	28 "		Seven Rft B.M.T. Dimensional 886 Coy R.F.C. to dispersal on becoming surplus to establishment of Cadre following manoeuvre reduction	
	29 "		Back to our peace camp - completed - conducted by demobilization	
			under I.B. arrangements etc.	
	30 "		Nothing worthy of note	
	31 "		Nothing worthy of note	

[signature]
Copy to OsmC
O/c 2/2 N. mid Fd Stub

11 140/3085

2/2 - 1st Ind. F.A.

June 1914

2/2 N. M.D. F.D. AMBULANCE Vol. VI

WAR DIARY

INTELLIGENCE SUMMARY
(Erase heading not required)

Army Form C. 2118.

JUNE 1919 Page 1

WO 29

Place	Date	Hour	Summary of Events and Information	Remarks and references to Appendices
DUNKIRK	1-6-19		Orders received from HQ 59 Division. Barracks alongside RASC personnel attacked	
			by 1 Sgt. and 10 R.V.s. Reply — Instructions asked for. memo of 9 GO 6902 of 30th at evening received 9 roughly 75% of original establishment.	
	2-6-19		Orders received from A.D.M.S. CALAIS. Force 194 — bath detached apart by 65 Gr. 27/6	
			Report contacts reinforcements — Reply — 25% increase 9 organised	
			complete. N/a.	
	3-6-19	13:00	Orders received from D.M.S. CALAIS that 9 S.M.O. DUNKIRK to attack reinforcements	
			in full to new establishment to No 4 Permit Advance Party in full strength of	
			6 men, 91 privates (9) Reinforcement camps — A.Div. J.J.	
	4-6-19		Military Reserve (9) — P.B.S engagement camp	
			a copy enclosed in margin 9 Employment Parties enquired 9 Reserves	
	5-6-19		Orders issued from D.M.S. to reinforce each through reinforcement 9 ROG. 6902. 30509A	
			re-orders appointed 9 men in "Equipment Permit Camp" J.J.	
	6-6-19		Nothing worthy of record.	
	7-6-19			
	8-6-19		A.D.M.S. of Dunkirk to Calais arrived (9) and on duty to No 4 General Hospital arrived at	
			instructions 9 A.D.M.S. CALAIS J.J.	
	9-6-19		Orders received to send one 9 (9) disease to camp Nos 13 Division 12:6 arrival	
	10-6-19		J-C. C. — Orderly 9 Sister.	
	11-6-19			
	12-6-19		Nos 4 & 6 GR continue "Guard" camp burnings and (?) getting beginning of	
			afternoon. D.O. 128 Inf. Bde. Instead a many grand to evening	

2/2 N.Md Fd AMBULANCE Vol. VI
JUNE
1919

Army Form C. 2118.

WAR DIARY

INTELLIGENCE SUMMARY.

(Erase heading not required.)

Instructions regarding War Diaries and Intelligence Summaries are contained in F. S. Regs., Part II. and the Staff Manual respectively. Title pages will be prepared in manuscript.

Place	Date	Hour	Summary of Events and Information	Remarks and references to Appendices
DUNKIRK	13.6.19		Nothing worthy of note	
	14.6.19		2 R.S.C. HT NCOs 1914 enlisted men sent to dispersal camp.	
	15.6.19		Application made for 4 drivers to replace NCOs sent home - fr HQ 59 Div Train.	
	16.6.19		Four received & future M.T. equipment placing vehicles & looking over was carried out.	
	17.6.19			
	18.6.19			
	19.6.19			
	20.6.19			
	21.6.19		Nothing worthy of note	
	22.6.19			
	23.6.19			
	24.6.19			
	25.6.19			
	26.6.19			
	27.6.19			
	28.6.19			
	29.6.19			
	30.6.19			

Alex M Biphter Capt
N.Z. M.S. 2/2 NZMd Fd Amb
6-7-19

160/3585
aust.

18 AUG 1919

2/2nd h. Mid. F.A.

July 1919

(6339) Wt. W160/M3016 1,300,000 10/17 McA & W Ltd (E 1898) Forms W3091.   Army Form W.3091.

Cover for Documents.

Nature of Enclosures.

Notes, or Letters written.

Army Form C. 2118.

2/2 N: MID: FD: AMBULANCE VOL VII

WAR DIARY
INTELLIGENCE SUMMARY.
(Erase heading not required.)

Instructions regarding War Diaries and Intelligence Summaries are contained in F.S. Regs., Part II. and the Staff Manual respectively. Title pages will be prepared in manuscript.

JULY 1919

Place	Date	Hour	Summary of Events and Information	Remarks and references to Appendices
DINGLE	1.7.19		Nothing to note to.	
	6.7.19			
	6.7.19		Inspection of received Equipment by 1st Offr i/c	
	7.7.19		Nothing to note t/c.	
	8.7.19		Letter from S.M.O. Dingle Rec'd -	
	9.7.19		S.M.O. Dingle received firing aerial. No telephone telephone etc this Unit. Serial No. Z.F.8.7. Destination CHILDWALL letter from H.Q. 59 Div. dy/Serving phone information. Wire from H.Q. 59 Div. R. morning alteration of destination to AINTREE. W.H. Confirmating S.M.O. letter of alteration of destination to AINTREE W.	
	10.7.19		Nothing to note t/c.	
	11.7.19			
	12.7.19			
	13.7.19		General Holiday for Peace Celebrations of France. P.H.	
	14.7.19			
	15.7.19		Nothing to note t/c	
	16.7.19			
	17.7.19			
	18.7.19			
	19.7.19		General Holiday for Peace Celebration. U.K.	
	20.7.19			
	21.7.19		Nothing to note t/c	
	22.7.19			
	23.7.19		Lecture from head of Peace Corps for landing on paper towel	
	25.7.19			
	26.7.19		Nothing to note t/c	

Army Form C. 2118.

9/2 N Mid Fd AMB Vol. VII
WAR DIARY JULY 1919 / PAGE II
or
INTELLIGENCE SUMMARY.
(Erase heading not required.)

Place	Date	Hour	Summary of Events and Information	Remarks and references to Appendices
DUNKIRK	27.7.19 28.7.19 29.7.19 30.7.19 31.7.19		Nothing to report. Orders received for Equipment found Stores and Extra equipment made for transport to the store at 9.0 am on 1.8.19.	

JM Campbell Capt.
O/C 9/2 N Mid Fd Amb

72. N.Mid. Fd. Ambulance. Vol XIC

Army Form C. 2118.

WAR DIARY
or
INTELLIGENCE SUMMARY.
(Erase heading not required.)

AUGUST 1919 / B.E.F.

Instructions regarding War Diaries and Intelligence Summaries are contained in F. S. Regs., Part II. and the Staff Manual respectively. Title pages will be prepared in manuscript.

Place	Date	Hour	Summary of Events and Information	Remarks and references to Appendices
DUNKIRK	1.8.19		Inspection & Dental of two O.R. 175 F.Bde. reporting to safe Keep until in charge Red Personnel, and remainder originally handed over to under whose camps NSFA Camps a.m. sent Personnel to Depot south of experience (illegible) where men join HMSO Dover West Harbour etc & others a party of reinforcements to the (illegible) Personally responsible for civing etc?	
				[signature] Gibbs Capt OC 72 F.C. 72 N.Mid.Fd.Amb

(3) No. 417256 Sgt. HENRY R. HILL

For consistent good work & devotion to duty during the two years that he has been with this Unit in France. On the many occasions he has been N.C.O. in charge of Bearers he has invariably displayed great courage and good judgment & by his fine example has obtained the utmost work out of the bearers working under him.

(4) No. M/282290 Pte CHARLES SYDNEY FORD
59th Divl. M.T. Coy A.S.C. attached.

For consistent good work & devotion to duty. Pte Ford has at all times shewn the utmost keenness in his work, and an utter disregard for danger in the carrying out of his duties. He has always been ready and willing to go along heavily shelled roads to evacuate wounded. Particularly was his courage commendable in the fighting round BAILLEUL in April 1918 and near the SCHELDT in November 1918.

(5) No 390049 Private WALTER LEO BAKER

For consistently good work as a Stretcher Bearer Pte Baker has at all times worked with commendable willingness & energy and by his untiring devotion to duty, cool courage and cheerfulness has set a fine example to those working with him in evacuating wounded, particularly was this noticeable in the fighting round WEZ MACQUART in October 1918.

www.ingramcontent.com/pod-product-compliance
Lightning Source LLC
Chambersburg PA
CBHW080906230426
43664CB00016B/2738